Advance Praise

Customer value, its delivery and management are words used very liberally in management jargon. However its definition, measurement and on ground delivery always left me with many open ended questions. These got addressed when we applied Total CVM described in Gautam's book very successfully by putting Total CVM in our balanced score card, measuring value we deliver, rolling out Customer circles in various States, and measuring Customer Value and driving value through our delivery chain and channel partners, using the concept of dealer brand equity. I strongly recommend Gautam's pioneering book, because it has potential to transform your thinking and significantly improve your business results.

—Kapil Mehan, Executive Director, Tata Chemicals Limited

Total CVM is a pathbreaking concept guiding the company, and the employees to become Customer-centric, and by so doing create shareholder wealth. Total CVM is the latest management practice that should make the Customer revolution happen much like the quality revolution. It will transform the reader's thinking and will benefit corporate returns by making value creation the prime task of employees and the company.

—Patricia Seybold, CEO, Patricia Seybold Group and Author, *Customers.com, The Customer Revolution* and *Outside Innovation*

Gautam's book on Total CVM is a classic, and makes a valuable contribution to managerial literature and transformation. It is easy to read, understand and most important, effectively implementable. To win in business you must create value, value for the customers, employees and shareholders. Beating the competition at creating value requires focus and alignment of all departments of a company. Gautam's book brings new principles and practices such as continuous customer improvement programs, customer performance management system, circle of promises and the MBA of the future. Driving your business strategy from a customer value first strategy will help you create a winning sustainable competitive advantage. The Total CVM approach and the case studies in this 'how to' book make it a must read for all managers.

—Ray Kordupleski, President, Customer Value Management, Inc.; Author, *Mastering Customer Value Management*

In a global and increasingly competitive marketplace, creating customer value is not an option — it is imperative to sustainable profitability and competitive superiority. There are two reasons that most companies struggle to create customer value. First, their definition of customer value is company-centric. Second, they fail to coordinate all of the moving parts that yield value in the customer experience. Gautam's Total CVM provides the practical know-how for meeting these pitfalls head on. If you're looking for a guide to optimize value management in your organization and get results, this is it.

—Scott M. Broetzmann, President & CEO, Customer Care Measurement & Consulting

I was a fan of CVM, but reading Gautam's innovative ideas on Total CVM and transforming business thinking to build a 360 degree focus on Customers and driving shareholder wealth tells me that CVM as known before is passé. This is the next significant management technique since Total Quality Management, and all managers should read this book to create value for themselves and their companies.

—Arvind Pande, former Chairman and Managing Director SAIL

I believe "Total Customer Value Management" is certainly the next practice in Customer focus and at setting best practices in "Customer Experience". Starting with novel ways of ensuring Do's & Don'ts in serving customers to building customer circles, establishing customer strategy and bill of rights for customer to ensure innovation in customer service and enhancing customer experience. This definitely is the way to learn and adopt to meet rising legitimate customer expectations.

— Ashok Sothi, Vice President — Mumbai Operation, Tata Power

Total Customer Value Management

Business Planning based on Customer Value Management at Tata Chemicals Crop Nutrition and Agri-Business (with their permission)

Total Customer Value Management

Value Management

Transforming Business Thinking

Gautam Mahajan

Response
Business books from SAGE
Los Angeles ▪ London ▪ New Delhi ▪ Singapore ▪ Washington DC
www.sagepublications.com

First published in 2011 by

Response Books
Business books from SAGE
B1/I-1 Mohan Cooperative Industrial Area
Mathura Road, New Delhi 110 044, India

SAGE Publications Inc
2455 Teller Road
Thousand Oaks, California 91320, USA

SAGE Publications Ltd
1 Oliver's Yard, 55 City Road
London EC1Y 1SP, United Kingdom

SAGE Publications Asia-Pacific Pte Ltd
33 Pekin Street
#02-01 Far East Square
Singapore 048763

Published by Vivek Mehra for SAGE Publications India Pvt Ltd, typeset in 11/13pt Book Antiqua by Star Compugraphics Private Limited, Delhi and printed at Chaman Enterprises, New Delhi.

Library of Congress Cataloging-in-Publication Data
Mahajan, Gautam, 1946–
    Total cutsomer value management: transforming business thinking/ Gautam Mahajan.
        p. cm.
    Includes index.
    1. Relationship marketing. 2. Cutsomer relations. 3. Total quality management. I. Title.
HF5415.55.M3264   658.8'12 — dc22   2010   2010037278

ISBN: 978-81-321-0312-7 (PB)

The SAGE Team: Rekha Natarajan, Aniruddha De, Nand Kumar Jha and Deepti Saxena

To my wife Veena and sons Karan and Shiv for their long
lasting, tireless and uncomplaining support

AND

to my readers, and many friends who have helped
me through good and difficult times, and friends
at my publisher's.

Contents

Foreword

Transforming a business or an organization is never an easy task. In a world where business moves at the speed of thought, realigning business processes with an organization's aspirations can often be a treacherous and unpredictable pursuit.

The fundamentals of Customer Value Management (CVM) offer a robust and dependable alternative to do precisely this. By allowing its customers to create and define its actions, a business hands over the reins of value creation to the only people who can truly augment a business' worth.

Total Customer Value Management (Total CVM), started by Gautam Mahajan, adds even greater emphasis on making this precept holistic and all-encompassing. While other business transformation strategies tend to view business re-engineering in a linear fashion, Total CVM addresses every constituent within a business simultaneously.

Increasingly, such a customer value perspective can result in the unlocking of value from every part of the business with each function and department working in concert to achieve a common and profitable goal.

At Godrej, when we applied the guiding principles of Total CVM to a service business, the results allowed us to draw a direct link between managing customers correctly and deriving greater, more sustainable value. In fact, our focus on this aspect has led us to pioneer the concept of a 'Chief Customer Officer' in our properties business.

I recommend that every organization in pursuit of greater value adopt these methods and practices.

Read this book to learn more about bringing Total CVM into your organization and helping you to create more value for your company and customers.

Adi Godrej
Chairman of Godrej Group

Preface

The Customer Revolution is here to stay. Companies practising Total Customer Value Management (Total CVM) and Customer[1] strategies that respond to Customers' increased awareness, demands and changing needs will forge ahead of competition and become more profitable.

To paraphrase Charles Schwab, the recent financial meltdown occurred because the financial community forgot that they were handling Customers' money and started to take unnecessary risk. (They forgot the Customer!) Joseph Stiglitz[2] laments that Wall Street did not come up with a single good mortgage product to help homeowners manage the risk of homeownership; instead the financial institutions looked at maximizing their own returns, whereas they should have looked at what their Customers really wanted from the mortgage products! Business and profit strategies had overtaken Customer strategies. Total CVM would have put a greater focus on the Customer and may have prevented the kinds of problems that the world economies had to face.

Companies are spending more money on Customers through processes such as Customer Relationship Management (CRM), but the impact from a Customer perspective has been negative, according to US National Customer Rage Studies.[3] This *Total Customer Value Management* book helps

---

[1] I use the capital C for Customers to show their importance, and to show eventually that they are individuals and have a special place.

[2] Joseph Stiglitz, *Freefall: Free Markets and the Sinking of the Global Economy* (Allen Lane, 2010).

[3] Customer Care Alliance published this study first in 2003, then in 2004 and 2005. Arizona State University published one in April 2008.

businesses understand Customers' needs and prioritize Customer efforts and build lasting competitive advantage.

Total CVM is the logical sequel to my previous book, *Customer Value Investment.*[4] Total CVM builds on the known models of Customer Value Management (CVM) through more holistic and all embracing means to transform the entire organization to be Customer-led and Customer-motivated. It goes beyond CVM because Total CVM aligns the entire company (whether frontline employees or top managers) to the Customer. Business strategy flows from the Customer strategy and the Customers drive the organization to greater profit. (Remember, profits come because of Customers.) Total CVM goes beyond the hitherto known techniques of CVM which were restricted to Customer Value measurement, and Customer focus (including service, loyalty programmes and CRM), generally limited to a few departments.

To my knowledge, this book is the first to articulate the Total CVM concept globally.

BENEFITS OF TOTAL CVM TO YOUR COMPANY

Companies such as Tata Power, Tata Chemicals Crop Nutrition and Agri-Business, and Godrej HiCare have embraced Total CVM concepts leading to an organizational transformation and improved Customer Value, efficiency, teamwork, lower complaints, higher referrals and sales, and thereby increased profits.

In the past, Customer Value Foundation (CVF) and its global associates had been running truncated programmes focusing on only a few aspects of Total CVM (which we called CVM). Such programmes have been carried out in many more companies, ranging from financial institutions

---

[4] Gautam Mahajan, *Customer Value Investment: Formula for Sustained Business Success* (New Delhi: Response Books, 2008).

like Chase Manhattan, GE Capital, State Farm Insurance to manufacturing and consumer goods, from utilities to white goods, service industries, research organizations and retailers among other companies (like Mercedes Benz, Disney, Johnson and Johnson, Whirlpool, Philips, Wisconsin Energies, British Petroleum, Vodafone, AT&T, etc.). However, the entire gamut of transforming an organization to be driven by the Customer has been tried first in India in large Indian companies. CVF is now rolling out Total CVM programmes globally.

Just as the converted companies discovered, practising Total CVM revolutionizes corporate thinking by focusing on the key reason for your company's being: the Customer (rather than processes), and transforming your business towards market leadership and increased profits by creating a proactive Customer-focused company. Look at the quantifiable results companies have had by starting Total CVM programmes:

Marketplace

1. Measuring Customer Value Added, the ratio of the value you add to your Customers, versus the value your competitors add to their Customers.
2. Why people buy from you and not from your competitors, and vice versa, predicting loyalty, market share and improving business results. Increase market share and reducing pressure on price. De-commoditizing products.
3. Total marketplace assessment: Voice of the Customer and Voice of the Competitor.
4. Increased loyalty (it is a well known fact that a 5 per cent increase in loyalty increases profits from 25 per cent to 95 per cent, depending on industry).
5. Increased referrals, word of mouth sales, sales per salesman (as much as 30 per cent), less pressure on pricing, pricing from a Customer Value perspective.

6. Reduction of complaints by 70 per cent in the quarter following the Total CVM intervention. Customer satisfaction scores have improved by over 10 per cent.
7. Changing the rules of the marketplace, and making price less of an issue. Pricing from a Cutsomer value perspective, and getting more for your offerings.
8. Growing brand equity by building brand equity of employees and delivery chain.
9. Converting call centres to Action Centres.

Employees

1. Measure Voice of Employee, increase employee self-esteem, awareness, proactiveness and engagement. Using value to reduce employee and Customer churn. Build individual promises to ensure Customer's Bill of Rights. Build employees' brand equity.
2. Equate improvements in Employee Value, business processes, and Customer products and services to increased Customer loyalty and bottom line business benefits.
3. Helping CXOs[5] align better with Customers. For example:

   - For CFOs, measuring Customer Capital, Customer Assets, correlation between value and share price, pricing techniques based on the Customer and perceived value, segmenting Customers from Shareholder Value viewpoint, reporting CVA scores with financial data, looking at financial systems and billing/credit from convenience of Customer, etc. CFOs should become the Chief Shareholder Value Creators.

---

[5] CXO: A Chief Officer of a function, such as Chief Financial Officer, CFO.

Or

- For HRD heads, assessing Customer needs and providing education based on this, hiring based on Customer Value, measuring and adding Employee Value added, correlating Employee Value to Shareholder and Customer Value, reducing employee churn, improving Customer engagement, etc. The HRD head becomes the Chief Employee Value Creator and builds Customer tasks for his function.

4. Providing education to all levels of employees including touchpoints, and certifying them for their ability to handle and work with Customers.
5. Increase of teamwork and employee happiness, building of employee self esteem, awareness. Establishing a pro-active Customer-centric and Customer aligned organization.
6. Putting a Customer Performance Management System into place.
7. Using Customer Value metrics for rewards and recognition. Often Total CVM forms a major part of the Balanced Scorecard.

Within the Company

1. Improving service quality.
2. Building Customer-Centric-Circles, Customer Conduits and the Circle of Promises among employees to deliver the Customer's Bill of Rights. This also institutes a Continuous Customer Improvement Programme.
3. Understanding competitive strategies and pre-empting competitive moves by competition. Building Customer strategies to drive business strategies.
4. Using Customer Value to decide on product and technology offerings, using Customer Value for valuation

Total Customer Value Management

in M&A. This is necessary for telecom companies, pizza companies, because their valuation depends on Customers they have and their buying ability.
5. Understanding the deterioration in touching and Customer Value in the delivery chain. Improved Customer focus and Customer Value by channel partners leads to an increase of value in the distribution chain.
6. Using Customer Value for product decisions.

Shareholder Value

1. Increasing profits and Shareholder Value.
2. Make investors desirous of investing more with your company.

BOOK LAYOUT

This book is about explaining Total CVM, how it works, how it is implemented and the business results that ensue. It has been tried out in companies where strong quality, business excellence, business process re-engineering and satisfaction programmes exist. Total CVM has led to organizational transformation and change in business thinking, and will also alter your business's thinking and move your organization towards pro-active success, allowing you to re-define marketing paradigms. It will give you quantifiable success in loyalty, market share, improved price, and profits and shareholder value. It also improves Employee Value, their awareness and pro-activeness, teamwork, channel and distribution performance and internal Customer Value.

My earlier book described how Doug Evert, then a Sales Manager at Glacier Products, a packaged food company, changed from being a pure sales-oriented manager to a Customer-focused manager (and transformed from being a hunter to a farmer of Customers). The book describes how

Krish Kumar, the Customer Guru, guides Doug through this change. The book outlines the phenomenal results seen at the Newark, Ohio store of Grocery World, a retailer for Glacier. Customer Circles were first exposed in this book. The concept of Total CVM was touched upon, as the next management practice.

I learnt from feedback on this book, that my readers were able to relate to the characters and their roles, and learn positively from the experiences described in the book. The current book follows the same storytelling approach as the earlier book.

Doug, who has been promoted to President and CEO of Glacier's, and Krish Kumar are the main characters. Doug wants to make his company Customer-focused and Customer led. He asks Krish to guide him and his staff through this organizational transformation.

The book describes the transformation of Glacier Products to Total CVM. Different chapters enunciate what Total CVM is, how it compares to existing programmes in the company including Total Quality Management, Business Excellence, Satisfaction, CRM and loyalty programmes. The book also describes how Total CVM can help you change the rules of the marketplace by better Customer insight. Through real life examples, the book shows the success of Total CVM at various companies.

Total CVM concepts such as the Customer's Bill of Rights and the Customer Circle of Promises are described. Other new concepts include the Customer Performance Management system, driving Business Strategy from Customer Strategy, Continuous Customer Improvement Programmes and Task Audits.

The book progresses on to organizations of the future, and the MBA of the future. We argue that value creation should be the overarching goal for MBA teaching. The book shows how every department can be aligned to the Customer, and what their Customer-related tasks can be. Krish also educates the senior managers of Glacier on their Customer roles.

The book then describes the alignment of the frontline people to the Customer, and how a bottom-up Customer organization works, giving case studies.

The book goes on to explain certification processes for employees and for the company. The book addresses impediments to the installation of a Total CVM programme. In the Appendices, the book discusses a real case study on a Total CVM, examines the barriers to implementation of Total CVM and suggests solutions to overcome such barriers.

How is this book designed to deliver value to the Customer, the reader? Readers are at all levels of management, and so some parts of the book are elementary for some readers and advanced for others. However, remember that top management has to increase market share, profitability and Shareholder Value which are driven by Customers. Functional managers want to maximize their operations and this requires adding Customer Value, though most of the functional strategies do not mention the Customer. Remember what Peter Drucker[6] said? "What the Customer thinks he is buying and considers Value is decisive: it determines what a business is, what it produces and whether it will prosper!"

---

[6] Peter F. Drucker, *Management: Tasks, Responsibilities, Practices* (Harper Paperbacks, 1993). The late Peter Drucker is arguably one of the greatest management thinkers of all times.

1

Prologue: From Best Practices to Next Practices

Doug stretches himself in his new office. He has just been appointed President and CEO of the retail food division of Glacier Products,[1] a packaged food company selling ready-to-eat foods. Over the last few years, he had made remarkably fast progress from a marketing manager to Head of Marketing, Chief Customer Officer and now the President!

He remembers that much of his success could be attributed to the Customer focus that he had learnt from Krish Kumar, the Customer Guru. As Chief Customer Officer, he had not been able to get all the functions aligned to Customer-centricity as well as he would have liked. This was because Bob Ostrofsky, his predecessor and former boss, had been old-fashioned in his thinking, and was more engrossed in increasing profits. If you asked Bob if Customers were important, his response was, "Heck, yes!" But truly, Customers were never his focus. Doug's own efforts on making Glacier focus on Customers, setting up Customer-Centric-Circles, and understanding Customer needs and competitive data, such as Customer Value Added (CVA)[2] had resulted in improved market share

---

[1] Much of Doug's success is portrayed in Gautam Mahajan, *Customer Value Investment: Formula for Sustained Business Success* (New Delhi: Response Books, 2008).

[2] See Gautam Mahajan, *Customer Value Investment*.

and profitability. This had been demonstrated conclusively and had led to his meteoric rise within Glacier.

If you are a president of a business, even one recently appointed, how can you make a tangible and measurable difference to your employees, to the business and the shareholders? How can you change the rules of the game you have learned through years of experience and extensive study in business administration, where processes and business process re-engineering become the prime objective? How do you stop chasing best practices and build next practices? You need Customer programmes focusing on Customer Value and Employee Value leading to Shareholder Value. This includes value creation for employees, Customers and shareholders in tandem.

And if you, as the president of a business, wanted to re-focus your business, where would you start? You would start with your Customers, winning them over to your side and getting their heart-share. And to do this you would add value to your employees, and build their awareness and self-esteem. And you would drive the business from these. No one would say you were wrong. But people will look at you quizzically. After all, this is not what is normally done. But, if measuring Customer assets were mandated by law (and their reporting was necessary on balance sheets), you would do this diligently, and develop means to improve Customer assets.

Doug continued his thought process. Was the route to the top through normal functions? How many Chief Customer Officers like Doug had made it to the top? Or, thought Doug, how many companies even have this function? Why not? Because the Customer activities were considered adequate, and other functions were more important. He had been one of the exceptions who had been a Chief Customer Officer.

Doug starts thinking. How is he going to make Glacier Products a dominant company, which will sustain market and business leadership for a long time? Profits are healthy. Market share has been increasing. However, competition was

catching up. Glacier has to think of staying ahead of competition. Processes can be copied. It is much more difficult to
emulate mindset changes, and these are tangible competitive
advantages. This calls for new and improved practices or
next practices, not just best practices.

He looks at the plaque on his desk. It says Customer-in-
Centre© (see Figure 1.1). He needs to find a way to place the
Customer in the centre of the business. But to do so, he has
to change the thinking of many of his CXOs.

FIGURE 1.1
Customer-in-Centre©

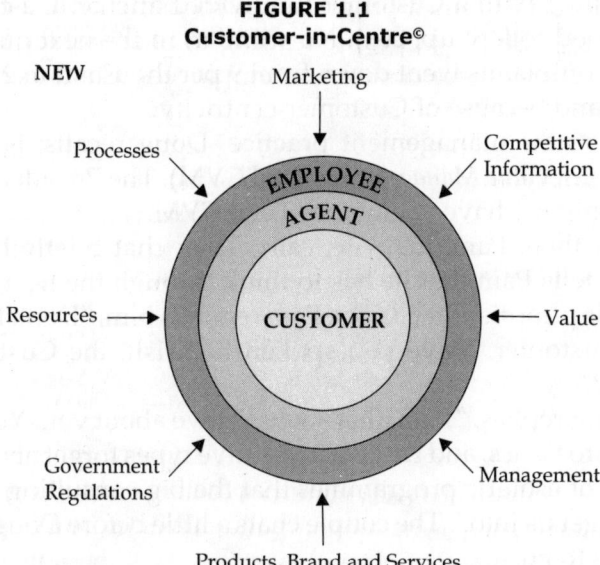

Source Gautam Mahajan, *Customer Value Investment.*

He remembers various success stories of companies
who attributed success to the Customer focus. In the recent
economic downturn, one of the Tata company's market share
had gone up, and they partially ascribed this to Customer
Value Management. This Tata company has set up Customer-
Centric-Circles, and understanding Customer needs and
competitive data (CVA) had resulted in improved market
share and profitability, and less price pressure.

Another example is where Tata Power's Customer Circles discovered obvious Customer-related activities and suggestions that were being overlooked because there was no such Customer focus. One example was that it was difficult for Customers to visit the Customer Relations department in the head office to correct their bills or to transact other business. Members of the Customer Circles put up direction signs leading to the Customer Relations office (the members were actually seen putting up signs), assigned an area for Customer meetings, and ensured basic hygiene in dealing with a Customer (undivided attention, a cup of tea, good follow up, etc.). No wonder, in the next quarter, their complaints went down from 9 per thousand to 2.7 per thousand because of Customer-centricity.

This new management practice, Doug recalls, is *Total Customer Value Management* (Total CVM). The President and his company have to embrace Total CVM.

Just then, Pam, his wife, calls. They chat briefly before Doug tells Pam that he has to think through the next steps and his priorities for Glacier. Pam reminds him, "Don't forget the Customer. Have you spoken to Krish, the Customer Guru?"

Doug replies, "Pam, that's what I love about you. You get down to basics, and make us executive types forget about all kinds of esoteric programmes that the big consulting types try to get us into." The couple chats a little before Doug says he has to go.

Doug starts to think about what Pam had said.

Doug is now sure. He remembers what Krish had told him about Total CVM. He and Glacier have to introduce Total CVM. He recalls what he has learnt through his previous work on CVM (some of these are shown in Appendix III: "Where We Left Off with *Customer Value Investment: Formula for Sustained Business Success*" at the end of this book).

This is going to take some doing. He is sure he will need help. And who better than the Customer Guru who had got him going earlier?

Doug calls Krish Kumar, the Customer Guru, to set up a meeting. Krish says he will send a discussion paper to him. The following are excerpts from what Krish sends Doug:

TOTAL CVM DISCUSSION PAPER
FOR GLACIER PRODUCTS

The focal Customer is generally the person who is paying the bills, but is also the end Customer or even the consumer. There are channel partners or channel Customers, internal Customers and in a sense stakeholders who are also Customers. Bomi Shroff, VP of Corporate Communications at Tata Power, looks at the company's shareholders as Customers to interact with, keep informed and happy. There are instances in any company where the external Customer is difficult to define, for example, in a company's project division. Here we have internal Customers or sometimes non-Customers (people who are not Customers but need to be treated as Customers).

Tata Power is looking at introducing Total CVM even in its Project Division where there are no external Customers. What are they trying to achieve? It is organizational transformation, which requires an attitudinal change in the company, starting with the employees' attitudes. Total CVM seeks to change attitudes towards being positive to one's Customers, whoever they be. It seeks to get self-driven employees focusing on Customers. It builds an awareness of the employees about themselves and what is happening around them. It develops a sensitivity for fellow employees, and in fact for everyone they interact with, whether suppliers, colleagues or Customers. It is the building of a community spirit within and outside the company, while growing Customer-centricity. Of course, there are measurable results, such as reduction of complaints almost threefold.

Attitudes are more difficult to alter, especially where companies are profitable, growing, or where their market share is increasing, or where habits and methodologies are well established. It is often easier to change attitudes where the employees are younger, looking for leadership and to learn.

Mindsets are historically harder to change at the top levels than at the bottom levels. This is a sad commentary on top management who often feel they "know it all!" and do not see the need to change. Also, they are caught up so much on their traditional and functional roles that they really do not have time for nor see the need to change from what has been a "successful" approach to business. The CEO's role here becomes very significant to make a Customer-centric change occur.

Value Creation for Stakeholders

Total CVM creates value for all stakeholders by first creating value for:

- Employees or Employee Value, engagement and employee brand quity
- Internal Customers
- Channel Partners or Channel Value
- Non-Customers like suppliers
- External Customers, and thereby to the
- Shareholders

Total CVM also builds value for suppliers, because they are treated as partners; also because they are dealing with a company which will become healthier and stronger! Total CVM increases the value creation (or stops value destruction) in the delivery chain and builds brand equity of the employees and the channel partners.

As value increases, the Customers reward the company with loyalty (because of the value and the delight they receive in dealing with or associating with the company, and the trust they now have in the company based on their positive experiences), improved brand image, market share and profits. Shareholder Value and stock prices increase disproportionately to the value increase (a 1 per cent increase in value increases share prices by 4.6 per cent).[3]

You have to be a first mover in building a value chain from employee to shareholder. Change attitudes in the chain, thereby forming an organization that consistently and continuously builds Customer Value, hence ensuring the future of the employees, managers and CEO, and the future of the owners!

Customer Value Metrics

Many managers are more interested in the metrics when they are sceptical of Total CVM. Metrics (these are defined later in the book) that improve with implementing Total CVM are:

- Employee attitude and teamwork, measured by employee churn, and by Employee Value added (the latter is a better metric than mere employee retention).
- Customer churn, measured by retention, but better still is CVA and Customer loyalty. Other than loyalty metric, such as referrals, wallet share, market share, total number of Customers and the increase of value of Customers are useful metrics.
- Better pricing, and seen by lower price pressure.
- Higher market share.

---

[3] Claes Fornell, Sunil Mithas, Forrest V. Morgeson III and M.S. Krishnan, "Customer Satisfaction and Stock Prices: High Returns, Low Risk," *Journal of Marketing* 70 (January 2006): 3–14.

- Improved profitability.
- Increased CVA and Customer satisfaction.
- Increased Business Excellence scores.
- Increased value of Customer, and Customer Lifetime Value.
- Value to company, and Return on Customers (ROC).
- Higher Shareholder Value.

Eventually we need to have a Customer Performance Management System based on people performance on Customer interaction, including number of times a Customer needs to contact a company for an interaction, whether systems work or not, correcting system and systemic problems, and on Customer delight. For many companies, the fact that Customers do not need to contact them is the best metric, because Customers contact companies if they have a problem or if they cannot understand something.

OUTLINE OF WHAT TOTAL CVM IS

As I stated earlier, if there were a Customer rating of your company (not just your products or services), where would Customers put your company on a 1 to 10 point scale? If you never touch the Customers, or Customers anticipate poor experiences or attitudes, or they do not trust you, they may rate you closer to 1. However, if Customers experienced all or even more than what they want in treatment—fairness, partnership, being viewed as individuals, being given customized offerings, proper warranties and servicing, guaranteed to get the best and in co-creation of Customer experience—you would probably get closer to a 10 from them.

In addition, if there were this rating, you might be shocked at the difference between where you expect to be rated versus what Customers think. Moreover, if the rating were on a global basis, not just based on where you are versus competition (for example, if you were the best in a poor

Customer-centric industry) your rating will not be 10 because you are the best of the lot (the cream of the crap); it might be a 3 or a 5.

Moreover, getting this rating up towards a 10 requires an all-round effort to become Customer-centric and Customer-friendly. Additionally, the business returns to the company, and to shareholders and change in organizational thinking are tremendous. This has been demonstrated case after case. It is known that a 5 per cent change in the rate of Customer retention swings profit increase from 25 per cent all the way to 100 per cent. Customer service is an important part of Total CVM. Great Customer service is not just the effort of a Customer Service department (and Customer service should not always be outsourced as Delta Airways found[4]), it requires a total focus on the Customer, from leadership, flowing through various departments, a shared purpose, vision and culture to make the Customer happy. That is what Total CVM achieves.

Generally, doing things correctly for the Customer doesn't cost much. It is often just doing the right things, which you should be doing in any event. Unfortunately, you often take your eyes off the fundamentals as you become far too busy with other "more urgent" priorities than the Customer priority.

All business people will agree that the Customer is important. Yet many do not give them any importance and often treat them purely as "sales". Examples include Indian white goods retailers who only want to immediately "sell" and not create a relationship with the Customer. Then they wonder why Customers become price sensitive.

Some companies do far more for the Customer, but often are process driven, not Customer driven. Customer Relationship Management (CRM), for example, is a passive process. Measuring satisfaction is a form of feedback but is an

---

[4] Delta pulled out of outsourcing to call centres overseas because of the negative impact on North American Customers.

incomplete measure. Satisfaction measurements have been proven not to reflect true Customer Value and do not relate to loyalty.

Take travellers who are loyal to one airline. They may travel sometimes on other airlines, and may be very satisfied. Do they switch their loyalties? What happens when the airline they are loyal to lets them down or dissatisfies them? Do they stop using the airline? Probably not. At best, satisfaction is a necessary condition but not sufficient to ensure loyalty.

Then there are companies who believe they are doing everything for the Customer. Their knowledge of what they could do for the Customer is limited to currently available techniques. Total CVM has been shown to increase their repertoire of Customer Value knowledge multifold.

Some companies bring in Customer service processes. But they do this without changing the attitudes of the people charged with systemically solving problems for Customers. Credit card companies, airlines and telecom companies are generally guilty of this.

Then, why don't companies change?

I don't think any business executive is so callous as not to care for the Customer in his heart. He simply does not know all that he could and must do to make his organization Customer-centric.

First, it all starts with an attitudinal change at the top, where CEOs have to stop being gods, because an organization can have only one god: either the CEO or the Customer. The choice is often not that simple. Total CVM helps organizations understand why the transformation is necessary, and how to do so. Leadership transformation is a key to Total CVM.

Second, an alignment of all top managers, employees and functions towards Customers becomes necessary. Saying or thinking "I have nothing or very little to do with the Customer in my job" really means you are not ready to start on a Customer-centric process. Total CVM helps executives and employees align to the Customer, not just the organization.

Third, the key to Total CVM is mindset. A great attitude only at the top towards Customers is not enough. You also need a great attitude at the bottom and in the delivery chain. Total CVM helps companies by encouraging their employees to not only build self-esteem, awareness and caring, but also to be self-driven and proactive to do the right things for the Customers.

Total CVM helps bring in self-esteem and awareness of, and a focus on Customers by employees. This bottom-up approach has been tested at Tata Power, Tata Chemicals Crop Nutrition and Agri-Business, and Godrej, through setting up Customer Circles, and has brought tremendous enthusiasm and change.

The Customer Circle of Promises is instituted through the Customer Bill of Rights, which ensures co-ordination of individual team players in ensuring the Customer's rights are maintained.

The key is not to dampen this new enthusiasm by putting these Customer Circles under traditional project management, but to allow the roll out to be employee-driven and driven by the employees' hearts, thereby changing organizational culture.

Fourth is capturing the Voice of the Employee, Voice of the Customer and Voice of the Competitor. The Voice of the Employee is measured by Employee Value Added (EVA), and by conversational means. The Voice of the Customer and the Voice of the Competitor are captured not through satisfaction but through value surveys and using a metric called CVA. Other Customer metrics are also necessary to get to a Customer Performance Management System.

$$\text{Employee Value Added (EVA)} = \frac{\text{Perceived Value your company adds to its employees}}{\text{Perceived Value competitors add to its employees}}$$

$$\text{Customer Value Added (CVA)} = \frac{\text{Perceived worth of your offer}}{\text{Perceived worth of competitive offer}}$$

CVA is an important concept. Just like companies do not wish to have negative, or lower than industry economic value added, they cannot afford to have lower than par for CVA. If CVA remains lower than this for two years, companies have to either close down or change management.

CVA relates to loyalty, market share, ROI and wallet share. CVA is used in Balanced Scorecards and goal setting.

Fifth is Customer-centric education and certification of frontline employees (and all employees if possible). This includes sales clerks, marketing people, service persons and many more.

Sixth is the manner in which you roll out the Customer mindset with the development of Customer-centric and flexible processes. Once you have the fundamentals in place, then you are ready to rework your processes to give you competitive advantage. Every effort should be to make them Customer-driven processes. Companies, such as American Express, strive to have Customer-driven processes, but do not always succeed, because there is such a deep-seated focus on the company itself and on overall efficiency instead.

Seventh, you embark on co-creating Customer experience. The Customer is your business partner. You should co-control the business with the Customer. Gone are the days where companies could control their suppliers, and could attempt to control their Customers (whose suppliers companies are). How many times do you hear a company or a store tell you, "This is our policy or this is our process"? (As a Customer, I would like to impose my process on my supplier, that is, your company.)

Why can't I charge them my fees for the harassment and time? I don't want to sound like a consumer advocate, but I most certainly would like companies to think about co-controlling and co-creating experiences, and establishing more of a partnership (and an equal partnership) role. A student–teacher partnership or an employee–company partnership are not equal partnerships. Attaining an equal Customer–company (or should I say supplier?) partnership is the goal!

So that leads us to the Eighth precept where you start to customize and begin to treat each Customer as an individual with customized needs.

Ninth, companies have to be prepared to be judged as companies, and not for their products alone by their Customers. This includes Customer trust, the perception Customers have of the company's fairness and the treatment they can expect from the company. And this judgement can finally change the company's Customer thought processes and build the brand further.

And lest we forget, the Tenth factor has to be the value to the company. Is this value increasing? It undoubtedly will if the precepts detailed in this chapter are followed. Value to the company includes total shareholder value, Customer Lifetime Value, ROC and even value to the employee.

All these have to be put together into a Customer strategy, which is aligned both to the Customer and to the corporate strategy.

Unfortunately, companies pick up bits and pieces of the Customer-centric actions and miss the fundamentals. Most often, they chase the tenth factor (increasing value to the company), which most large consulting houses espouse. But they inevitably neglect many of the key concepts that make up Total CVM.

Often, companies believe simply having good processes will drive them to success. And they become process driven and system driven. A form of process bureaucracy creeps in, making the process more important than the people or the Customer. Sometimes they believe having a call centre is akin to Customer friendliness or Customer focus. (One other task we achieve for companies is to convert call centres to Action Centres.) Or others believe that great Customer service will balance everything and put service standards in place without changing attitudes or culture.

Therefore, there is a litany of well-meaning but insufficient or poorly thought-out actions, which lead companies to wonder why such highly touted initiatives don't deliver promised results.

Total CVM will help companies design a strategy to become Customer-centric by taking a holistic view of the Customer and build profitability and shareholder value.

2

Total CVM and the Company

K rish Kumar and Doug are sitting in Doug's new office. Krish is admiring the office, its sheer size and elegance.

"*Boy, you sure have come a long way from being a hunter.[1] Recall that we really had to work together to strike a balance between hunting and farming.*"[2]

Doug adds, "I do remember that we put together the focus on Customers in Newark, Ohio in the Grocery World[3] store, by using Customer-Centric-Circles or as some people prefer, Customer Circles. In addition, I recollect the great results we got and how we converted Bob Ostrofsky, the former CEO, to start taking Customers more seriously. And we put together the Customer Strategy session and the roll out of our Customer focused ideas into all of Ohio."

"*That was the start of your meteoric rise,*" says Krish Kumar, "*as you changed the rules of the game in the retail world, by introducing and practicing Customer Value and using the concept of Customer Circles for the first time.*"[4]

---

[1] That is, a marketing person adding new Customers to increase sales; see Gautam Mahajan, *Customer Value Investment: Formula for Sustained Business Success* (New Delhi: Response Books, 2008).

[2] A farmer is a marketing person who nurtures his Customers to grow them and his business with them, described in Gautam Mahajan, *Customer Value Investment.*

[3] See Gautam Mahajan, *Customer Value Investment.* Grocery World is a retail store that was used for piloting CVM work by Glacier, which is a packaged foods company.

[4] See Gautam Mahajan, *Customer Value Investment.*

Doug interrupts, "But I now realize that is not enough. We still do not have everyone aligned and pulling in the Customer's direction. Glacier is ahead of competition, but competition is catching up as they incorporate our ideas and the learnings from our Customer Value work. We are in a competitive world, and the competition is not standing still. We have to find better ways to look after the Customer.

"Our results have shown that the investment in Customer Value makes eminent sense.[5] The bulk of the investment in Customer Value costs us nothing, because we are aligning many of our people, including frontline people to understand the Customer, and to think through, and do the right things for the Customer. In addition, the frontline people brainstorm what annoys Customers, and then figure out how to first understand and then avoid the Customer's DNA (Do Not Annoy) factors. They even went further and thought about the Customer's delight factors. Every time we annoy the Customer, say the wrong thing such as 'this is our policy' or 'this is the way we do things', the Customer gets his back up and the value we are providing decreases.

"I am convinced when we all pull together and truly put the Customer-in-Centre,[6] we will improve the value we add to the Customer. This will make the Customer more loyal to us, and want to do more business with us.

"When that happens, our market share increases, and because we are more Customer-focused, we make fewer mistakes in dealing with Customers. We become more efficient and so our costs are reduced. Higher market share, better efficiency means higher ROI. Couple this with increased wallet share and we keep getting ahead. No wonder CVI or Customer Value Investment gives higher ROI."

---

[5] See Gautam Mahajan, *Customer Value Investment*.

[6] See Gautam Mahajan, *Customer Value Investment*, a concept first outlined there. The Customer has to be in the Centre of any business, and not a corollary to it.

$$CVI = Higher\ ROI^{©}$$

Doug continues, "But I wish to add even more value to the Customer. Moreover, I want to be successful. The new initiative I want to bring into Glacier and prove at the retail level with our eventual Customers (the person who buys and consumes our products) that we are a superior supplier to others in competition with us and that we can change the rules of the game in our business and in the retail chain. This is the concept of Total CVM. I truly believe this will revolutionize management thinking and transform business thinking."

Krish interrupts: "*I don't think we should do this at Grocery World yet. Let's keep it focused to transform your organization to be Customer-led. In any event, Grocery World will start to see an impact automatically as we change to deliver more value to the Customer.*"

"I agree. To get started internally, I will have to get our top managers, and our CXOs to embrace Total CVM. We'll have to work with them and show them what role they have with the Customer.

"Krish, you have always talked about Total CVM. What do you think? Are we ready to implement it? Can we really be successful at it?"

The Customer Guru enthusiastically responds, "*You're dead right. Total CVM will put you miles ahead of the competition. But, first, you'll have to change your own thinking. Simultaneously, your top officers must understand this. I suggest we discuss this together, and later with your officers.*

"*Second, you will have to review the tasks people in Glacier perform from a Customer perspective.*

"*What you did earlier were bits and pieces of what we call Total CVM. Customer Value Management was what we knew, when we started our journey at Grocery World, and now we are starting to learn how much more CVM can be. In fact, it pervades the whole organization. And to make this happen we move on to Total CVM which helps convert the entire company and its strategy to be driven by the Customer and his needs, and the pursuit of Customer happiness!*

"Total Customer Value is about revolutionizing and transforming management and business thinking. You have to modify your traditional management learning and experience to get long-term success. Profit no longer drives your philosophy. Profit is a result of your new thought process, one where Customer thinking guides your business ideas and leads you to profits and success. In fact, it creates organizational transformation. Witness that Deming[7] stopped using the term Total Quality, replacing it by 'transformation of the prevailing system of management', the real work of a company. Total CVM does just this.

"As you do this, you'll have to make certain to differentiate Customer Management from Customer Value Management and eventually from Total Customer Value Management."

CUSTOMER MANAGEMENT OR CVM?

Doug says, "I also remember why Total CVM is *Total Customer Value Management* and not Total Customer Management. The aim is not to manage the Customer but to add value to him. In the past, we tried to control the Customer, and manage him. Now we need to let the Customer manage us into providing him with more value. We need to put the Customer-in-Control."

Krish adds, *"Top leadership buy-in is absolutely crucial to the transformation of a company to be Customer-focused. The entire team has to believe in Customer Value leading to alignment and*

---

[7] William Edwards Deming was an American statistician, professor, author, lecturer and consultant. Deming is widely credited with improving productivity in the United States during World War II. Deming made a significant contribution to Japan's later renown for innovative high-quality products and its economic power. He is regarded as having had more impact upon Japanese manufacturing and business than any other individual not of Japanese heritage.

a strategy that enunciates a Vision, Mission, Values, Goals, and then leading to proactive action.

"Customer-focused attitudes of the organization and its people create Customer-centricity. Making the frontline people responsible for and thinking about the Customer is a crucial step.

"Values (just like Customers) cannot be delegated.

"Also, remember, the world is changing. Nothing is constant. We tend to be reactive in business, and we react to problems that seem big. We tend to ignore issues that creep up slowly.

"For example, take slow loss of Customers. You think you can make up the loss through acquisition and you do not do anything drastic. I'll give you examples of state-owned (or public sector) companies in India, two telephone companies, MTNL and BSNL, and the other, an airlines company, Indian Airlines (now merged with Air India). Both had dominant shares and were virtual monopolies. When private companies were allowed to enter these sectors, the dominant public sector companies did not react swiftly, and initially their market shares eroded slowly. By the time they reacted, their market shares had eroded considerably, and it is doubtful if they can regain lost ground. To do this, their organizations will have to transform themselves into being proactive and Customer focused to add more value to their Customers.

"What happens is the well known Boiling Frog Principle (see Box 2.1).

BOX 2.1
Boiling Frog Principle

A frog thrown into a pan of boiling water will try to jump out of the pan and escape. However, if it is put into a pan of cold water, which is slowly heated up, it does not react until the water becomes too uncomfortably hot. By this time, the frog has become lethargic and finds it difficult to jump out, even though he attempts to.

"Total CVM would have helped these companies to be more aware of the Customer, thereby becoming proactive, not reactive. Keep in mind that Total CVM is becoming not purely a 'local' management technique, but should be applied globally by a variety of companies."

Doug gives an example, "I read in the US in 2009, the focus of the financial sector in the wake of the current financial crisis will move from fire-fighting to fire-prevention, which is what they would have done in the first place were they following the Boiling Frog principle."

TOTAL CVM

"I agree," says Doug, "I see Customer Value becoming more and more recognized globally. Although more companies are using it, the fact is that Total CVM as described here is not currently prevalent."

"Why I wish to explain this," Krish says, looking Doug in the eye, *"is because many people will say we are practising CVM. Some companies have many elements of Total CVM in use. However, I know of no company in the world other than a few companies in India such as Tata Power, Tata Chemicals Crop Nutrition and Agri-Business and Godrej HiCare who have Total CVM programmes in place."*

STEPS TOWARDS TOTAL CVM

Total CVM requires that the company becomes totally Customer-centric and builds a Customer culture. The elements outlined below are ongoing, and must be practised incessantly. Krish hands Doug a folder called **Steps towards Total CVM**.

A. Business Strategy must be Customer-driven

Krish states, *"In the final analysis, a business strategy should follow a Customer strategy and a shareholder strategy. Kanazawa and Miles[8] make a case for more focus in a company, and the focus to be Customer-led. In fact, well-focused companies, according to them, drive to set (not meet) best practices, which provide the highest value points for the Customer. They build a Customer Vision, Mission and Strategy first. Examples of companies who use Customer strategies are Cigna, Netezza and American Family Mutual Insurance. Cigna's Customer strategy puts the Customer in the centre of their universe!"*

Doug agrees, "You've always said, 'Move from Best Practices to Next Practices. Set the standards that are Customer-led.' In fact, I would call our Customer Vision our Passion!"

Krish nods in agreement. He continues, *"Absolutely right, Doug! A company has to build a unique standing in the eyes of a Customer or it is nothing!*

"Today there is overload on executives with too many competing priorities. Driving the Business strategy from the Customer strategy puts the focus on the most important part of your business, and then there is no excuse not to have time for the Customer. Focus, according to Kanazawa and Miles, is not doing less work overall but about doing more on fewer and focused tasks. In fact, they say CEOs are afraid that if they admit the organization is doing too many things, they will not be able to motivate the team to do more!

"Normally business strategies are postulated by looking at the market place and the competitors, and a SWOT analysis (basically Strengths, Weaknesses, Opportunities and Threats) is conducted. In a company led by Total CVM, we start with the Customer. We examine why we cannot get close to him or how we can. We investigate if we do get close to the Customer and understand him, how can we change the rules of the marketplace by providing the Customer what he wants, and not just what he needs

---

[8] Michael T. Kanazawa and Robert H. Miles, *Big Ideas to Big Results: Remake and Recharge Your Company, Fast* (Financial Times Press, 2008).

(latent or otherwise). The change of rules of the game results in your providing the Customer what he truly demands (in goods and services), to the detriment of your competitors, who have been following traditional practices. Remember, it is easier to copy products than to copy attitudes."

Why Customer-led Strategies and Marketing-led Strategies Might Lead to Different Business Strategies

Doug does not agree, "Wait a minute, Mr Customer Guru. In all of our strategy sessions, we look at the marketplace, and therefore the Customer is taken into account. You know as well as I do that strategy is all about making choices with incomplete data, and uncertainty. However, we all make our best-reasoned guess of the future and the risk, and trade-offs, and base our strategy on that. One important reason to have a strategy is to not only understand competition but also get ahead of and out-manoeuvre them. That means if we all have the same strategy, then it is a toss-up on who wins. It perhaps is the one with the best implementation. But to increase your chances of winning you have to have a differentiated strategy stating what you want to do or be, and what you don't want to do or be. In fact, strategies become more important when you have a commodity product, and you try to differentiate it."

Krish responds, *"Absolutely right. And certainly one way of differentiating is on the way you view the Customer. You build a Customer strategy, because you want to focus your thinking on the most important piece of your business, the Customer. You make a choice on whether you want to view your Customers as a faceless mass, or differentiate them by segments based on size, product use, needs, etc., or whether you can differentiate yourself by attempting to view each Customer as an individual. You want to change the attitudes in and the culture of your company.*

"*Next, you start to look at the various needs of the Customer, using the hierarchy of needs, including the unmet needs (and beyond wants).*

"*You assess the price sensitiveness based on the value perception of the Customer, the product aptitude based on needs. In India, some large unmet wants were entertainment, and hence the ingress of the TV in the home, not just black and white, but also high-end colour TVs. Cell phones are a classic example of unmet needs, and therefore the fast penetration in the country of such phones, including in remote areas. The phone is not only a status symbol, but helps people keep in touch, small business people become more accessible and so on.*"

Doug says, "So what I am hearing is that you start with your Customer or potential Customers.

"So, first, look at existing Customers. We spend 80 per cent of our advertizing on attracting new Customers, but hardly any money on existing Customers. A Customer strategy will make us rethink this. Moreover, Charles Schwab said that in the financial crisis, investment firms forgot they were handling the Customer's money. They were too busy driving their business from their profit and the market strategy.

"With a Customer strategy, we could ask if we could expand geographically with Customers, can we provide more products to them and whether we can customize. How do we make them accessible to us? How do we make them loyal? What are the strategies to do this? And how will they drive the business strategy in incorporating these as a pillar of business success?"

Krish agrees, "*Yes, absolutely. It takes away the age-old focus on profits and traditional internal thinking. We also move from product-centric to Customer-centric.*"

"Quite right," adds Doug. "Nestle is a product-centric company and Proctor and Gamble is a Customer-focused company. Both are in consumer-packaged goods. P&G's strategy translates to a closer relationship with retailers and global supply chain partnerships."

"*Yes, I accept this,*" says Krish. "*But another difference is that product-centric companies try to sell the same product to as many*

Customers as possible, regardless of how different those Customers were. The product-centric model is based on an efficiency model, to maximize its own revenues. This was how Glacier was when we first met.

"A Customer-focused strategy maximizes revenues from Customers rather than products. A Customer-focused strategy delivers different services to different Customers based on how unique the Customers are. The Customer-centric strategy builds efficiency with growth."

Doug states, "One can start with a product and find as many Customers as possible. Or the other (Customer) strategy is to start with the Customer's needs and find as many solutions for that Customer. I can see this difference is not just words, but represents different value pro >ositions, a different organizational structure, a different pricing model and different methods of connecting with the Customers. A truly Customer strategy driven company will do things completely differently and not marginally differently from the old product-centric business strategy led company."

Krish agrees, *"You are right. More important, the Customer strategy and the shareholder's strategy must be put together in determining business strategy. A large firm may dictate their division remains only in the software space and not in hardware, even though Customer needs may go beyond that. Another thought the shareholder may have is that they want to be focused in a particular geography. Some shareholder's strategies prohibit entry into tobacco and liquor, whereas our Customer strategy may try to lead us there.*

"It is possible that your view of the marketplace is in sync with that of the Customer. But often we have Customer myopia, and we look at the Customer through our impression of the marketplace. Take the sub-prime crisis. The banks took their eyes off the Customer, and what happened? The strategies were led from a market potential to consolidate mortgages, and the focus was to sell these, and not to see if the Customers were creditworthy and whether they were too stretched. In addition, there was an over-reliance on external

credit ratings and models, rather than a true view of the Customer, the homeowner.

"According to Joseph Stiglitz, Customers wanted products that would protect them when interest rates went up or housing prices dropped. The mortgage companies' strategy ignored the Customers' needs and focused on bundling mortgages, so that they could recycle their loan funds.

"The Customers did not care about bundling of mortgages, did they? Charles Scwab said that we all forgot that the money we were risking was not ours but our Customers'!

"In addition, without a Customer strategy, we tend to forget Customers. Rick Germano of Comcast, when their business was hurt by Customer discontent, said that Comcast's business reputation had been harmed. He stated companies cannot hide their problems any longer, and that now Comcast was going out and trying to listen to Customers, and ask what they needed to do to get their reputation back.

"This is why you must have Customer-led business strategies."

Doug, who has listened intently, remarks, "In the aftermath of the recent global financial crisis, one of the recommendations for the future to financial institutions is to focus on cash/capital, conservatism, closeness, convergence, consolidation, cost consciousness and communication. *The most important 'C', the Customer is missing!* However, I would suspect though, closeness means closeness to the business model and the Customer through simplicity and transparency, and could also mean Customer-centricity. I would have preferred the 'C' word to have been spelled out as opposed to sounding as an after thought.

"And if it meant Customer-centricity, why wasn't that a strict norm during the start of the subprime crisis?"

Krish is grinning, *"You just made my point!*

"The marketplace for a fertilizer company may be fertilizer and allied products, but the real need to be addressed is that of the farmer. Small farmers need help with farm income improvement, and for better advice and knowledge, and help in marketing their produce. Such focus might throw up different opportunities."

"Changing communications available to the farmer, such as mobile phones, can provide different selling opportunities. Farm insurance is a selling opportunity. Helping farmers get subsidized products, such as pipes, in a corruption-prone environment is another opportunity. Another need is crisis support. Currently, credit needed in a crisis, for example, is given by the moneylender in India, or the retailer, or a middleman. Maybe supporting microfinance is a possibility," adds Doug.

"Then the strategy becomes dynamic and can take advantage of the Customer's changing needs, well before competition becomes aware of the changing nuances and wakes up to the new reality."

"This is the fundamental strength of the Total CVM approach. We do not have to play catch up. Others (our competitors) do!" articulates Krish.

"I just got off the phone with a Godrej executive, after discussing the action steps from the CVA study, and the Customer Circles. The executive reminded me that they were driven by their strategy, which focused on the bottom-line, the profit, and processes. Can the Customer compete with these priorities? The priorities and strategy have to be devised differently for the Customer to have his rightful place in the organization.

"For a long time, we have been used to driving businesses in a certain way. We have vision statements and mission statements. We derive our strategy from them. This has been accepted as the norm.

"However, today the relevance of the Customer is becoming increasingly clearer. So much so that there is a profound understanding that the Customer is the reason for the business to exist. Therefore, the vision of the Customer and his mission should drive our strategy.

"For many, this is heretic. However, stop and think about it. If we truly understand the Customer, we will devise strategies to meet his needs for now and the future. We will understand the marketplace. We will temper our strategy to allow for customization, and co-creation of Customer experience.

"We will then work out the business strategies and the financials based on this deep Customer understanding and Customer-driven strategic thrust.

"We want our functions to be in harmony with our strategy. If our strategy is in accord with the Customer, won't all our functions, too, be in harmony with the Customer? Moreover, the stranglehold on strategy of the Products, Profits, Price and Processes will decrease.

"The first step for building a business Strategy is:

1. Build a Customer strategy that ultimately translates (along with the shareholder's strategy) as a Customer-led business strategy. In any event, the business strategy is driven by the Customer, his changing needs and competitive action (the marketplace!).

   a. Define Customer.

      "Customers are internal and external, or shareholders or other stakeholders or channel partners. See if Customers can become partners. We must start the exercise by defining our Customer. The Customer, of course, is the external Customer who buys our product, and sometimes the consumer. An example of a consumer is a person who receives a greeting card from the purchaser or Customer. Fish is the consumer of the lure the angler buys, and so fish is the ultimate Customer of the lure manufacturer. Why? Because if the fish is not attracted to the lure it will not bite, and the angler will not buy the lure.

      "Another example is the greeting cards we buy. We buy them to send to others, and if the recipients do not like them, then are they worth buying?

      "For a fertilizer, the ultimate consumer is the plant, and if the fertilizer helps the plant to grow well and the farmer to make money, then the farmer will continue to buy the fertilizer.

      "Channel partners are also Customers. Many companies duck this by thinking that by calling a dealer or *a retailer a partner takes them off the hook in thinking of them as Customers. Generally, dependent channel-partners treat the supplier as the Customer, not the reverse.*

"Internal Customers should also be treated as external Customers. I was with the Human Resources department of a company who were in a Customer Circle. Their reputation was one of being distant, and employees had difficulty getting help. During the Customer Circle meeting, they were reluctant to treat the other employees as Customers, until I reminded them that their jobs could become redundant if the services they provided were outsourced. If they were to provide the same service as an outsourced agency, they would be judged by their (now) external Customers. They got the message and got down to the job of figuring out how they should change to make their internal Customers happy."

Doug, who has been listening intently, says it is also necessary to understand what prevents us from treating people like Customers. "For example, take channel partners. We often say they are our partners, but the partnership is often unequal. The company (supplier) often is dominant. This changes when you sell through a powerful retailer like Wal-Mart. Assuming the company is the dominant partner, it calls the shots and often even defines the partnership. It becomes difficult for the company's people to treat them as Customers!"

"That is absolutely right. Doug, we ought to incorporate this in our strategy brainstorming session," adds Krish. *"This includes not having a choice of service provider. This is especially true when you are an internal Customer. And the realization that you are captive often prevents a true Customer focus."* He continues to refer to his notes.

b. Strategy for each segment of Customers including channel partners and internal Customers.

"Eventually we have to try to customize offerings for every single Customer. Often, this is not possible nor is it easy to do. Therefore, the least we can do is to define the Customer segments as finely as possible and define the value of each Customer segment, pruning back on those giving us poor value."

Doug mentions, "Each set of Customers requires a different strategy, which is then built into the corporate strategy."

Krish continues:

c. Replace profits as the purpose of an organization with Loyal Customers being the purpose.

Doug interjects: "Doesn't it make sense to replace profits as the purpose of an organization to having Loyal Customers and increased Customer Value Added (CVA)?

"To get true loyalty from a Customer requires that your strategy is firing on all cylinders, whether it is co-creating or customizing, whether it is seeking to delight or avoid the Customer's DNA, or whether the products are Customer designed. Profits will follow increases in loyalty and CVA. In any event, profits is the reward that Customers shower you with."

Krish answers, *"Use loyalty or other Customer metrics to define the purpose of the organization. Remember profits have to be there to have a healthy organization. However, to have a superb organization, we must deliver Customer Value, thereby increasing value of Customers and Return on Customers (ROC) and, of course, profits.* **Profits are a result, not the cause of success."**

d. Use the Customer strategy to build with employees their Customer Mission.

Doug says the employee must drive his Customer mission. "It could be:

"We want to give the Customer a great and memorable experience, so that he remembers us, and reminds others of us and the experience. Remember he funds our paychecks, and therefore make him come back, and hopefully with new Customers.

"An example," continues Doug, "is Nordstrom. You do not need to stand in line to pay your bill; the sales clerk does it. Hopefully while waiting you look around a little more in the store. A win-win for the store and for you."

Krish continues by pointing out the next steps in the folder he had given Doug.

2. Devise Customer-centric rewards, incentives and bonus systems.

"Incentives must reflect the true increase in CVA, loyalty and, of course, certain functional goals and loyalty. Profitability is a short-term incentive, Customer Value a long-term motivation," remarks Doug.

"Good," grins Krish, *"you really don't need me!"*

"This is just the result of your educating me," asserts Doug. "We must have a celebration system to highlight the good actions we have taken or individuals have taken for Customers. We must have a multitude of recognition and reward systems to adorn our office walls to remind everyone that the Customer is important."

Krish moves on:

3. Have Customer-centric tasks in each department.

"Many departments and function think they are too far removed from the Customer and so they have no role to play with the Customer. They believe their operational and functional tasks are more important than trying to become Customeric. We advise all such departments, such as finance, HRD, to have at least two customer-related tasks for external

or internal Customers. This book outlines the Customer role
of various departments and functional heads.

"Next, we have to change mind-set at all levels, including
the frontline people. Build awareness and pro-activeness
towards the Customer in all parts of the organization.

B. Build the Culture by Ensuring Attitudes are Customeric

"Culture is a shared system of values, beliefs and what is meaningful
to the organization. An ideal Customer culture is putting people
first (your Customers and your people), and performing to do
so. The key to Total CVM is mindset. A great attitude at the top
towards Customers is not enough. You also need a great attitude at
the bottom and in the delivery chain. Total CVM helps companies
by encouraging their employees to not only build self-esteem,
awareness and caring, but also to be self-driven to do the right
things for the Customers.

"Attitudinal changes start at the top and with employees.
Many employees are there just to do their job, not to look out for
improvements or making a change."

1. Change attitudes at the top, where CEOs have to stop
   being gods. The organization can have only one god,
   and that is the Customer.

   Doug says, "I understand this. You have already told
   me that the Customer is god. To make this a reality,
   I cannot be a competing god! Thus, the CEO has to set
   an example.

   "Bureaucracy kills Customer culture, and the CEO
   should watch out for this. Krish, I am going to repeat
   what I learnt from you. We should therefore,

2. Appoint a Chief Customer Officer (CCO).

   "Changing the mindset is not an easy job. It is not a one-
   time job. It requires full time attention. Many companies

having Business Excellence programmes employ VPs for Business Excellence. That is why the implementation becomes possible and is company-wide. Total CVM also requires full time attention. The CCO will:

a. Align all top managers, employees and functions towards Customers and build Customer Conduits.

"Customer Conduits are a top-down initiative required to support the CEO in making Total CVM a reality. This also helps in aligning all levels of personnel to the Customer. The CCO also builds apex Customer Circles and helps build Customer strategy. In fact, Yum! Restaurants (owners of Taco Bell, Pizza Hut and KFC) converts managers into Coaches, and we need Customer Champions or Coaches from company managers.

b. Change mindset at all levels, including the frontline people. Build awareness and proactiveness towards the Customer in all parts of the organization.

"Customer Circles and providing departments with Customer tasks help in this attitude change at all levels. The Customer's Bill of Rights and the Circle of Promises also lead towards a changed mindset. Orchestration of and monitoring of such programmes is the realm of the CCO.

"The main pre-requisite is Customer-centric people. And to get people to focus on the Customer you have to create a motivating environment for them, and give them treatment that you expect them to give Customers. Treat them right and as valuable. Give them the tools and the information in the right environment, and watch them use their brains to perform.

"As an example, Walt Disney said he was in the Happiness business. Shouldn't we all be? Shouldn't smiles and memories (good ones, of course) be important? Disney also emphasizes the importance of leadership in a Customer-centric organization.

c. Align all functions to the Customer, with Customer-focused task building.

"This starts with a Customer-centric strategy. It stops when some function says the Customer is not my job. The Customer belongs to someone else! Thus, the alignment to the Customer must happen, and it occurs with an alignment of all employees and functions with the Customer. We have used Customer strategy and Customer Circles to involve people with the Customer and also to gauge how well the company performs for the Customer. Customer alignment works best where people are self-motivated, and so changing mind-sets is important.

3. Build frontline and employee self-esteem, employee engagement and Employee Value. Educate all Customer-related personnel, be they sales, information, marketing, technology, service people, complaint handlers, call centres, etc., on being Customeric, and certify them.

"Before we can make employees responsive to and caring for the Customer, the employees must feel that the company cares about them, and builds their self-esteem and image. The Customer Circles approach builds this image and brings out an awareness of the Customer, and pro-active tasks to make him loyal. Capturing the Voice of the Employee helps here. In India, we call this a 'Chalta Hai'[9] attitude, meaning let things move as they always do, or do not rock the boat. However, Total CVM installs a courtesy system in the company, builds the employees' self-respect and awareness, and this leads to their becoming more aware of the Customer and his needs, thereby shedding the Chalta hai attitude.

a. Sponsor Customer-centric education and certification of frontline employees.

---

[9] *'Chalta Hai' is a casual attitude which means anything goes.*

"Here we have to recognize that Customer skills are just as important as business or technical skills. Certifying employees for Customer skills requires education and testing leading to certification, which has to be an ongoing process.

"Customer-centric education and certification of frontline employees (and all employees if possible) is a key component to establishing Total CVM. This includes sales clerks, marketing people, service persons and many more. Many companies train and certify employees and service people for the technical skills. A TV service man is perhaps certified to repair TVs. Unfortunately, he is not taught how to handle Customers, nor is he certified to do so. Customer Value Foundation does this certification.

4. Start and propagate Customer Circles.

"When we put employees into Customer Circles, we find that they take a leadership role, become proactive towards the Customer and devise things to do for him, and go into a self-learning and self-management mode. Continuous Customer Improvement Programmes, better teamwork and awareness of other employees and Customers also ensue:

a. For brainstorming Customer needs
b. For Customer's DNA and Delight factors
c. For Customer's Bill of Rights and for the Circle of Promises
d. For Continuous Customer Improvement Programme and to maintain Customer focus

"The participants in Customer Circles not only are asked about what to do for the Customer (few companies formally ask their frontline people on their view of the Customer), but also the pain and pleasure of dealing with Customers. How can they avoid the pain and increase the pleasure. It turns out that most of the factors on doing so vest in the frontline people. This awareness prompts them to suggest and do the right things for the Customer. This cooperative effort can be spread throughout the company."

Krish says, *"Total CVM helps bring in self-esteem and awareness of, and a focus on the Customers by employees. This bottom-up approach has been tested at Tata Power, Tata Chemicals Crop Nutrition and Agri-Business and Godrej, through setting up Customer Circles, and has brought tremendous enthusiasm and change.*

"The challenge is not to dampen this new enthusiasm by putting these Customer Circles under traditional project management, but to allow the roll out to be employee driven and driven by the employees' hearts, thereby changing organizational culture. Let's look further at the steps, Doug.

C. Make Customer Excellence the Cornerstone of Your Organizational Transformation Process

"That Business Excellence is meant to change attitudes is partly true. However, fundamental and attitudinal changes do not appear as important as processes in such excellence models, because pro-cesses are easier to change than attitudes," continues Krish.

"What is clear is that if the fundamentals are not in place and the employees are not self-motivated and incented to do the right things for the Customer, all the processes and all the other initiatives like Customer Relationship Management (CRM), call centres and the like fall by the wayside (they become less effective). On the other hand, great motivation can do wonders, but without proper process, support will also be insufficient.

"Fundamentals imply good professionalism, employees with self-esteem and value added, and Customer focused.

1. Use Customer excellence as your organizational goals.

"If a company strives for Customer excellence, it must imbibe professionalism and Business Excellence as pillars. This

implies a Customeric attitude, an organizational alignment, professionalism and processes to work together. In a sense, Customer excellence will drive Business and Business Process Excellence and it will make your quality and Six Sigma programmes significant."

D. Understand Your Customer and His Needs

1. Segment your Customers.

   Krish goes on, *"While Prahalad[10] suggests a Customer segmentation of one, this is not always possible. However, we should drive towards this and try to customize our offerings to the Customer.*

   "In any event, proper segmentation is necessary. And this segmentation should be Customer approved. We should ensure that the Customer wants to be in the segment.

   "Measure and add value of the Customer to the company, increase value of the Customer and Return on Customer (ROC). Get rid of non-profitable Customers.

   "Most companies have a right to choose their Customers, market segments and Customer segments. Exceptions are where regulations prevent you (for example, as a water utility) from selecting Customers.

   "The right to select Customers has to be exercised. We should get rid of our non-profitable Customers or segments, particularly where we see no potential to make this segment more profitable.

2. Measure and add value to the company, increase value of the Customer, Return on Customer. Get rid of non-profitable Customers.

   "We also need to understand if the value of Customer to the company is increasing. It undoubtedly will if the precepts detailed above are followed. Value to the company includes

---

[10] C.K. Prahalad and M.S. Krishnan, *The New Age of Innovation: Driving Cocreated Value Through Global Networks* (McGraw Hill, 2008).

Total Shareholder Value and Customer Lifetime Value. Return on Customer (ROC) is another measure defined later. We should even measure value to the employee."

Doug repeats, "The Value of the Customer to the company is measured by Total Lifetime Value or Return on Customer,[11] and financial parameter improvements on Customer segmentation should be done also by value.

"Also, I believe, we must differentiate between market share and Value of the Customer,[12] and Customer Value. Our aim is to maximize the last two. Market share will follow. We should also,

3. Measure Customer Assets and Customer Capital.

"Customer Assets, also defined later, or Customer Capital should be measured and reported on monthly or quarterly reviews along with CVA measurements. Just seeing these parameters rise or fall will force questions and a focus on parameters creating these measurements. This will then ensure a focus on Customer-related tasks.

"It is a matter of time before the USA's Security and Exchange Commission (SEC) moots this kind of data is put on the balance sheets. For many companies, their Customer assets are bigger than their physical assets. Very often, companies are valued on the Customer Assets when they are being sold, because Customer assets take into account the numbers of Customers, their profitability, their rate of growth, acquisition cost, retention cost and rate of attrition.

4. Capture the Voice of the Employee, Voice of the Customer and Voice of the Competitor (CVA). Use this data to understand the Customer needs, and use this insight to build Customer strategy and tasks.

"Capturing the Voice of the Employee, Voice of the Customer and Voice of the Competitor is paramount

---

[11] A registered service mark of Peppers and Rogers Group.

[12] See Gautam Mahajan, *Customer Value Investment*, 47.

to success. The Voice of the Employee is measured by Employee Value Added (EVA), and by conversational means. The Voice of the Customer and the Voice of the Competitor are captured not through satisfaction but through value surveys and using a metric called CVA.

$$\text{Employee Value Added (EVA)} = \frac{\text{Perceived value your company adds to its employees}}{\text{Perceived value competitors add to their employees}}$$

$$\text{Customer Value Added (CVA)} = \frac{\text{Perceived worth of your offer}}{\text{Perceived worth of competitive offer}}$$

"Other Customer metrics can also be used to arrive at a Customer Performance Management System. CVA relates to market share, ROI, wallet share, and is used to measure the health of the company. CVA is used in the reporting metrics along with financial scores, and for bonus systems."

E. Treat Every Customer as an Individual

Doug says, looking at Krish, "So that leads us to the precept where you start to customize and begin to treat each Customer as an individual with customized needs.

1. Customize.

"Our strategy has to be to customize for individual Customers. Give him what he wants. We start by customization of Customer segments. When building segmentation models think of the smallest discrete segments possible."

2. Think of the Customer size of one.

Krish quickly interjects: *"This is the customization and looking at a Customer as an individual and co-creating value with and for him through co-creating Customer experience. C.K. Prahalad has best espoused this.[13] Prahalad suggests that the Customer segment size N = 1.*

"Prahalad gives examples in India where diabetes insurance is personalized and the insurance premium depends on the lifestyle of the patient and how his diabetes is in control. A patient controlling his diabetes partly with medication and partially with lifestyle changes (diet improvement, exercise) is incented by lower insurance rates, as his risk drops versus a patient whose diabetes is out of control.

"He is suggesting that our focus should be on each individual Customer using global resources and innovative ways to get the sample of N = 1 (that is, looking at Customers as discrete individuals, and designing offerings and co-creating Customer experience and co-controlling the business with them).

"Another example is satellite mapping of individual farmlands, enabling suppliers to customize agri-inputs on a customized basis."

3. Co-create Customer experience and co-create profits.

Doug takes over: "As you embark on co-creating Customer experience, we must keep in mind that the Customer is our business partner. You should co-control the business with the Customer. Gone are the days when companies could control their suppliers, and also control their Customers (whose suppliers companies are). How many times do you hear a company or a store tell you 'this is our policy or this is our process?' (As a Customer, I would like to impose my process and my policy on my supplier, that is, your company).

---

[13] C.K. Prahalad and M.S. Krishnan, *The New Age of Innovation.*

"Co-creating profits means that the Customer and the company work together in reducing costs, so that both can profit. The classic example is Fedex shifting the tracking of parcels to Customers, thereby cutting costs."

Krish chimes in: *"I just had a recent experience with a credit card company, where they misplaced my check, charged me interest for late payment, waived it in return for my re-making a full payment (which I did). Soon after that, they found my check that they had misplaced and deposited it, only to find a stop payment on it (which they had advised me to place) and charging me for the old check that bounced because of the stop payment, and rescinding my membership privileges.*

"Note that all this happened because of their own mistakes. Why can't I charge them my fees for the harassment and my time? I don't want to sound like a consumer advocate, but I most certainly would like companies to think about co-controlling and co-creating experiences, and establishing more of a partnership (and an equal partnership) role. A student–teacher partnership or an employee–company partnership is not an equal partnership. Attaining an equal Customer–company (or should I say supplier?) partnership is the goal!"

F. Processes must be Customer-driven and Customer-friendly

1. Roll out the Customer mindset with the development of Customer-centric and flexible processes.

   Doug relates to the processes: "The manner in which we roll out the Customer mindset with the development of Customer-centric and flexible processes will directly impact success. Once we have the fundamentals in place, then we are ready to rework our processes to give you competitive advantage. Every effort should be to make them Customer-driven processes. Companies such as American Express strive to have

Customer-driven processes, but do not always succeed, because there is such a deep-seated focus on the company itself and on overall efficiency instead."

The Customer Guru adds: *"This is generally accompanied by processes, supposedly Customer-centric. A former American Express executive told me that most processes truly are not Customer-centric or Customer-friendly, (and often the failure is in process-scripted responses, and that often non-scripted responses depending on the Customer-Centric human being is better)."*

G. Customer-centric Reporting Systems

Doug has started to take over, because he has been educated in the past years by Krish on the Customer:

1. Report CVA scores along with quarterly reporting.

   Krish suggests that CVA scores should be reported along with quarterly reporting. In addition, he felt that Customer Value discussions are part of the review meetings. We could add Customer assets to the reporting system. Doug continues,

2. Ensure Customer Value discussions are part of the review meetings.

   "Normal business reviews focus on generally accepted parameters such as new sales, market problems, Profit and Loss, financial issues, logistic problems, etc. Very few reviews have a section on Customer and Customer Value, CVA, EVA and the trends. Very few examine Customer assets and changes in these, and possible causes for changes and remedial action.

   "Customer Value Added and associated information should become a standard part of the review process.

3. Correlate CVA with market share, loyalty, profitability and Shareholder Value so that you have quantifiable results.

"Finally, we must correlate CVA with market share, loyalty, profitability and Shareholder Value so that you have quantifiable results. Correlations with Market share versus Value; ROI versus Value and Wallet share versus Value are shown in Figures 2.1, 2.3 and 2.4. In addition, we know price can be related to the perceived benefits and the value. An example is given in Figure 2.2 on CVA versus retention."

FIGURE 2.1
Market Share versus Value
(Example from Telecom Percentage Installs)

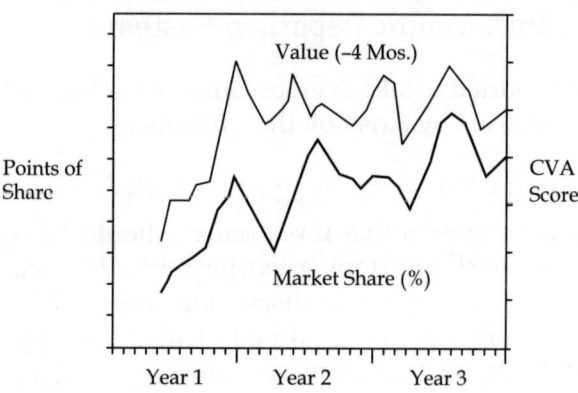

Source   Ray Kordupleski, *Mastering Customer Value Management* (Pinnaflex, 2003).

Using CVA for Benchmarking

Krish adds: *"One of Ray Kordupleski's[14] sterling contribution to creating Customer Value Management as an art and a science is a benchmarking system based on over 3850 companies. This gives companies a measure of where one's company is on a global scale. This is a powerful way of benchmarking (Figure 2.5). The actual data is confidential, but the curve gives you an idea that if your*

---

[14] Ray Kordupleski is the father of CVM and author of *Marketing Customer Value Management* (Pinnaflex, 2003).

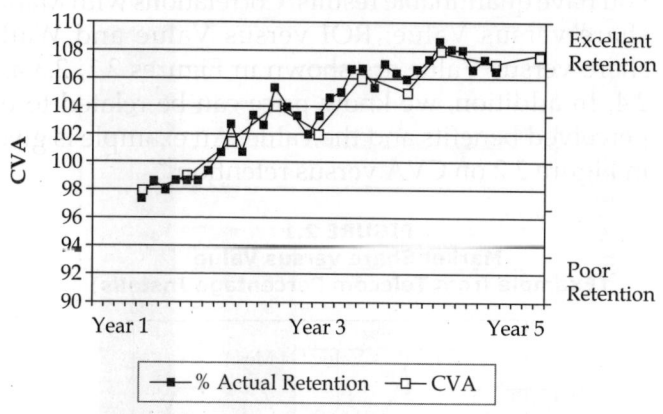

FIGURE 2.2
**Increases in Customer Value Added Followed
by Improvements in Loyalty and Retention**

Source   Customer Value Foundation Australia, available at http://www.cvm.com.
au/(accessed on 21 June 2010).

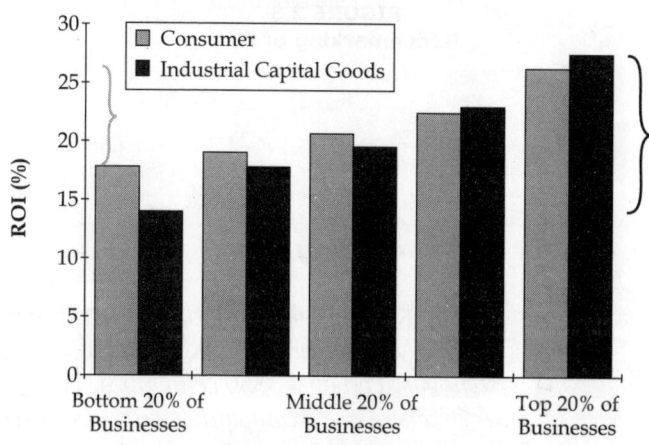

FIGURE 2.3
**ROI versus Relative Customer Value
(PIMS Data Over 1000 Companies)**

Source   Ray Kordupleski, *Mastering Customer Value Management.*

company is consistently below a CVA of 1, you need to rethink
your business, or change your management, just as you would do
if your economic added value is unacceptable.

FIGURE 2.4
Share of Wallet versus Relative Customer Value

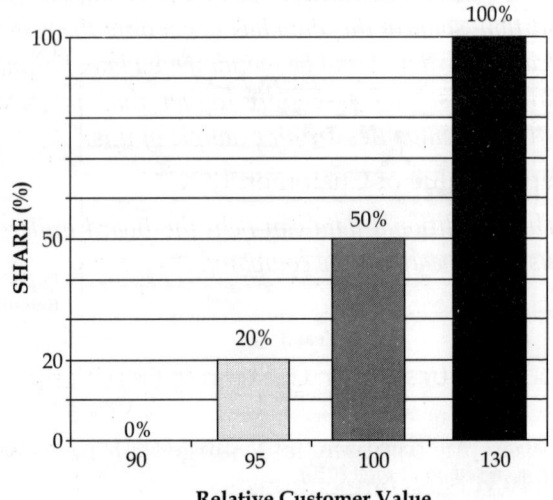

Source   Ray Kordupleski, *Mastering Customer Value Management.*

FIGURE 2.5
Benchmarking of CVA

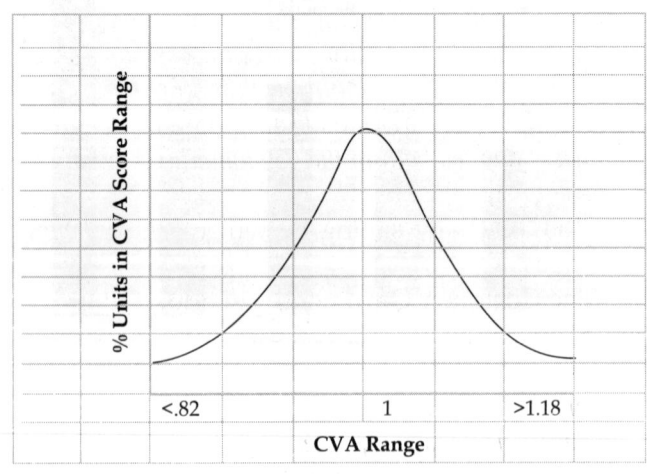

Source   Ray Kordupleski, in correspondence with author.

4. Put Customer Assets on Financial Balance Sheets.

"As we discussed earlier, such data should be reported. In addition, some of this data has to get onto the balance sheet, because one day it will be mandated by law. For many companies, Customer assets are higher than physical assets. Software companies are an example of this.

5. Report Value of Customer, ROC.

"These additional data can help the Board understand the Customer health of the company.

H. Prepare Yourself for Customer Certification

1. Prepare the company to be judged by Customers positively versus competition.

"Companies have to be prepared to be judged by the Customers for all they stand for and are, and not just for their products. This includes Customer trust, the perception Customers have of the company's fairness and the treatment they can expect from the company. Trust is another important factor. And this judgement can finally change the company's Customer thought processes and build the brand further.

"All these have to be put together into a Customer strategy, which is aligned both to the Customer and to the corporate strategy."

Doug ends by saying he will work towards these changes.

The Customer Guru nods and adds: *"Unfortunately, Customer-related work in a company is practised again in bits and pieces, where some companies work on service excellence, others on Customer loyalty or CRM. Hardly anyone focuses on departmental and top level attitudinal changes. Some will argue that business excellence models do some of this.*

2. Certify the company from a Customer's view point.

   "Eventually, you will need to be able to certify your company from a Customer's viewpoint and advertize good certification scores, and work on poor certification scores."

"Just to recap", says Doug, "Total CVM focuses on Customer-led business strategy, Customer-required products and features, Customer Value-based pricing, Customer-admired brands and the best Customer services. These come from CVA studies, Customer focus or a deep understanding of Customer needs through targeted research.

"Total CVM helps you synchronously optimize all of the company parameters. It implies that corporate strategy and Customer strategy are in harmony. An emphasis on Return on Customer (ROC) and Customer Lifetime Value, and Total Shareholder Value is necessary (it has been shown more and more that increased CVA increases Total Shareholder Value and ROC). CRM in itself has to be modified to collect data that will help a company add value to the Customer.

"More importantly, companies have to change from being profit-led to Customer-led. Being Customer-led makes us ask questions like: if it is ok for us to control our suppliers, why don't we let our Customers (whose suppliers we are) control us?

"Customer-related tasks and initiatives cannot be mandated and instituted using top-down edicts and project-related methodologies. They have to be adopted and be adaptable; they require supportive leadership, incentivization and a change of culture. They call for a bottom-up approach. The analyze/think/aim/fire approach has to give way to the feel/see/believe approach. The approach has to be one of human orientation and not of project orientation, of enabling not ordering, and supporting not mandating. This is accomplished through Customer Circles or Customer-Centric-Circles." He tells Krish he will send him a chart (Box 2.2) showing the difference between Total CVM and the conventional business approach.

BOX 2.2
Existing Customer Approach versus Total CVM Approach

Existing Customer Approach	Total CVM Approach
Business Philosophy	
1. Profits are the purpose of a business	1. Profits are a result of a higher purpose of the business, to have Customers who are your partners
2. Business strategy is driven from the market assessment	
3. Price is the main driver of purchase	2. The Customer strategy along with the shareholder strategy drives business
4. The bottom line improved by better processes, and a focus on costs	3. The main driver of purchase is CVA
	4. CVA builds loyalty, market share, higher profits and Shareholder Value
Conventional Business Thinking on Customer	
1. The Customer is important. This is said but not truly meant	1. The Customer is important. The Customer is put in the centre of our business thinking
2. The front facing departments take care of the Customer. They are responsible for the Customer, and the rest are onlookers	2. Everyone in the company must have a Customer focus
3. Business needs supersede Customer needs even in these departments	3. The Customer needs come first
4. Greater focus on price type issues and not on Customer Value creation	4. Customer Value creation is an important topic of discussion
5. Business thinking clouds focus on problems perceived by or enunciated by Customers and channelpartners. "This is the way we do things" syndrome	5. Open approach to recognizing Customer problems is the first step in resolving them. Examples are logistic issues, accounting and settlement issues
6. CXO's for important fuctions	6. Chief Customer Officer needed

(Box 2.2 continued)

(*Box 2.2 continued*)

Existing Customer Approach	Total CVM Approach
Channel partners	
1. No clear emphasis on role of channel partners in Customer Value creation. Generally channel partners are convenience partners 2. Whether channel partners with brand equity is important or not	1. Customer Value has to be created or co-created with channel partners 2. Serious thought to be given to role and brand equity of channel partners in value creation 3. Build Brand Equity of channel partners.
Top Management and non-Customer Facing Departments	
1. Top management involvement in the Customer thinking is small. There is little discussion of the Customer in top management reviews 2. Customer roles of non-Customer facing department not clear 3. The frontline people are hampered by lack of self-esteem, awareness and Customer proactiveness	1. Top management involved and drive Total CVM 2. All departments have clear cut Customer roles 3. Focus on making frontline people pro-active to Customers and enabled
Frontline and Entire Company Focus	
1. Managing the entire organization to look at the Customer is limited 2. Conventional approach to employees and their Customer focus	1. Customer Circles are a great starting point, and bring in a Customer focus, a continuous Customer Improvement Programme, and the Customer Bill of Rights and the Circle of Promises 2. Focus on Employee Value, awareness and pro-activeness. Frontline driven

(*Box 2.2 continued*)

(*Box 2.2 continued*)

Existing Customer Approach	Total CVM Approach
Employee Focus	
1. Employees are to be motivated	1. Employees are the key to Customer focus
	2. Employee self-esteem, awareness, proactiveness, involvement and engagement is necessary
	3. Build Employee Value Added
	4. Put frontline employees into Customer Circles
	5. Build Employee Brand Equity
Competitive Marketplace Assessment	
1. Customer satisfaction is a surrogate for Customer Value	1. CVA/loyalty important. Satisfaction is for transactions
2. Too much focus on products and processes	2. More focus on Voice of Customers and Voice of Competitor
	3. Build Brand Euity
Pricing, New Products	
1. Pricing from a value consideration not done	1. Price using Customer Value and needs
2. New Products selected from business and market considerations	2. In addition, new products to be selected from Customer Value considerations

Source   Author.

CHAPTER SYNOPSIS

This chapter talks about adding value to Customers and not managing them. In fact, we should co-control the business with the Customer. The status of Total CVM at a few companies in India is outlined.

$$CVI = Higher\ ROI$$

This is to remind the reader that most Customer Value interventions are for free. They do not require any investment, as we start to do the right things right from the Customer's viewpoint.

- **Customer Management or Customer Value Management?**
  We want to ensure that we are not managing the Customer, just adding value to him. The Customer must feel he is controlling (Customer-in-Control).
- **Total CVM Status**
  Total CVM is being practised in limited number of companies, because it is a relatively new concept. However, bits and pieces are being conducted around the world, with many companies, under the name of CVM.
- **Steps towards Total CVM**
  There are several steps towards Total CVM, which are outlined as follows:

A. Business Strategy must be Customer-driven

Here we make a case for a Customer strategy for driving the business strategy.

  a. Define Customer
  b. Strategy for each segment of Customers including channel partners and internal Customer
  c. Replace profits as the purpose of an organization with loyal Customers being the purpose

d. Use the Customer strategy to build with employees their Customer Mission
e. Devise Customer-centric rewards, incentives and bonus systems
f. Have Customer-centric tasks in each department

B. Build the Culture by Ensuring Attitudes are Customeric

The key is to work on mindsets and attitudes to make the employees Customeric. Steps include:

1. Change attitudes at the top, where CEOs have to stop being gods.

   i. Appoint a Chief Customer Officer who will assist top managers, employees and functions to move towards Customers and to build Customer Conduits
   ii. Change mindset at all levels including the frontline people. Build awareness and proactiveness towards the Customer in all parts of the organization
   iii. Align all functions to the Customer, with Customer-focused task building

2. Build frontline and employee self-esteem, Customer awareness and proactiveness.

   i. Start and propagate Customer Circles.

C. Make Customer Excellence the Cornerstone of Your Organizational Transformation Process

Use Customer Excellence as your organizational goals. To do this build on Business Excellence programmes.

D. Understand Your Customer and His Needs

It is paramount we understand our Customer and his needs.

E. Treat Every Customer as an Individual

Essentially, we have to treat every Customer as an individual. Here, we need to:

- Customize offerings to Customer
- Think of the Customer size of 1
- Co-create Customer experience and co-create profits

F. Processes must be Customer-driven and Customer-friendly

Roll out the Customer mindset with the development of Customer-centric and flexible processes. This is a crucial exercise looking at the needs and the convenience of the Customer.

G. Customer-centric Reporting Systems

- It is essential that Customer value results and data be reported and discussed at monthly meetings, quarterly reviews, at Board level and that data be put on balance sheets
- This is a key step for Total CVM
- Prepare company to be judged by Customers positively versus competition
- Certify the company from a Customer's view point

3

The Fundamentals

THE CUSTOMER COMES FIRST: NO CEO GODS

Krish continues, *"Doug, do you truly believe that the Customer comes first?"*

"But, of course, there is no doubt in my mind."

Krish persists, *"You remember Bob Ostrofsky, your predecessor at Glacier, used to say the same thing. But when he wanted something from you, he expected you to jump to it. It did not matter if you had to ignore a Customer or give the Customer a lower priority.*

"There cannot be two gods in an organization. Either the Customer or the CEO is the god. It is a choice you have to make. And this means you will have to change your style of managing and dealing with your employees to make everyone respond to the Customer first and to you second! Not being a CEO god sends a very powerful message to the organization...but, remember, abdicationg godhood is not easy! Can you do this? Especially when the boss of your group calls? And wants some numbers right away? When bosses change to become more democratic, the company becomes better organized and more efficient since bosses and employees are forced to plan their days better and can adhere to their planned work better.

"Deming says that people learn to please their teachers as kids, and please their bosses as employees. Culturally, they do not view their role as changing the system to please Customers."

Doug smiles. "I have an advantage. I've just come into this job, and don't have to change a known way of behaviour. I imagine Bob would have had a tougher time changing himself and his style. People would still try to treat him as numero uno, even if he said otherwise.

"I have no problem in discussing Total CVM with my boss (the Chairman of the Glacier Group) and explaining to him my focus on the Customer and the Customer priority, and the benefit of this approach. He pretty much knows about our Customer Value initiatives and how beneficial they proved to be for Glacier at Ohio.[1]

"I want to implement Total CVM. I will let my people know that the Customer comes first, and I truly believe this. The Customer's priority will take precedence over the CEO's other priorities. The Customer's needs will have to be handled first."

"Actually the Customer's needs and the Customer's priority must match the CEO's priority," adds Krish. *"When this happens, there is true alignment in the organization."*

"The CEO has to turn the company upside down:

"The Customer has to come first, and the Customer focus has to flow upwards to him from the CEO, as shown in Figure 3.1. This is a classic invented pyramid, and we all know about this.

"Vineet Nayar in his recent book, *Employees First, Customers Second,*[2] suggests that enabled and empowered employees can deliver better to Customers, provided managers act not as gatekeepers or bosses but as enablers and resource people."

Necessary and Relevant Tasks from a Customer's perspective: Task Audit

Krish smiles, *"I am glad to hear this. We are doing well. But, a Total Customer Value Management programme is not a passive programme. It requires proactive effort. This means people have to*

---

[1] See Gautam Mahajan, *Customer Value Investment: Formula for Sustained Business Success* (New Delhi: Response Books, 2008).

[2] Vineet Nayar, *Employees First, Customers Second* (Harvard Business Press, 2010).

FIGURE 3.1
The Customer Pyramid

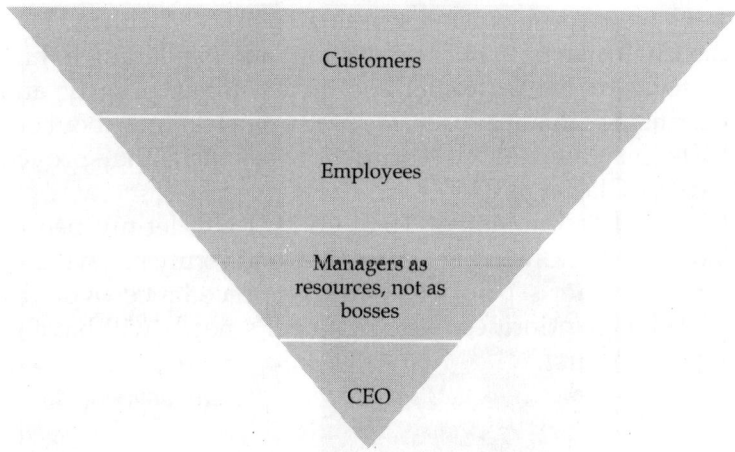

Customers

Employees

Managers as
resources, not as
bosses

CEO

Source Author.

find the time to work on Total CVM. Many times, we inherit many
programmes where effort has to be expended. Some are employee-
bonding programmes; others have to do with reach out and so on.
The Tatas are an example of a company with many programmes
and initiatives. To bring in a Customer initiative requires the exe-
cutives to have time, and often, they throw up their hands and say,
'Oh, no! One more initiative!'

"*You have to view corporate initiatives and programmes*
from a Customer's perspective: Are they relevant and necessary
for the Customer? Are they unnecessary and irrelevant to the
Customer?"

Krish shows Doug the chart (Figure 3.2).

Doug says, "Krish, I believe we also have to look at tasks
that are necessary and relevant for our business, not just
for Customers. We should eliminate those tasks judged
unnecessary and irrelevant from the point of view of the
Customer and the business. I agree this step has to be taken
to free time for the employees so that they can work on
Customer issues. I would imagine reading unnecessary and

FIGURE 3.2
Mahajan Task Matrix

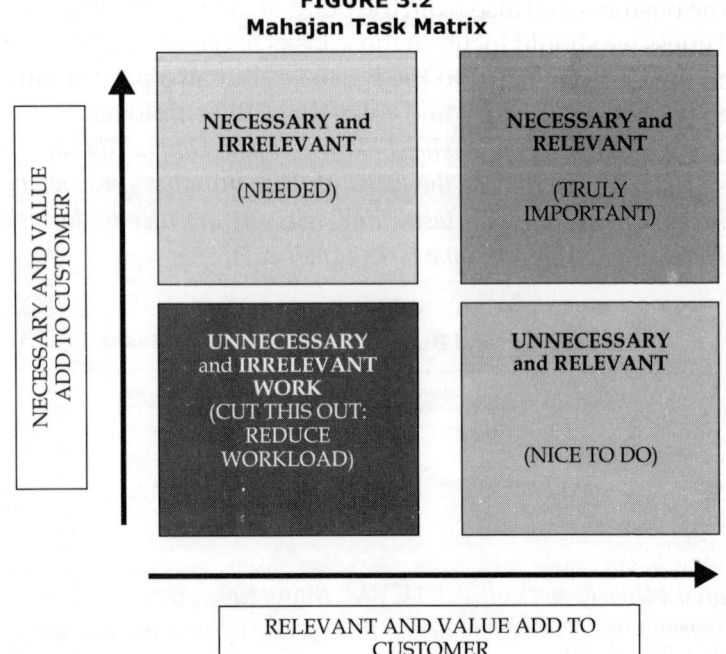

Source Author.

irrelevant e-mails takes a fair chunk of every employee's time. I spend two hours a day on reading e-mails and at least 40 minutes of these e-mails I could do without. Can you imagine 100 of my senior staff saving 30 minutes a day or 50 man-hours a day! Wow, how significant!

"I never thought of this. Now that I am aware, I can start working with my colleagues to reduce unnecessary and irrelevant e-mails (at least internal e-mails). An easy example of each internal e-mail is to have a subject, and based on that subject you can ensure you do not get an email on that subject. Or you can ask the sender to remove you from the mailing list. Once we know what else is unnecessary and irrelevant, we can eliminate these tasks also.

"I think tasks also have to be looked at as necessary and relevant not only from the point of view of the Customer and the business, but also from the point of view of the employee. I guess we should focus on those tasks necessary and relevant to the Customer and to the business, but also pay attention to the tasks necessary and relevant to the employee."

Krish says, *"This is what I like about you, Doug. You catch on so fast and you can see the merit of these initiatives. Remember, necessary are must-do tasks, and relevant are nice-to-do tasks. Here's an example of some tasks (Table 3.1):*

TABLE 3.1
Customer and Business Importance of Tasks

Customer Related Tasks	Customer		Business		Net Importance of Task
	Necessary to the Customer	Relevant to the Customer	Necessary for the Business	Relevant to the Business	
Meeting Customers at his request	√√√√√	√√√√√	√√√√√	√√√√√√	√√√√√
Meeting Customer to maintain contact	–	√√	√√√	√√√√	√√
Preparing note for Boss on Customer	–	√	√√	√√√	√

Source   Author.

"Let me leave you a note for your reference:

Task Audit

"Companies, unwittingly or otherwise, sometimes cause employees to perform unnecessary and irrelevant work. Sometimes employees are guilty of doing this (repeating themselves, not being to the point, not being able to find information, re-doing work done before, spending time socializing at work, etc., not planning properly) so that work is not done in a timely manner (sequentially and/or simultaneously).

"By eliminating unnecessary and irrelevant work (from the Customer's viewpoint), people and companies become more efficient. In times of difficulty, companies tend to reduce the work force; reducing the work load would have been better and would add to profit. Work is divided into:

- Necessary work and relevant to the Customer
- Necessary work but irrelevant to the Customer
- Unnecessary work but relevant to the Customer
- Unnecessary work and irrelevant to the Customer

"This will help people focus and cut down on non-value-creating (unnecessary and irrelevant) work! This task audit is the first step in understanding tasks that could be eliminated without impacting the Customer, or efficiency.

"As definitions:

"*Necessary work* is essential for, vital to, indispensable to, important to, crucial to, needed by, compulsory required by or requisite for the Customer.

"*Relevant work* is pertinent to, applicable or germane to, or appropriate to the Customer. This is work that can be eliminated without deterioration of present service or product.

"What work is the Customer willing to pay for?

"Every business enterprise has at least eight stakeholder groups, whose concerns must be considered when analyzing business processes: customers, suppliers, managers, employees, creditors, investors, governments and community groups.

$$\text{Customer Value Added of Task} = \begin{array}{l}\text{(Value to Customer}\\ \text{after the task) MINUS}\\ \text{(Value to the Customer}\\ \text{prior to the task)}\end{array}$$

"Who is the Customer? Are some classes of work for internal customers necessary. If such work is free now, would someone pay for these services or work?

"It is the final bill paying Customer at the end of the entire value chain who determines if the work/task adds value.

Identifying Necessary and Relevant Work

"In this exercise, we are focusing in on identifying unnecessary and irrelevant tasks from a Customer's perspective that can be eliminated.

"First, look at each activity and argue the merits of the activity versus its objective, that is, adding value to Customers.

"Now, look at the same activity as a Customer: discuss the value of the activity from the Customer's viewpoint (or will the Customer pay for this).

"This way you look at each activity from two different view points!

"When you set tasks, ask what goal they will meet. Let's say you are assigned a task: Beautify a park. What is the goal? Beautification or making it good for the community, and what impact on your Customers?

"Look at these classes of work and ask if the work is necessary and relevant to the Customer (or the business) or not:

- Overhead costs
  - Audit
  - Legal
  - Administrative
- Costs of meetings
  - Useful
  - Meaningless
  - Setting up a meeting
  - Waiting for meetings to start
- Management reviews
- Employee churn
  - Keeping employees increases value to Customer

- Presentations
    - Making irrelevant presentations/repeating yourself (call center data is often relevant but much of it is unnecessary)
- Reports
    - Reviewing and reworking
- Questions asked by a call center to a Customer
    - Relevant
    - Necessary to Customer?
- Filling forms
- Meeting government regulations
    - Necessary for Company
    - Only sometimes necessary for Customer
- Selling
- Travel
- Research and Development (R&D) expense
- Quality Control
- Crisis Management
    - Responsible people avoid crisis
- Troubleshooting/chasing problems
- Other causes of work and costs

Make a value added work index: It has two parts:

- The quality of your work
- Its relevance and necessity to Customer

Quality can be poor because of:

- Incomplete information
- Poor communication
- Poor understanding
- Poor execution

The quality of your work:

- Poor work in your control (avoid)
  - making appointments late
  - not planning trips for maximum impact
  - going on a trip and not utilising time effectively
  - not planning and thereby not being able to finish action because of missing input
  - repeat meetings
  - not being ready for meetings
  - not getting information ready in time
- Incorrect deliveries (not correct address)
- Ineffective negotiations
  - Poor order processing
  - Incorrect quotations
  - Inconsequential demonstrations
  - Ineffective relationship building
  - Revisiting Customers
  - Correcting work caused by others
  - Wasted travelling time

Value Added Task Background

Value add of the task: "The value-add assessment of the Task identifies a Task as one of the following:

- a Customer-value-added (CVA) Task to the Customer,
- a business-value-added (BVA) Task,
- an employee-value-added (EVA) Task
- a non-value-added (NVA) Task

"We will evaluate these criteria from a Customer's perspective.

"A task is classified as CVA if it satisfies the customer's expectations. Any task which improves the customer's perception of the product or service is a CVA Task. Production type activities are CVA activities (for example, taking customer orders, receiving materials, assembling materials and shipping).

"Most importantly, would the Customer be willing to pay extra or prefer us over the competition if he or she knew we were doing this task? (Sometimes, communicating the task and its relevance/necessity to the Customer is important.)

"BVA activities are those activities which satisfy business requirements but add no value from the Customers' viewpoint (for example, preparing financial reports, maintaining human resources records and ordering business supplies). You should ask if the process would break down if this task were removed? Or is this task required by law or regulation?

"NVA activities are activities which do not enhance the Customer's image of the product or service and do not support the business process. If the task can be removed, with no effect on the end-product or service, it is a NVA Task. NVA activities, also referred to as waste activities, often indicate deficiencies in the process design. These types of activities include storage, transportation, approval and inspection type activities. Waiting, over-processing and re-working are examples.

"Customer complaints are non-value adding (listening to them is not NVA. The complaint should not have happened)...therefore, eliminate (or do whatever you can so that complaints are reduced or eliminated). Customer complaints can be converted to CVA activities if we learn and improve ourselves, and make systemic and process changes to prevent recurrence. Waiting for meetings and unnecessary travel are other examples of NVA.

"Factors such as company culture, hiring practices, management styles, turnover rates and morale can all contribute to this waste—not using your employees' abilities to their fullest potential. I am sure you can think of examples of culture and hierarchy impacting work (waiting for a meeting with the boss).

"Why do we have unnecessary or irrelevant work? Lack of role clarity is a main cause. Much time is wasted and the 'somebody, nobody and everybody' game gets played over and over again. Another aspect is to ensure there is value addition in the management. Some middle management positions not only carry little value, they also tend to be counterproductive. This is manifested in the bureaucracy by status reports, meetings, lengthening the chain of written and verbal communications (with all the negative implications), requiring justifications for proposed actions, pitches, and just 'keeping the boss informed'. Why? Because it has always been that way. It is part of the bureaucratic process. Managers are merely performing the traditional management command and control functions required of the position.

"Staff jobs add to non-value added work. Examples are powerful, protected, policy-setting functions such as human resources, administration and the many staff functions.

"Next," continues Krish, *"We need to look at the role of the CEO. He comes behind the Customer. He has to ensure employees are doing necessary and relevant work, thereby reducing the work load; and he has to build the Organization of the Future."*

A Moment with Pam

Just then, Pam, Doug's wife walks in. After saying hello, Krish leaves. Pam complains to Doug that he has more time for work, and even for Krish, than for her. Doug smiles and says, "Krish has told me about the task audit: a sure-fire way of saving time and getting time for the important things in life, you!"

Pam smiles wryly and leaves, mumbling, "We'll see!"

THE ORGANIZATION OF THE FUTURE

A few days later, Krish Kumar is back again with Doug. Krish remarks, *"The purpose of any organization is to create value: value to its employees, to its Customers and thereby to its shareholders and owners.*

"So in a sense the CEO is the Chief Value Creator, and reporting to him are three people, the Chief Customer Value Creator, the Chief Customer Officer and the Chief Shareholder Value Creator. Generally, the role of the employee is crucial to the Customer and the Chief Customer Value Creator becomes also the de facto Chief Employee Value Creator."

"The job of the CEO is optimizing Shareholder Value and Customer Value. In the long run, both of these are one and the same. We all know life is about managing value conflicts. Moving from value conflicts to value synergism makes more sense. Adding Customer Value increases market share and loyalty, and ROI. Increasing Customer Value increases ROC, which increases Total Shareholder Value (TSV). The optimization and prioritization comes from managing the dilemma of increased future cash flow with decreased current cash flow. Looking at the Customer is a long-term view. However, most managers are incentivized to maximize the short run because that is how the stock market perceives their success. Now, not later!"

Doug remarks, "I read somewhere the principle of conservation of value says that value cannot be destroyed, and Customer Value is equal to Business Value. Using buzzwords, CV = BV."

The Customer Guru agrees, *"But he says value can be destroyed by ignoring the Customer or doing unnecessary work. This is like destroying energy during motion through friction."*

He then shows Doug a proposed organization chart (Figure 3.3) for the organization of the future.

"In addition, the CEO has to balance short-term and long-term goals. Short-term ROI and Customer Value growth are equally important. A cross-functional approach is necessary.

"The CEO has to get cross-functional CXOs to work together. As an example, the Chief Financial Officer and the Chief Marketing Officer have to get together to measure and report Customer Value. How often do you see these two meet to discuss Customers?

FIGURE 3.3
Organization of the Future

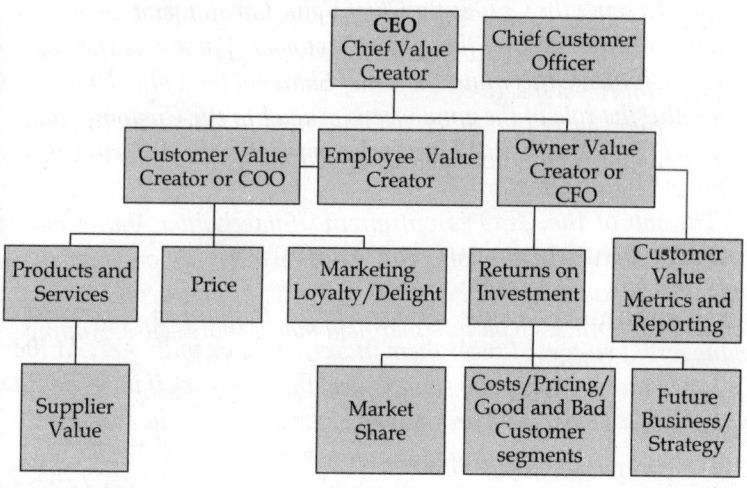

Source   Author.

In the organization of the future, there will be more Customer interactions, and building long-term Customer Value will become more prevalent."

The Business School of the Future

Krish continues, *"So if you accept the concept of a CEO being the Chief Value Creator, then are we really looking to employ business administrators, or value creators? The MBA in the future will be replaced by Masters of Value Management (MVM), or Masters of Value Creation (MVC). The business schools will become value creation schools, teaching executives about value creation for the shareholder and for the Customer, and to teach them that this is natural and the two are complementary. Using your analogy, $CV = BV$!*

"Students will be taught to manage short-term value and long-term value. They will also look at optimization between Customer Value and the Value of the company, the Customer Lifetime Value,

and learn how to measure CVA, Return on Customer (ROC) and Customer assets, how to increase these and the relationship between Total Shareholder Value, the Customer Value and ROC.

"Some MBA courses will be modified from a value, shareholder and Customer perspective.

"Once you agree that this is what we need to follow, we can then talk some more about your role as the CEO."

Getting Buy-in of Your Top Managers

Krish continues, *"Doug, we need to get the buy-in of your top managers. I suggest I meet them individually or with you. At the end of all our sessions, you should meet them and ask if they should embark on a Total CVM programme. I am leaving some sheets with notes on how some existing programmes co-exist with Total CVM. This is because many people will ask you why you need Total CVM when you have:*

- *Total Quality Management*
- *Total Business Excellence*
- *CRM*
- *Customer Satisfaction*
- *Customer Retention and Customer Loyalty*

"Meanwhile, don't forget Customer Strategy and Non-Customers."

Later on, Krish will tell Doug that to get top manager alignment, an apex Customer Circle, consisting of the VPs be instituted, and that the leader of this should be from a traditionally non-'Customer' function. Such a function can be IT, strategy, HRD or the like.

CUSTOMER STRATEGY

Krish is now discussing Customer strategy: *"To kick off Total CVM, it is necessary to build a Customer strategy, involving the top management. This is a way of not only getting their buy-in, but also of building a road map, a combined focus on the culture that has to be built, the tasks that have to be achieved and in what time frame, and the measurement metrics. The strategy meshes into the Corporate strategy, and modifies the Corporate strategy to recognize the role of the Customer and Customer parameters, and their relationship to what were hitherto more important corporate objectives. The Customer strategy encompasses milestones, review mechanisms, and how to bring the entire company and channel partners into the Customer-centric culture. It builds Customer-centric goals, engenders Customer related discussions, and increases inter-departmental interaction and teamwork, all building a Customer-focused organization.*

"Eventually, business strategy has to be led by the Customer strategy and the shareholder strategy. At Tata Chemicals Crop Nutrition and Agri-Business, the business strategy will be based on the Customer strategy, which is the right way to go, but requires revolutionary thinking that Kapil Mehan, CEO of the business, and Alok Tyagi, the head of strategy and business development for the business, had displayed.

"If there is a Customer Bill of Rights supported by a Circle of Promises, then the administrative methodology can be created for having people take responsibility for their part of keeping the promise, so that the Customer sees an intertwined promise from those responsible for delivering the promise.

"The different aspects of Customer strategy have been discussed in detail in Chapter 2 in the section Steps to Total CVM.

"Just remember, before making the Customer strategy, one needs to have a Customer Vision (some people prefer to call it the Customer Passion Statement), and a Customer Mission. For example,

---

Tata Power's Customer Vision

*To be the most **Customer Caring Company** delivering sustainable Value to Customers.*

"Yum! has a Customer Vision which they call Customer Mania.[3]

---

[3] Ken Blanchard, *Customer Mania!* (Harper Collins India, 2005).

> **Customer Mania**
>
> *We not only listen to and respond to the Voice of the Customer, we are obsessed to go the extra mile to make our Customers happy.*

"Customer strategy when developed properly, goes into tasks and tactics with responsibilities that spread throughout the company including HR and Finance as shown in Box 3.1 in a sample of one task:

Box 3.1: A Customer Strategy Sample

Mission: *At our company, the Customer is Job 1*

  Strategy: *Highest Customer Priority at all level*

   Tactics: *1. Top led Customer results in reporting system, review Customer Value metrics and Customer Assets. Implement Total CVM*

   Tasks: *Priority to be given to customer related issues in all the review meetings.*

- *Adequate resources to be provided as per the approved customer acquisition and network augmentation plan.*
- *Schedule of Authority to be refined to expedite the resolution of customers commercial complaints and budget release.*

   Responsibility: *VP(HR), VP(Operations), VP (Commercial), Dir. (Project), SHE Head, other functional GMs, Communication Chief, Strategy Chief, co-ordinated by GM (HR) & DGM (Customer Services), DGM(Logistic), VP Finance.*

Source   Author.

Non-Customers

"Whenever we have talked about Total CVM we have talked about Customers as stakeholders including:

- *External Customers*
- *Shareholders/owners*

- *Employees*
- *Internal Customers*
- *Channel partners*
- *Other stakeholders such as suppliers*

"As you know, in our marketplace, we have our loyal Customers, and loyal Customers of competition. We have floaters, who may not be Customers presently, or retained Customers of competition who are not shifting because of inertia. How do we use Total CVM to work on these non-Customers?

"The most obvious is to build our own Total Customer Value programme and Customer loyalty, and thereby build referrals and viral marketing, which will bring in non-Customers. Customer loyalty will build our brand image and trust will improve, drawing in non-Customers.

"The other way is to look for any possible interaction with non-Customers, be they through solicited or unsolicited enquiries, trade show visits, visits to your showrooms, offices, websites, and social media. We need to look at adding value to them and to these interactions, making them pleasant, easy and useful experiences.

"Often departments or businesses of a company do not have a direct Customer. For example, much of Tata Power's business is in new projects, with no external Customer. Here Total CVM focuses on internal Customers, and builds the base for Total CVM when external Customers are acquired after the projects are completed. Total CVM also builds teamwork and efficiency.

"We also teach companies such as Tata Power to view many suppliers as Customers. A good example is a farmer from whom you buy land. Traditional thinking would suggest that Tata Power is the buyer and the farmer is the seller. However, the seller has an emotional bond to the land; he also has long-term economic needs. Tata Motors learnt, to their chagrin, that the Nano project had to be relocated from West Bengal because politicians could muster somewhat disappointed farmers (even after they received the financial compensation) to renege on the land deal.

"Understanding the farmers' needs, focusing on them and working together with them, and building a value proposition for them would have negated a retreat from Bengal. Tata Power has started to recognize this early on."

Doug says he remembers Val and Jeff Gee[4] describing a Customer for a Customer Service person as "My Customer is anyone who isn't me."

CHANGING THE RULES OF THE GAME

Krish continues, *"Very few managers are proactive, nor are they willing to change the rules of the game. Instead, they bemoan the current market place and its dynamics. Normally, the market place dynamics are their perception of the market place. And generally, where the market is not growing, or where price pressure seems to be a factor, sales and marketing people tend to blame the market (and, of course, the Customers: the Customers buy on price, or are price conscious!)*

"When you ask them what they aim to do, they talk about cutting price and changing products. They rarely think about or talk about increasing value and beyond, and in changing the rules of the game. (See Box 3.2)."

Decommoditizing a Commodity Business

"Jeff Immelt, Chairman of GE, said that businesses are in danger of becoming commodity businesses. He states, 'The only way to climb out of the commodity hell is by adding Customer value...'. The following two examples show how," remarks Krish (See Boxes 3.2 and 3.3).

---

[4] Val and Jeff Gee are Customer Service consultants.

BOX 3.2
Frank Perdue and the Chicken Business

The classic example of changing the rules of the game is one of Frank Perdue and the chicken business.

Frank Perdue inherited the chicken business from his father. He found that it was a real commodity business, with there being no importance to the brand. A chicken was a chicken was a chicken! Chicken was being sold frozen. Availability in the store was the most important buying decision. Given below is the purchase criteria.

Chicken Business: Customer's Purchase Decision

Key Purchase Criteria	Before Frank Customer Rating			
	Relative Weight	Perdue Chicken	Others	Rating Differential
• Product				
– Yellow Bird	5	7	7	0
– Meat-to-Bone	10	6	6	0
– No Pinfeathers	15	5	5	0
– Fresh	15	7	7	0
• Service				
– Availability	55	8	8	0
– Brand Image	0	6	6	0
	100			

Weight on Quality vs. Price Before Frank	
Quality	10
Price	90
	100

Source PIMS Principle.

He decided that he needed to change the rules of the game. He met consumers and found that the major need was for chicken to be yellow, fresh, with no pinfeathers and good meat to bone ratio. He, therefore, decided to sell his birds refrigerated and not frozen. You could then press the bird and it felt soft in contrast to a hard frozen chicken (which definitely did not feel fresh). He also fed the birds well with yellow corn and put them on yellow Styrofoam trays to enhance the yellowness, and took good care to get rid of the pinfeathers in the

(Box 3.2 continued)

(*Box 3.2 continued*)

production stage. Frank then went on TV and extolled the virtues of his birds, particularly freshness. The resulting purchase decision is shown to contrast original purchase criteria curve.

Chicken Business: Customer's Purchase Decision

Key Purchase Criteria	After Frank Customer Rating			
	Relative Weight	Perdue Chicken	Others	Rating Differential
• Product				
– Yellow Bird	10	8.1	7.2	+0.9
– Meat-To-Bone	20	9.0	7.3	+1.7
– No Pinfeathers	20	9.2	6.5	+2.7
– Fresh	15	8.0	8.0	0.0
• Service				
– Availability	10	8.0	8.0	0.0
– Brand Image	25	9.3	6.5	+2.8
	100			

Weight on Quality vs. Price After Frank	
Quality	70
Price	30
	100

Source PIMS Principles.

After some time, brand had become important (25 per cent importance) and availability had dropped to 10 per cent. More importantly, his product got a positive differential rating versus competition, showing consumers preferred his product. In 1971, he started his ad campaign built around changing the rules of the game and the rest is a history of Perdue's success. From a negligible market share (3 per cent), they went on to become a leading national chicken player.

You too, can change the rules of the game if you know what Customers truly want, and not falling into the trap of thinking that you have to compete in what is perceived as the conventional marketplace.

Source Ray Kordupleski, *Mastering Customer Value Management* (Pinnaflex, 2003).

BOX 3.3

Decommoditizing Business: Tata Chemicals Crop Nutrition and Agri-Business Example

An example is where Tata Chemicals' Crop Nutrition and Agri-Business decided to decommoditize their business, by starting a loyalty programme and franchised stores which would provide a range of agri-solutions under one roof. The loyalty programme called for farmers to be enrolled in a programme called Tata Kisan Parivar (TKP), literally, Tata's Farmer Family, and the franchisee store is called Tata Kisan Sansar (TKS) (or Tata Farmer World). The normal sales pattern involved traditional channel partners — dealers and retailers, both of whom were multi-brand.

In 2006, the question came whether these were cost programmes or gave real benefits to the Customer, and thereby to the company.

In a Customer Value Study by Customer Value Foundation, it was proven that these two programmes were seen as giving immense benefits to the farmer and to the company. Even a non-TKP member found the TKS stores adding value to them. TKP members going to normal stores seemed to derive more benefits and had higher brand loyalty to Tata than normal farmers. The biggest payoff came when TKP members dealt with TKS stores.

Based on this study, Tata Chemicals decided not only to continue growing the two programmes but also decided to increase the focus on TKP through the TKS stores.

The loyalty curves are not true loyalty curves, but are curves based on the per cent that would recommend the brand or the retailer. True loyalty curves are based on re-use likelihood, not on recommendations. Recommendation based loyalty curves tend to be more stringent than when you ask people if they would re-purchase. You can see the remarkable improvement in loyalty on TKS and TKP.

(Box 3.3 continued)

(Box 3.3 continued)

ANALYSIS OF TATA FARMERS: NON TKP and NON TKS vs. all Other Combinations

Only for TATA

Non TKP and Non TKS	Normal Tata Farmer buying from normal retailer
TKP	All TKP (buying from normal retailer and from TKS)
TKS	Tata Farmers Buying from TKS (includes TKP buying from TKS)
Non TKP, TKS	Normal Tata Farmer (non TKP) buying from TKS
TKP, TKS	TKP Farmer buying from TKS
Impact weight TKP*	Impact weight of TKP shown where there is a significant difference

Value

	Impact weight for all (non TKP, non TKS)	TKP vs. Non TKP/Non TKS			Impact wt TKP*	TKS vs. Non TKP/TKS		Non TKP, TKS vs. Non TKP/TKS		TKP, TKS vs. Non TKP/TKS	
		Non TKP and Non TKS	TKP	Ratio TKP vs. Non TKP and Non TKS		TKS	Ratio TKS vs. Non TKP and TKS	Non TKP, TKS	Ratio Non TKP, TKS vs. Non TKP and TKS	TKP, TKS	Ratio TKP, TKS vs. Non TKP/TKS
Overall Quality	22%	6.32	7.16	1.13	20%	7.01	1.11	6.68	1.06	7.2	1.14
Urea Brand image	45%	8.20	8.74	1.07	62%	8.55	1.05	8.21	1.00	8.89	1.08
Overall Price	33%	5.67	6.34	1.12	18%	6.35	1.12	6.35	1.12	6.35	1.12
Overall Value	100%	7.40	7.98	1.08	100%	7.89	1.07	7.63	1.03	8.04	1.09

Price

	Impact weight for all (non TKP, non TKS)	TKP vs Non TKP / Non TKS				TKS vs. Non TKP/ TKS		Non TKP, TKS vs. Non TKP/ TKS		TKP, TKS vs. Non TKP/ TKS	
		Non TKP and Non TKS	TKP	Ratio TKP vs Non TKP and Non TKS	Impact wt TKP*	TKS	Ratio TKS vs. Non TKP and TKS	Non TKP, TKS	Ratio Non TKP, TKS vs. Non TKP, TKS	TKP, TKS	Ratio TKP vs. Non TKP and TKS
Competitive Price	30%	7.07	7.68	1.09	33%	7.65	1.08	7.51	1.06	7.73	1.09
Discounts	18%	3.60	3.85	1.07	23%	3.72	1.03	3.86	1.07	3.64	1.01
Credit Terms	52%	5.02	6.00	1.19	44%	5.93	1.18	5.80	1.15	6	1.19
Overall Price	**100%**	**5.67**	**6.34**	**1.12**		**6.35**	**1.12**	**6.35**	**1.12**	**6.35**	**1.12**

Quality

	Impact weight	TKP vs. Non TKP / Non TKS				TKS vs. Non TKP /TKS		Non TKP, TKS vs. Non TKP/ TKS		TKP, TKS vs. Non TKP/ TKS	
		Non TKP and Non TKS	TKP	Ratio TKP vs. Non TKP Non TKS	Impact wt TKP*	TKS	Ratio TKS vs. Non TKP TKS	Non TKP. TKS	Ratio Non TKP, TKS vs. Non TKP and TKS	TKP, TKS	Ratio TKP vs. Non TKP and TKS
Overall Urea	27%	9.10	8.98	0.99	4%	9.03	0.99	8.91	0.98	9.1	1.02
Overall Retailer	73%	6.97	7.46	1.07	96%	7.43	1.07	7.18	1.03	7.58	1.09
Company's Services											
Overall Quality	**100%**	**6.32**	**7.16**	**1.13**		**7.01**	**1.11**	**6.68**	**1.06**	**7.20**	**1.14**

means poor, irrespective of rating versus competition

means better than competition

means equal to competition

means worse than competition

(Box 3.3 continued)

(Box 3.3 continued)

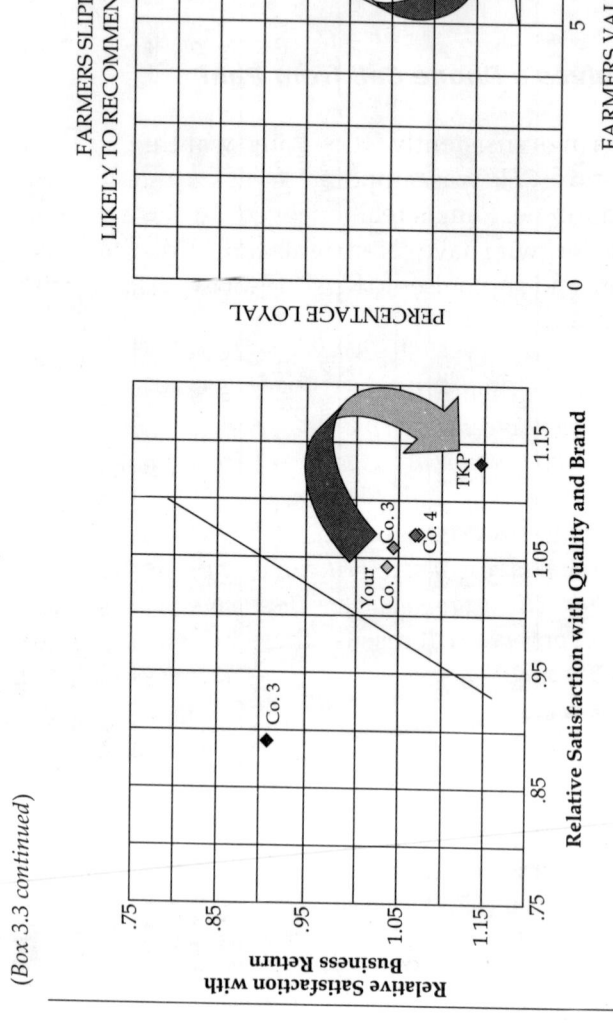

FARMERS SLIPPERY SLOPE
LIKELY TO RECOMMEND BRAND OF UREA

The end-result was that brand became important, price became immaterial and a methodology for improving loyalty, and validating the loyalty programmes was installed. Also, it told Tata where to improve to increase value.

Source Customer Value Study by Customer Value Foundation.

Changing the Rules of the Game in a Service Business

Giving another example, Krish says, *"Very often, we are followers in a business. As we showed earlier, one can change the rules of the game, by using Value data and understanding Customers and their changing needs. The following example (Box 3.4) shows how."*

Doug Receives a Phone Call from Pam

The phone rings insistently. It is Pam, wanting to know where Doug was. He was supposed to pick up some guests for dinner at home. Pam is really peeved: "You know your friends and your wife have some rights too." Doug promises to leave soon, and apologises to Krish, "Got to go. Pam insists on her rights!"

Krish is pleased, *"So she should. Your Customers also should demand their Bill of Rights. Total CVM builds the Customer Bill of Rights through interconnected promises, or what I call the Circle of Promises, established through Customer Circles. Next time, we will discuss The Customer Bill of Rights."*

Handing Doug a few sheets of paper, (shown in Appendix I), Krish says, *"I am giving you a write up on these topics so that you can discuss with your managers these points, should they arise.* In any event, we will discuss these in detail when we meet next."

The list includes:

- Total Quality Management
- Total Business Excellence
- CRM
- Customer Satisfaction and Total CVM Customer retention versus Customer loyalty

Krish says goodbye and leaves.

BOX 3.4
Changing the Rules of the Game: Godrej HiCare

Godrej HiCare was a late entrant in the pest control business. This business was the domain of what in India is called the unorganized sector. That means a sector literally run by mom and pop operations and where no real large, organized players existed. A few years earlier, one organized player had entered, called Pest Control of India.

When Customer Value Foundation started work at Godrej, we were convinced that Godrej would have to change the rules of the game. The majority of Godrej people agreed that brand would play a role, but were unable to think that brand would reduce the importance of price. A Customer Value Foundation study showed how it was possible to change the rules of the game, and how unconsciously, Godrej was actually doing this. We showed Godrej this through our study.

Value

In the marketplace, we see ourselves as we want to. And when we come up against a seemingly price conscious market, we tend to think the market works only on price. We are not willing to change the perception. But through a value study, we can start to understand how benefits can become more important than price. The following table vividly portrays this.

Attribute	Entire Industry	PCI and Godrej	Only Godrej
		Impact Weight	
Overall Benefits	33%	45%	64%
Overall Image	5%	0%	0%
Overall Cost	63%	55%	36%
Overall Value	**100%**	**100%**	**100%**

Even with limited Customers, the actual cost in the case of Godrej is less important.

What does this tell us?

It tells us that the majority of the Customers in the un-organized segment view cost as important as they do not see the benefit of pest control service as high. Godrej has to find a way of letting them know the importance of the pest control service and the advantages of using Godrej over competiiton.

In addition, this tells us that by adding value, you can make the price less important in the eyes of the Customer. Over a period of time, brand and image will be built up. Why is it not important now? The reason

(Box 3.4 continued)

(*Box 3.4 continued*)

is that, currently, service execution (that is, the pest control service works to my satisfaction in the elimination of pests) is more important than the HiCare brand, which has to be established.

Similar results were seen in Overall Benefits.

Overall Benefits

It is likely, as Godrej becomes more important a service provider, the package and people will become more significant. If we look at only the organized sector, we can see the weights (importance) change from the perception of the overall market.

The people become more important (34 per cent versus 19 per cent for the entire industry). Thus, teaching our frontline people Customer Value will help as the industry seeks more organized players.

	Entire Industry	PCI and Godrej
Attribute	Impact Weight	
Pest Control Package	34%	37%
People	19%	34%
Service Execution	47%	28%
Overall Benefits	**100%**	**100%**

Pest Control Package

In an effort to understand what drives the pest control package, we went beyond what HiCare executives had suggested. The pest control package has to have a warranty and a service execution declaration or history that Customers can see and derive satisfaction from.

Pest Control Package Importance from Customers	
Attribute	Impact Weight
Understands my Needs	23%
People	23%
Service Execution	33%
Warranty	21%
Overall Pest Control Package	**100%**

The pest control package should include people, service execution selling, warranty and, of course, show an understanding of the needs of the Customer. Is HiCare too rigid?

(*Box 3.4 continued*)

(*Box 3.4 continued*)

People

Actually, within PCI and Godrej, Customers want more skilled people. This is different than the un-organized sector where people are not that important.

	Entire Industry	PCI and Godrej
Attribute		Impact Weight
Skilled	24%	45%
Responsive	22%	0%
Knowledgeable	22%	18%
Accesible	10%	18%
Prompt	21%	19%
Overall Benefits	**100%**	**100%**

In trying to understand the people equation, one also sees how the actual service execution impacts the Customer. Skilled people will execute the job better and be more responsive! And what does the Customer equate sevice execution with? It is the lack of any pests during the contract. If this is not done properly, the service package and people are perceived to be poor.

People Importance from Customers	
Attribute	Impact Weight
Skilled	21%
Responsive	12%
Knowledgeable	18%
Accessible	6%
Prompt	9%
Service Execution	34%
Overall People	**100%**

People are reviewed on their service execution, something missed out in looking at how Customers perceive people.

Service Execution

Going further, Crisis Management is a very important part of the service execution, even more so in the organized sector (PCI and Godrej). We can see the market needs shift from reliable and effective to crisis control, as the previously important factors become more common and expected in the organized sector.

(*Box 3.4 continued*)

(*Box 3.4 continued*)

Attribute	Entire Industry	PCI and Godrej
	Impact Weight	
Reliable	22%	14%
Effective	13%	7%
Quality Assurance	10%	15%
Timely	10%	3%
Technical Support	23%	19%
Crisis Management	21%	43%
Overall Service Execution	**100%**	**100%**

Overall Image

Image is currently not important but is bound to become so.

If we look at the organized sector, trust in the company becomes more important, showing Customer's latent need coming out.

Attribute	Entire Industry	PCI and Godrej
	Impact Weight	
Brand	0%	0%
Trust	5%	25%
Ethics	44%	45%
Concern for Safety	51%	30%
Overall Image	**100%**	**100%**

Overall Cost

Non-price terms make up 60 per cent of the price and the actual price is 40 per cent of the importance in the perception of overall cost.

Payment terms become less important in the organized sector. Actual price is more important, because people suspect that the organized sector will be more expensive.

Attribute	Entire Industry	PCI and Godrej
	Impact Weight	
Price itself	44%	60%
Payment Terms	56%	40%
Overall Price Terms	**100%**	**100%**

Non-price terms are more important than the price terms.

Price justification does not showup as being important. Yet, when we look at the organized sector, price justification becomes a significant factor! Not as significant as warranties but important enough.

(*Box 3.4 continued*)

(*Box 3.4 continued*)

Attribute	Entire Industry	PCI and Godrej
	Impact Weight	
Crisis Support	12%	16%
Partnership—Training, Updates, Safety, Health	37%	13%
Warranty	47%	44%
Price Justification	4%	28%
Overall Non-Price Items	**100%**	**100%**

The end result is that Godrej was able to increase referrals, reduce pressure on price while improving on branding.

Source Customer Value Total Customer Value Management programme at Godrej. See Appendix II for greater detail.

Note Sometimes the impact weights do not add up to 100 per cent because of rounding errors.

CHAPTER SYNOPSIS

In this chapter, we look at the fundamentals that have to be in place for the Total CVM programme becoming effective.

The Customer comes First: No CEO gods
The CEO must change, and be Customer led. We have to dismantle the CEO god syndrome, a difficult thing to do.

Necessary and Relevant Tasks from a Customer's perspective: Task Audit
We also find that managers in a company are often "overworked" and do not have time for new programmes and Customer transformation. Task audits can pinpoint unnecessary tasks and release time for more necessary and relevant tasks, by eliminating unnecessary and irrelevant work like looking at unnecessary mails you get.

The Organization of the Future
If one accepts Value creation as a goal for the shareholder and for the Customer, then the organizations have to be structured to deliver value by having the CEO become the Chief Value Creator and have a Chief Customer Value Creator and a Chief Shareholder Value Creator. The CEO has to balance and maximize the value creation between the shareholder and the Customer.

The Business School of the Future

Likewise the business school of the future will change to being a Value creation school, giving Masters in Value Creation.

Getting Buy-in of your top Managers

For Total CVM to take hold in an organization, there has to be a buy-in by the top managers. Participating in Customer strategy, and in Customer Circles and developing Customer oriented roles for themselves and their departments along with Customer focused incentive systems builds this alignment.

Customer Strategy

As discussed earlier, the Customer strategy has to be built as a precursor to Business strategy. It should include Non-Customers who are:

- *External Customers*
- *Shareholders/owners*
- *Employees*
- *Internal Customers*
- *Channel partners*
- *Other stakeholders such as suppliers*

Changing the Rules of the Game

Marketplaces have perceived rules which are often accepted. Our job is either to excel at these rules or attempt to change the rules of the game. To do so, one must understand the Customer's evolving needs and play to them.

Next we look at:

- Decommoditizing a Commodity Business: Here we look at Tata Crop Nutrition and Agri-Business.
- Changing the rules of the game in a Service Business is yet another example through Godrej.

Thus, with the CVA data and the understanding of Customer's needs, we can change the rules of the marketplace. We can convert a price sensitive or commodity market place into a value or brand driven market. These are great benefits to an organization.

4

Existing Programmes and Total CVM

TOTAL CUSTOMER VALUE MANAGEMENT AND TOTAL QUALITY MANAGEMENT

Vikki Solomon, Glacier's Head of Quality, is meeting with Jimmy Vaidya, Head of Manufacturing, Jack Griswold, the COO, and Krish Kumar. Jack asks Vikki, "How often have we talked about the Voice of the Customer? We have been working together on the quality front and improving products and processes. Customer complaints are examined, but you have not really instituted any Customer Value or needs analysis beyond product and service quality. I know you are copied on the satisfaction studies."

Vikki agrees. "We have been focusing, as you said, on the product and process quality, and on building quality circles. The direct contact with the Customer has been through marketing, generally."

Krish says, "*Deming stopped using the term 'Total Quality Management' or 'TQM' because he thought that it had become a process or a tool. He started saying that* transformation of the prevailing system of management *is the real work of a company. Total CVM does just this. Nevertheless, the TQM movement has been a fantastic example of human endeavour in improving employees and their organizations. The improved products and service quality is a reflection of the yeomen work this movement has achieved for companies and their Customers. In addition, the discipline and employee involvement TQM brings to an organization is exemplary.*

"Total CVM is complementary and should be viewed with the TQM movement and many of the principles followed should be merged into a Total CVM programme. For example, one could make a case for quality circles becoming Customer-Centric-Circles, or both should be followed simultaneously.

"Very often, I find TQM devotees very defensive when we discuss CVM. They firmly believe TQM is based on Customer needs and feedback, and therefore does everything Total CVM can deliver. I am glad you are being honest and saying you have little contact with the end Customer. I am sure you meet the retail chain's quality people, though."

Vikki nods her head in assent.

Krish says, *"First looking at the Customer feedback, I can only repeat what I found at GE, namely that Six Sigma, also supposedly driven by the Customer, does not necessarily reflect the Voice of the Customer, unless you use Customer Value Added (CVA). GE now uses CVA as the Voice of the Customer, before converting it into Net Promoter Score (which is another measure of loyalty).*

"The other day, I spent time with a Motorola executive, who at one time had been in charge of quality and Six Sigma. He kept telling me that Total CVM was no different than TQM and Six Sigma because the Customer drove them both. Forty-five minutes into the discussion, he said he could see the difference. Predicting why people buy from you, or pricing using value, or looking at the relative importance of brand, quality and price go well beyond Six Sigma and TQM. Building total Customer-centricity is beyond what TQM is delivering.

"According to many recent studies, Total Quality is no longer adding value to the corporation. An Arthur D. Little study on over 100 British firms concluded that there was no significant impact of TQM. Further, the study quoted that over two-thirds of 500 US companies studied, found zero competitiveness gains. Generally first and early movers get an advantage which diminishes as competition catches up.

"Peter Senge[1] says most managers regard the Quality Management revolution like the organizational learning fad of the early 1990s. I do not subscribe to this.

"Nevertheless, we should use TQM and Total CVM together to build a class, Customer-centric organization."

Jack says, "This is a good idea." He asks Vikki to become part of the Customer Circles and use her experience in Quality Circles to guide the Customer Circles.

THE TOYOTA WAY AND TOTAL CVM

The driving principles of the Toyota Way and the Toyota Production System which have led to the great innovation are:[2]

- *Long-term Philosophy*
- *The Right Process Will Produce the Right Results*
- *Add Value to the Organization by Developing People and Partners*
- *Continuously Solving Problems Drive Organizational Learning*

Using these, operational excellence becomes a strategic weapon. Of course, doing the right thing for the Customer and putting the Customer first are important.

Total CVM imbibes all of this. It assumes that process excellence and efficiency are in place. Customer excellence and Customer focus and partnerships drive everything. Continuous improvement is replaced by Continuous Customer Improvement Programmes, and everyone becomes a value creator building their own and the company's brand equity. So Total CVM goes far beyond the Toyota Way in organizational transformation.

---

[1] Peter Senge, *The Fifth Dimension* (Doubleday, 1990).
[2] Jeffrey K. Liker, *The Toyota Way* (Tata McGraw Hill, 2004).

TOTAL CVM AND BUSINESS EXCELLENCE

Krish is addressing Doug's question about Total Business Excellence. Jack Griswold is also present.

"The problem with businesses is that they embrace processes better and faster than they embrace Customers. By thinking that they are putting into place programmes such as business excellence, businesses think they have achieved the right thing from the point of view of the Customer. I am afraid the Customer does not see things this way.

"Implementing Total CVM is easier when business excellence processes are in place to help. Customer excellence is the goal, and business excellence is a good path. As long as there is no understanding that Customer excellence builds business excellence and great business results, business excellence will be seen as the overriding organizational challenge.

"Business excellence can only work when the managers are truly professional. This means, they come to meetings on time, they keep appointments, they do not keep visitors waiting, they have basic courtesy of acknowledging e-mails and answering calls, keeping promises and so on. Many such managers think they are the gods of their department. If fundamental business professionalism does not exist, how can you install business excellence? Companies (and I have such clients) spend money on business excellence without changing managerial attitudes. Total CVM builds professional attitudes, whereas Business Excellence focuses on processes and results.

"Advocates of Business Excellence will say it does do many things that Total CVM espouses. They will cite the Baldridge Award criterion.

"The core concepts of the Baldrige Criteria for Performance Excellence are:

- *Visionary leadership*
- *Customer-driven excellence*
- *Organizational and personal learning*
- *Valuing employees and partners*

- *Agility*
- *Focus on the future*
- *Managing for innovation*
- *Management by fact*
- *Social responsibility*
- *Focus on results and creating value*
- *Systems perspective*

"I believe," continues Krish, "the difference lies in the focus on the Customer and the methodology applied through Total CVM. Much less emphasis is paid to internal processes and measurements as on Customer measurements. The methodology also improves Employee Value, Customer Value and Value of Customer and Total Shareholder Value.

"This is the reason I keep saying, the concepts are all there, it is in the focus and the methodology to implement these where there is a difference.

"More importantly, many companies with elaborate and established Business Excellence programmes have started using Total CVM with success. Obviously, they are seeing the differences in the results and to the organization and are espousing Total CVM. Total CVM comes from the heart. Total business excellence is mandated in an organization. Business Excellence Scores improve with Total CVM.

"I think if Total CVM has TQM and Business Excellence as cornerstones and building blocks, the company will excel in its Customer and business goals, and move towards continued market leadership.

"A classic example is the Tata Group in India, one of Customer Value Foundation's clients.

"The Total CVM programme at this Tata company was a major success, first in converting frontline people into Customer Advocates. We had predicted Customer roles for the Head of Safety and Environment, and this was echoed by the Customers in the Customer Value study, where environmental and safety issues were considered a major part of the quality of supply.

"After our work was over, this Tata company instituted a seven-point business agenda, heading which was Total CVM, followed by increasing market capacity tenfold. And this division got the best TBEM (Total Business Excellence Management) score in the Tata Group.

"The VP of Business Excellence of another Tata company congratulated me on our report, which he termed as 'priceless'."

"You are right," says Doug. "Business Excellence and Total CVM go hand in hand, with Quality being an important component."

CUSTOMER SATISFACTION AND TOTAL CVM: CUSTOMER RETENTION VERSUS CUSTOMER LOYALTY

Krish continues: *"However, there are people who believe the purpose of any organization is to have satisfied Customers and so they say satisfaction is everything. Now we know satisfaction does not lead to loyalty. This is best exposed by Jeffrey Gitomer,[3] who claims Customer satisfaction is worthless, Customer loyalty is priceless. We are talking about true loyalty (not just retention). Satisfaction is a necessary (but not sufficient) condition for loyalty but does not ensure loyalty. Some people seem loyal but stay on with a company because of inertia.*

"That is why Peter Drucker[4] who expounded satisfaction some 50 years ago, changed to being a Customer Value exponent, saying around 15 years ago that Customer Value is everything."

---

[3] Jeffrey Gitomer, *Customer Satisfaction is Worthless, Customer Loyalty is Priceless: How to Make them Love You, Keep You Coming Back, and Tell Everyone They Know* (Bard Press, 1998).

[4] See http://homepage.mac.com/bobembry/studio/biz/conceptual_resources/authors/peter_drucker/business_functions.html (accessed on 21 June 2010).

Doug stops Krish. "Unfortunately people remember Drucker's statement on satisfaction. They do not remember that he espoused Customer Value, which is a more recent management tool started by Ray Kordupleski, and later by Brad Gale.

"Peter Drucker said the following:

- Only one valid definition of Business:
  - To create a Customer
  - The Customer determines what the Business is

- What the business thinks it produces is not of first importance, especially not to the future of the business and its success

- What the Customer thinks he is buying and considers *value* is decisive: it determines what a business is, what it produces, and whether it will prosper!

"I just read Jeffrey Wallman's *An examination of Peter Drucker's work from an institutional perspective: How institutional innovation creates value leadership*. Basically, this paper uses an institutional perspective to analyze Peter Drucker's contributions to management, marketing and marketing strategy. At the heart of each institutional comparison are the Customer and the value created for the Customer by the organization. Institutional comparisons help managers understand how the organization can create Customers by adjusting its Customer Value proposition. Drucker influences marketers by focusing on how the organization's values are used to develop the organization's Customer Value proposition. Further, he showed that the organization's values and its Customer Value propositions are manifested in its transaction rules."[5]

---

[5] Jeffrey Wallman, "An Examination of Peter Drucker's Work from an Institutional Perspective: How Institutional Innovation Creates Value Leadership", *Journal of the Academy of Marketing Science*, 37, no. 1 (2009).

Krish comments, *"You must send this to me. I have not seen it. However, such a recent article highlights Drucker's passion for Customer Value. Yet people continue only to measure satisfaction. I recall Tata's Business Excellence Programme called for ever-increasing value to the Customer. However, Tatas did not have a means of measuring value and, so instead measured a surrogate, satisfaction. Customer Value Foundation was able to measure Customer Value for Tata through the Voice of the Customer and CVA studies."*

Doug chips in, If you do not know how to measure value, you measure satisfaction. Satisfaction should be continued to be used to measure transactional interactions."

Krish offers one more thought: *"Actually, it is not satisfaction, but delight and value that come close to getting loyalty. Delight is not easy to deliver. I often challenge employees to think of one thing that could truly delight a Customer. I give them a month. Very few are able to come up with something that can cause true delight — something Customers would be wowed by, something they would talk about. Giving flowers to a Customer or a discount cannot be thought of as creating delight."*

Customer Surveys and their Usefulness

Doug shows the study conducted by Customer Champions in the UK (an associate of Customer Value Foundation) on the usefulness of Customer data. "While 95 per cent of the companies measure Customer metrics, less than 30 per cent of the companies plan action steps, and only 10 per cent actually act on such data, and only 5 per cent communicate back to the Customer (See Figure 4.1). Telling, isn't it?"

Doug continues: "In 2005, about USD 23 billion was spent on Customer surveys and market research initiatives. The usefulness of such surveys is low. Less than 30 per cent of such surveys are used, according to a *USA Today* article."

FIGURE 4.1
Maximizing the Value of Customer Feedback

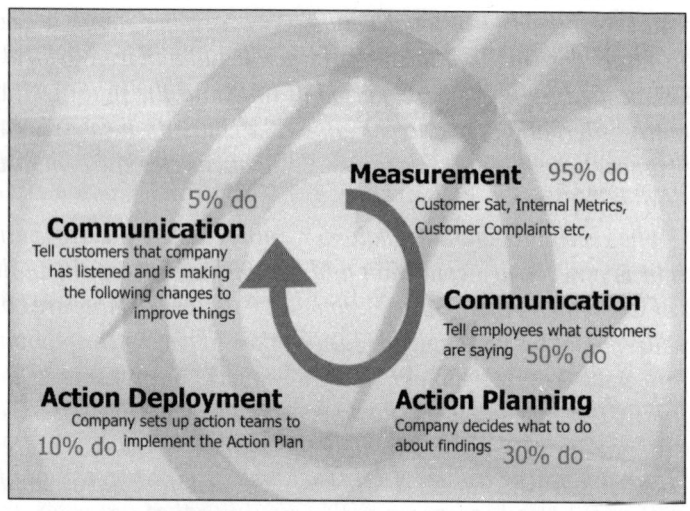

Source   Customer Champions Survey of 100 European Companies.

Krish says to Doug: *"You are right. Many of my clients tell me that the satisfaction scores make them look better than the value scores. Moreover, the value scores are versus competition. Value surveys focus on decision makers and buyers, whereas satisfaction surveys focus on the user of the product or the service, and look at transactions. Satisfaction surveys require three to four times the sample size that value surveys required, because in value surveys, we do not try to differentiate between frequencies of the responses. Value surveys do incorporate some aspects of satisfaction while going beyond satisfaction."*

Customer Satisfaction not Directly Linked to Loyalty

Doug reaches over to his bookshelf and pulls out a book called *Customer Satisfaction is Worthless, Customer Loyalty is Priceless* by Jeffrey Gitomer. "This says it all!"

Krish remarks, *"You are right. For example, mild irritants and transactional dissatisfaction do not necessarily lead to divorcing a brand, or breaking of loyal bonds. On the other hand, a great transaction does not lead to loyalty either. What will lead to loyalty are embedded feelings over a period of time and the juxtaposition of many interactions and experiences. Satisfaction measures just the transaction at hand. Customer Value measures the composite feeling and is more holistic.*

"It has been proven that Customer Value leads to loyalty. Satisfaction is a necessary condition and complementary to the building of Customer Value. Satisfaction and Customer Value are both measurements we recommend, satisfaction to check transactional improvements and Customer Value for loyalty improvements and changing Customer needs. Customer Value studies are done once a year or once in two years; satisfaction more often. The questions to be asked in a satisfaction study are best designed from the Customer Value study results. Only important items to the Customer (as assessed from the Customer Value study) need to be addressed and not trivial issues. For example, generally packaging satisfaction is measured, but often is not an important reason for purchase in a bulk commodity product like fertilizer. Yet satisfaction studies keep measuring it. Jagdish Khattar, former MD of Maruti Suzuki said to me that they were the only market leader that had the highest satisfaction scores in JD Power's surveys, the implication being that market leaders do not have the highest satisfaction rating. How is this possible, if satisfaction measures loyalty?"

Doug gets back to his desk and accesses the net from his computer. He shows Krish an article by Murphy Spoyles who puts it interestingly[6]: He says satisfied Customers usually seek your services first, and assuming you are competitive, and won't spend time shopping around. Still, they are vulnerable to competition and will often look elsewhere if your offer is

---

[6] See http://www.helium.com/items/657711-Customer-retention-versus-Customer-loyalty (accessed on 21 July 2010).

expensive or inconvenient. The satisfied Customer may give you a referral when you solicit it, but they are not inclined to refer you of their own initiative.

He also says that one has to remember that a satisfied Customer is never static. They will become either loyal Customers or dissatisfied Customers at some point in the future. The satisfied Customer is the easiest to convert to a loyal Customer. Make him loyal!

Doug surfs to yet another article, this time by Richard Fouts, who agrees:[7] Satisfied Customers may not necessarily be involved emotionally with the product. Retention does not equate to emotionally investment, which is critical for loyalty. He gives an example of your dentist whom you may not particularly like, but go back to him because you've neither the time nor energy to look for a new one.

However, if a great referral on a new dentist came your way, you might change. Your current dentist cannot understand. However, your perceived loyalty was actually nothing more than convenience. Maybe you complained about him to your spouse and friends, but you never really articulated your dissatisfaction with him.

Loyal patients tolerate any inconvenience to do business with their preferred dentist. In addition, they send him or her referrals.

To get loyalty you have to deliver a memorable experience rather than just service. Companies that create experiences have higher loyalty. Nordstrom sells the same clothes as its competitors, but its loyalty quotients are high because of the experience they create.

Loyal Customers give you *wallet retention*. This should increase over the previous year. Wallet retention ratio can be measured.

---

[7] See http://www.helium.com/items/491965-Customer-retention-versus-Customer-loyalty (accessed on 21 July 2010).

$$\text{Wallet Retention Ratio} = \frac{\text{Total client revenue this year divided by this year's number of clients}}{\text{Total client revenue last year divided by last year's number of clients}}$$

If your wallet retention exceeds client retention, it indicates that your high-value Customers are coming back. Your shareholders love this.

Richard Fouts quotes Vance Christensen, the CEO of Amae Software (specialists in interactive voice systems) who has a good list of loyalty signs:

- You negotiate prices with Customers. You negotiate costs with loyal Customers.
- Customers pay at their discretion. Loyal Customers pay on time.
- Customers become referrals of your competitors. Loyal Customers willingly provide referrals to you.
- Generally, you will experience turnover rates of 15 per cent or higher. The turnover rate of loyal Customers will be less than 5 per cent and will be for reasons out of your control.
- Most Customers seek competitive data. Loyal Customers share it.
- Loyal Customers perceive you as a partner, not a commodity provider.
- Contracts keep satisfied Customers in place. You have a virtual lifetime contract with your loyal Customers.
- Most Customers will leave you if they find a better offer. Loyal Customers will stay by your side.

The Customer Guru nods his head in agreement. *"'Brand Loyalty', as we once knew it, meant Customers being loyal to a specific brand. Patricia Seybold[8] says things have changed*

---

[8] CEO, Patricia Seybold Group and author, *Customers.com, The Customer Revolution, Outside Innovation.*

180 degrees in recent years. Today, the brand has to be loyal to the Customer (in other words, the brand must deliver on its promise, and meet the Customer's expectations and values if the organization is to expect loyalty and repeat purchases). The key to success is to build and maintain a brand that resonates with the Customer's own values. Often, Customers want to know if the supplier is loyal to the Customer!"

"Remember that in a seller's market or where there are shortages, Customers look for supplier's loyalty. Most suppliers forget this! I remember Dow, a major plastics resin supplier cut off Continental Can, a big Customer buying polystyrene for foamed cups and plates. Consequently, the Customer's plant had to be shut down. Guess what, the Customer had a long memory and for many years refused to do business with the supplier."

"Business is no longer Businesses selling to Consumers (B2C). Rather, it is Consumers buying from Businesses (C2B). How easy is it for the Customer to do business with the Business?

Customer Relationship Management (CRM) and Customer Value

Doug says, "First and foremost, managers must shift their mindset from CRM, which generally is a data management tool and not the ultimate relationship building tool, though it does assist in managing Customer Value. Managing Customer Value is a two-way street: it entails managing both the value provided by the company to Customers and the value of Customers to the company. Decisions are based on a detailed understanding of the value that Customers place on the benefits they receive and on the economics of delivering those benefits. Customer relationship is an essential part of Customer Value. However, CRM has by and large become data collection and a tool to help true relationship management. In most companies it is process or IT-led. It is not led from the heart and soft skills are considered to be distinct from the CRM department.

Krish says, "There are some exceptions, but by and large you are right."

"As I've mentioned previously, getting repeat and increased sales from existing Customers has generally been approached through various CRM programmes. Companies usually think CRM means 'Loyalty Programmes'. Customers consider loyalty programmes for the reward and discount elements contained in the programmes. However, these programmes have little or no individual touching element.

"In truth, most CRM programmes are process-centric. Often the processes are designed from the point of view of the company and purely for the convenience of the company (not the Customer) and are not Customer-centric (They don't focus on the 'C'). The majority of organizations treat loyalty programmes as 'Cost' programmes. For example, many hotel and airline companies feel their loyalty programmes are not increasing loyalty, and that they are stuck with them and the consequential increased costs and the need to match competitive offers without getting true loyalty from their passengers.

"You must know people who stay in New York in one chain hotel and in Chicago with another. Why aren't they loyal to one hotel chain?

"CRM should be led by CVM, which is akin to the Voice of the Customer and Voice of Competitor, and complemented by Customer Share Marketing (CSM), and by co-creating Customer experience.

"CRM loyalty programmes are usually the responsibility of sales and marketing and are generally administered by IT and call centres, while Customer touchpoints range throughout the organization. It is therefore imperative that the entire organization is energized to enhance and add value to the Customer. This is where CVM comes in. This is why we need to build a 'Customer Conduit' running through the organization.

"Examples of Customer Conduits exist. Lloyds Bank involved every employee from touchpoints to senior management to 'Deliver Service Excellence' and used teams such as those we have described.

IBM uses a similar approach when they want to roll out a service excellence model in many countries.

"Also, remember we normally outsource our touching (retailers, call centres, etc.). We must examine third party touching. And don't forget Customers' DNA (Do Not Annoy) and the need to avoid erosion touches.

"By the way, it's an established fact that many companies have not achieved a return on their CRM investment."

Doug adds, "For example, financial institutions such as banks spent USD 6.8 billion on CRM in 2002, and a third of all financial institutions use CRM for sales force automation and call centres. Only 8 per cent of these institutions have a 360 degree view of the Customer. Real and crucial information at their touchpoints (for example, the personal banker, who may not be in his job posting for long) is not available, reducing the ability of the institution to become a trusted advisor to its most profitable Customers, or to grow business with lower profile Customers."[9] Spending on all worldwide CRM programmes was over USD 25 billion in 2006 and expected to be USD 41 billion in 2010 (may not happen with the economic downturn).

"CRM is useful if defined as a creator of Customer Value as suggested by Vince Kellen, President, CRM Strategy, Blue Wolf. His definition is 'CRM is a business strategy that seeks to improve the company's profit and revenue generating ability by better understanding its Customers and delivering value to them'. Unfortunately, the bulk of the CRM programmes are passive information gathering systems and add limited value versus Total CVM."

TOTAL CVM AND CUSTOMER-CENTRIC PROCESSES

Doug continues, "It is not surprising that company processes are important if not sacrosanct. Sometimes even more important than people!"

---

[9] Fincentric article in *American Banker*, 2002.

Krish adds, "*While I agree with the need for processes, I would like to see processes that are Customer-friendly. To do this the design of processes has to be Customer-centric. Therefore, the designers or specifiers have to be truly Customer-oriented people, who examine the processes and systems from a Customer's point of view. They also need to put in the possibility of prompt systemic changes based on Customer feedback and Customer irritants.*

"*Customer Value Foundation, along with other experts, has been designing Customer-centric self-learning processes. In fact, they have been converting call centres to Action Centres. The idea is to see if a process is friendly, convenient and useful to a Customer and whether the process can adapt to a Customer's need, and if not, how can it be modified to do so?*

"The author recalls standing at a client's call centre focusing on a service business. One Customer called at 9.45 a.m. He said he was promised service around 9.30 a.m. He has to rush to office. Where is the service technician? The call centre attendant asks his name, and then she asks what plan he has signed for. What is his address? How many services has he had? She was going to ask more, but the Customer was getting upset. All he wanted to know was where the service person was?

"It turns out the service person is in the neighbourhood and has been searching for the Customer but had an incomplete address and so is late.

"We asked the call centre head about this, and he rolled out reams of graphs showing improvements. However, he could not show whether the Customer was getting results and fast, and what processes should be changed. There was no need to ask the process-driven questions. Once the attendant has the names, she should become event-driven and Customer-driven to give him information on the technician and where he is. Unfortunately, this is a call centre with no access to the technician, except through the company. So why even have such a call centre?

"In the end, our Total CVM programme corrected this situation of wrong addresses and better feedback. Moreover, we were able to change the script for such situations, so that simple questions were not answered by a spate of questions."

TOTAL CVM AND ORGANIZATIONAL TRANSFORMATION

Doug has always been irritated by the supremacy of processes. He suggests, "Companies need to go through a transformation and evolutionary process to improve. This requires the employees to be aware and have a positive, proactive, self-learning and self-managing attitude. Self-motivation to do the right things for the Customer is also important."

"Total CVM techniques do just these" says Krish. *"This includes setting up a Courtesy system, capturing the Voice of the Customer, building employee awareness and self-respect, understanding the employee's pain when Customers are angry with him, reinforcing his delight when Customers are happy with him and putting employees into Customer Circles, where they decide what they should do for Customers. In a Customer Circle, employees explore what to do to build such attitudes. Thus, Total CVM goes a long way to Organizational Transformation, transforming it into a Customer-focused, proactive, self-learning organization, with Continuous Customer Improvement Programmes. This is a Customeric organization."*

Doug interjects, "Deming said just this when he shunned terms like 'Total Quality' or 'TQM', replacing them by *transformation of the prevailing system of management,* the real work of a company. Deming said that employees go through their worklife by pleasing bosses and not improving systems that serve Customers. Total CVM is a Customer-focused continuous improvement technique. And it changes the organization, and is not just a process."

"Deming went on to say," according to Krish, *"The individual, once transformed, will:*

- *set an example;*
- *be a good listener, but will not compromise;*
- *continually teach other people; and*
- *help people to pull away from their current practices and beliefs and move into the new philosophy without a feeling of guilt about the past.*

"Further, in changing attitudes, we have to get rid of two aspects:

- *He did this or the enemy out there syndrome.*
- *He should do this.*

"And look at what I can do!

"People have to be encouraged not to look for fault and for blame, and for what others should do. Instead, they should also focus on what they could do, and must do and actually do these. They need to be proactive. True proactiveness comes from awareness, and in viewing and solving our problems, not only problems in front of us, but problems that we could anticipate.

"While we learn not to blame each other, we should not end up blaming the system."

CUSTOMER VALUE AND THE BRAND MANAGER—BRAND LOYALTY

Krish, Jack and Rita are having a very interesting conversation on the relative importance of brand loyalty and Customer loyalty. While Krish is of the view that he does not wish to split hairs, it is Customer Value that leads to brand loyalty. Rita thinks a communication, and public relations (PR) effort leads to it. Jack believes every function in a company tries to maximize their importance and impact on the company. Consultants suggest various approaches, and companies adopt bits and pieces that suit them or seem attractive to them. Total CVM avoids this problem by providing a holistic and overall view of the company and its stakeholders by adding value to all.

Jack says, "I don't think brand equity is an inanimate object. It is changing, and every Customer experience impacts it. Brand equity, among other things, also includes the sum of the brand equity of all the people in the company, and the Customer views this composite, which might change during an interaction.

"Thus, it is important that employees build their brand equity inside and outside their companies, so that their bosses and colleagues, and their Customers want to deal with them and even ask for them.

"Brand equity (or the value of a brand) is giving way to Customer equity (or the sum total of the Customer's lifetime value). At best, brand equity is a means to build Customer equity.

"Brand managers seek brand loyalty, and for this they require good products and a good image of the company. They ought also to look at increasing the brand equity of their people and processes too."

Krish nods in agreement and says: *"Without seeking to enter a debate, what is most important? The brand, the loyalty or the value? Or does the brand engender loyalty or the brand experience, or the Customer experience? Is brand equity the same as loyalty or is it a recognition feature? We can get into a semantics issue. I have the greatest respect for brand building.*

"However, in the Total CVM approach we are maximizing value to the Customer and to do this, we measure the benefits of the various components that are perceived as beneficial to the Customer, be it the product, the image (and in this we look at the brand of the product and the brand of the company, and the trust the Customer has for either, or the association he has with the brand or the company), the company itself, the people, the services, etc. This is shown in Figure 4.2. Sometimes the brand is more important than the image, and we look at brand at the same level of importance as

the benefits. Customer Value is then the aggregate of the perceived value of the benefits, the value of the brand and of the cost."

Rita agrees: "We can then determine how important the brand or the image is in the buying decision. For example, for a farmer buying a commodity, such as fertilizer, the brand assumes 45 per cent importance, suggesting that decommoditizing the product requires brand building, and so the sub-attributes become important, such as association with brand, trust, etc.

"In India, the cement industry tries to brand its commodity products, unlike in the West. Branding leads to faster inventory turns, lower discounting of price, etc.

"In the power industry in India, image forms 40 to 60 per cent of the benefits, showing how important this is to the consumer to be associated with a trustworthy, environmentally and safety-oriented and Customer-concerned supplier, and with a good company brand."

Krish adds, *"Brand loyalty will come as Customer Value increases. If brand means Customer Value then there is no difference. This is a wide definition of brand. In the narrower definition, as we have shown, brand has an impact on value.*

"Brand effort co-exists or in some cases is synonymous to value. Total CVM will improve both, as shown in Figure 4.2.

FIGURE 4.2

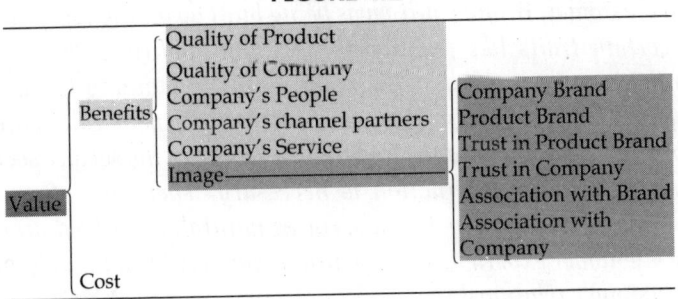

Source Author.

"Figure 4.3 shows where brand is significant or somewhat significant in importance."

Figure 4.3

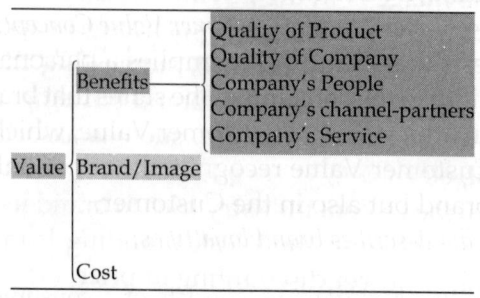

Source   Author.

ARE YOU BUILDING BRAND
LOYALTY OR CUSTOMER LOYALTY?

Krish continues, *"Do Customers want to be loyal to a brand? If you say Customers benefit from the value they get from the brand, then brand value and Customer Value are synonymous. Brand value essentially comes from increasing Customer Value. Customer Value creation is much more than building brand equity and brand recognition.*

"Most brand managers and product managers tend to be brand-centric, and are people with no direct contact with their end Customer. Brand equity was being built by giving recognition to certain traits like trustworthiness and quality to the brand. So the brand was used as the main means to building Customer loyalty. However, poor Customer interaction, poor call centers, can ruin the brand and the loyalty. Moreover in the service sector, direct Customer interaction is necessary. Therefore, efforts to improve Customer loyalty in services naturally revolved around the Customer experience, as the interaction could be thought of as a Customer relationship.

"Timothy L. Keiningham[10] *states that the goal of the two approaches is the same: to keep Customers coming back. The metrics of success are different."*

Rita says that Dr Gonca Telli Yamamoto of Okan University, in an article, *Understanding Customer Value Concept: Key to Success*, suggests that brand value implies a personality, which imparts utility to the consumer. She states that brand value is reducing in importance to Customer Value, which is a wider concept. Customer Value recognizes that not only must we invest in brand but also in the Customer.

"Wikipedia describes brand loyalty as:

Brand loyalty, in marketing, consists of a consumer's commitment to repurchase the brand and can be demonstrated by repeated buying of a product or service or other positive behaviours such as word of mouth advocacy. True brand loyalty implies that the consumer is willing, at least on occasion, to put aside their own desires in the interest of the brand.

Brand loyalty is more than simple repurchasing, however. Customers may repurchase a brand due to situational constraints, a lack of viable alternatives or out of convenience. Such loyalty is referred to as "spurious loyalty". True brand loyalty exists when Customers have a high relative attitude towards the brand, which is then exhibited through repurchase behaviour...

Perhaps the most significant contemporary example of brand loyalty is the fervent devotion of many Mac users to the Apple Company and its products.

From the point of view of many marketers, loyalty to the brand — in terms of consumer usage — is a key factor.

"On the other hand," Krish continues, *"Brand Builder*[11] *asks, 'Is there such a thing as brand loyalty anymore?' According to*

---

[10] Timothy L. Keiningham, *Are You Building Brand Loyalty or Customer Loyalty?* See *www.ipsos.com.*

[11] See http://thebrandbuilder.blogspot.com/2006/01/brand-loyalty-vs-brand-comfort.html (accessed in 2009).

them, 'the answer is yes, when you think sports teams or when you think of Ford versus Chevy, or of Playstation versus X-Box, or Apple versus Microsoft.

"Brand loyalty is likely to be about Customers' habits, and need for convenience and comfort. People (and Customers are people) like their routine and do not like change. Therefore, they tend to shop at the same place, or read the same newspaper, buy the same soap or go to the same pharmacy.

"If one day the pharmacy is closed, you may go to another one. What happens if you like this new store? After this experience, will you go back to the old store, or visit the new store? You'll go back to your original store if you are truly loyal to it.

"My take," continues Krish, "is very simple. You have to get Customer loyalty. However, when you have a large Customer base, you also need brand equity.

"The components of CVM include:

- **Transaction/Process 'Service Value'**
  - 'Moments of truth' touchpoints
  - Governed by processes
- **Product Quality/'Price Value'**
  - Product and Services quality balanced with price paid
- **Brand Equity/'Relationship Value'**
  - Former for large Customer bases

"So, one needs to build a Customer relationship when the Customer base is small. Where it is large, you need to build brand equity, including the other value builders shown above, which include Customer interaction and service, product and price value. For large Customer bases, Customer and brand loyalty are similar and complementary. Customer loyalty will then depend on brand loyalty to some extent, but is built by Customer Value."

Rita has the last word: "Branding minus differentiation equals nothing. Total CVM helps you to be different!"

CHAPTER SYNOPSIS

This chapter discusses existing programmes in companies that are synergistic to Total CVM. A case is made that Total CVM has to imbibe some of the lessons, and work hand-in-hand with these programmes, while becoming the lead programme, having quality and business excellence as its pillars. Much has to be learnt from these in making Total CVM a success. These programmes include:

- Total Customer Value Mangement (CVM) and Total Quality Management.
- Total CVM and Total Business Excellence Management.

Total Quality Management includes Six Sigma programmes, and examples are given where processes are perfected without impacting market share. Customer Value Added analysis showed what to do to increase market share.

Next, we look at satisfaction surveys and programmes as being measurements of transactions and not leading to loyalty. We discuss the role of CRM, brand and brand loyalty in Total CVM. We eschew processes that are not Customer-friendly and Customer-led.

Customer Satisfaction and Total CVM/Customer Retention versus Customer Loyalty

The differences between satisfaction and Total CVM are outlined. Often Customer retention is wrongly assumed to mean loyalty.

Customer Surveys and their Usefulness

Customer Champions UK data show that most Customer data is not acted upon.

Customer Satisfaction not Directly Linked to Loyalty

Here we show why Customer satisfaction does not relate to loyalty, though it is a pre-condition.

CRM and Customer Value

CRM is used as a surrogate for Customer Value, but mostly is a passive process.

Total CVM and Customer-centric Processes

Customer-centric processes are essential to make Total CVM a success.

Total CVM and Organizational Transformation

Finally, we explain how Total CVM brings about organizational transformation, because it touches everyone and builds awareness and proactiveness. Total CVM changes attitudes and mindsets.

Customer Value and the Brand Manager—Brand Loyalty

It is clarified that brand and image are a subset of Customer Value. Brand is often as high as 50 or 60 per cent of the importance Customers place to value. In addition, building brand equity of employees is a pre-requisite in building the company's brand equity.

Are you Building Brand Loyalty or Customer Loyalty?

Both have to be built, but finally it is Customer loyalty that is most material. The components of CVM include:

- *Transaction/Process 'Service Value'*
  - *"Moments of truth" touchpoints*
  - *Governed by processes*
- *Product Quality/'Price Value'*
  - *Product and Services quality balanced with price paid*
- *Brand Equity/'Relationship Value'*
  - *Former for large Customer bases*

5

The Customer Bill of Rights and the Circle of Promises

Krish, the Customer Guru, is meeting with Doug's staff. Present are Rita Timko, VP of Sales and Marketing; Shirley Madison, VP of Finance; Gyani Nayak, Head of Consumer Research; Avi Grandlay, Head of Customer Service; Cindy Pandit, VP of HRD and Training; Vikki Solomon, Head of Quality; Jack Griswold, COO; Jimmy Vaidya, Chief of Manufacturing and JoJo Mohindra, CIO.

Jack starts the meeting and says Doug, the CEO, couldn't make it, but that his staff has to consider an important issue of the Bill of Rights. He asks Krish to take over. Krish starts, *"The Customer Bill of Rights and the Circle of Promises is a confusing title!"*

"Not only that," remarks JoJo. "Many companies have Customer Bill of Rights. Often they are not worth more than the paper they are written on! Others frame the Bill of Rights and mount it on a wall, and everyone forgets about making it real. So why are you suggesting something that may not work?"

Krish smiles. He hands over some sheets to Doug's staff showing examples of Customer Bills of Rights.

Jack wrinkles his nose. "JoJo is right. Most Bills of Rights are framed and put on some wall. The Customer gets little of the rights!"

Krish nods in assent, *"We wish to have a Bill of Rights, which also translates to promises to the Customer. The Bill of Rights is* often deliberated and put together in the Customer Circles, (although this can also happen outside Customer Circles, for example, in a Customer Strategy meeting). Remember, most members of the Customer Circles are frontline people, closest to the Customer. Each right enunciated in the Bill of Rights is a promise made by and dependant on the company and the employees. The employee promises what he will do to make the Customers' Bill of Rights a true right. They take ownership of the Bill of Rights and its operation. Obviously, frontline people cannot directly promise to the Customer; the company can. For the frontline people to be able to promise (to the company and the Customer what they will do for the Customer as per the Bill of Rights), they need promises from those functions that must support them in keeping the promises and approval of top management. Thus, in turn, their colleagues and the company promise them the support they need to keep their promises.

"Once we publish a Customer Bill of Rights, we have to respect it. The Customer considers it a promise.

"Everyone in the company has to honour this Bill of Rights. To do this, the people responsible for fulfilling the rights have to promise and commit that they will do all that is necessary to respect the Customers' rights. In return, the company and the managers will have to promise and support the employees to fulfill their commitment to the Bill of Rights and to the Customer. This is the process of enabling the employees.

"The entire process starts with the Customer, and circles through the company back through top management to the Customer as his Bill of Rights! Generally, the promising process happens in the Customer Circles and is an interconnecting Circle of Promises from the company to the Customer, from the employee to the company and from the company to the employees and the support personnel, the support personnel to the frontline people; hence, the Circle of Promises! This is necessary because people who hear Customer problems are generally not the ones that have the responsibility for fixing them.

"Top management involvement is necessary for ratifying a Customer's Bill of Rights as this forces them to look at the Customer more seriously.

ADVANTAGES OF THE CUSTOMER BILL OF RIGHTS

"Of course, there is an advantage to the Customer, since he is the end beneficiary of the Customer's Bill of Rights. There are other advantages to this." He hands out the sheet titled, Advantages of the Customer Bill of Rights backed by the Circle of Promises.

Aligning of Top Managers to Customers

These managers are often too busy and so deeply immersed in meeting their functional goals that they cannot change. Having to sign off on the Customer's Bill of Rights will make them participate in it and become more aligned to the Customer. Before publishing a Customer's Bill of Rights, top managers must examine it, agree with it, promise to make it a reality and get legal opinion before implementing it.

Building an Interconnection between Internal and External Customers

By focusing on promises made by different parts of the organization to the channel partners and the frontline employees, and the touch points, we are building an interconnection between employees, internal Customers, channel partners, frontline employees and touch points with the External Customer. Such an interconnection (see Figure 5.1):

FIGURE 5.1
Customer's Bill of Rights and the Circle of Promises

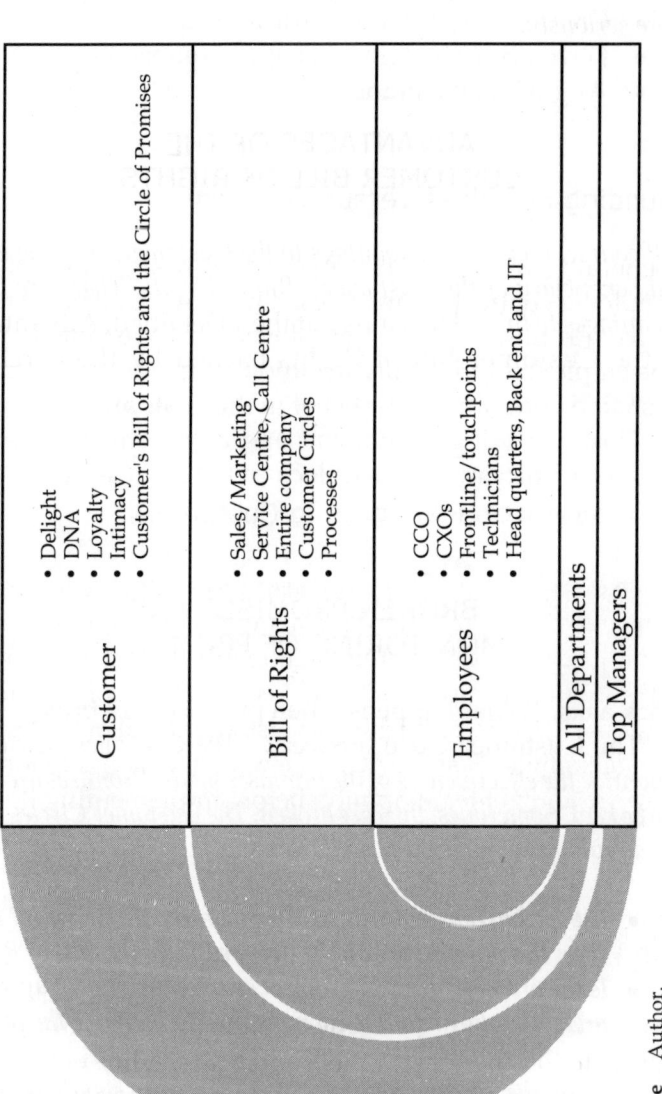

Customer
- Delight
- DNA
- Loyalty
- Intimacy
- Customer's Bill of Rights and the Circle of Promises

Bill of Rights
- Sales/Marketing
- Service Centre, Call Centre
- Entire company
- Customer Circles
- Processes

Employees
- CCO
- CXOs
- Frontline/touchpoints
- Technicians
- Head quarters, Back end and IT

All Departments

Top Managers

Source   Author.

- Engenders teamwork
- Builds a culture of making and keeping promises
- Creates a Customer-centric attitude
- Develops a Customer-focused organization
- Augments the brand

Building Promises versus Contracts

Generally, we work on a contractual basis, an employee–employer contract, or an honest day's pay for an honest day's work. Promises between employees or covenants between the employee and the organization, or the Customer, means a shared commitment or belief in the goals and the values.

This also brings alignment and commonness in shared beliefs. Cynicism is a roadblock to the success of the Circle of Promises.

BROKEN PROMISES AND MONITORING OF PROMISES

Jack asks, "What happens when promises are broken?"

The Customer Guru answers, *"The Customer Circles will monitor the effectiveness of the promises made. Promises are meant to be kept. Sometimes, they are broken. The Customer Circles, which is a cross functional team, will examine:*

- *Is the team not able to or not ready to keep the promise? In this case, the promise should be dropped from the Bill of Rights.*
- *Is the promise broken because of some let up or goof up, or misunderstanding? In this case, we have to reinforce the promise.*

"Lastly, the Customer Circles of the company should be looking for corrective (and not punitive) action, unless there is some serious infraction of ethics or company policy. The best action is corrective action and punitive action is an extreme step.

"Note, we are examining promises made, kept or not kept. We are not looking at this as a process, but as a delivery and human chain working for the Customer. With Total CVM we depend on people for making things happen, and processes to support them and the Customer."

Krish hands out Bills of Right from JetBlue Airways, the City of Seattle, Travelocity and Massachusetts Bay Transport (see Boxes 5.1, 5.2, 5.3 and 5.4).

BOX 5.1
JetBlue Customer Bill of Rights

Above all else, JetBlue Airways is dedicated to bringing humanity back to air travel. We strive to make every part of your experience as simple and as pleasant as possible. Unfortunately, there are times when things do not go as planned. If you're inconvenienced as a result, we think it is important that you know exactly what you can expect from us. That's why we created our Customer Bill of Rights. These Rights will always be subject to the highest level of safety and security for our Customers and crew members.

INFORMATION

JetBlue will notify Customers of the following:

• Delays prior to scheduled departure
• Cancellations and their cause
• Diversions and their cause

OVER BOOKINGS (As defined in JetBlue's Contract of Carriage)

Customers who are involuntarily denied boarding shall receive USD 1,000.

DELAYS (Departure Delays or Onboard Ground Delays on Departure)

For Customers whose flight is delayed by three hours or more after scheduled departure, JetBlue will provide free movies on flights that are two hours or longer.

ONBOARD GROUND DELAYS

JetBlue will provide Customers experiencing an Onboard Ground Delay with 36 channels of DIRECTV®,* food and drink, access to clean rest rooms and, as necessary, medical treatment. For Customers who experience an Onboard Ground Delay for more than five hours, JetBlue will also take necessary action so that Customers may deplane.

(Box 5.1 continued)

(*Box 5.1 continued*)

Arrivals:

1. Customers who experience an Onboard Ground Delay on Arrival for 1–1: 59 hours after scheduled arrival time are entitled to a USD 50 voucher good for future travel on JetBlue.

2. Customers who experience an Onboard Ground Delay on Arrival for two hours or more after scheduled arrival time are entitled to a voucher good for future travel on JetBlue in the amount paid by the Customer for the round trip (or the one way trip, doubled).

Departures:

1. Customers who experience an Onboard Ground Delay on Departure after scheduled departure time for 3–3: 59 hours are entitled to a USD 50 voucher good for future travel on JetBlue.

2. Customers who experience an Onboard Ground Delay on Departure after scheduled departure time for 4–4: 59 hours are entitled to a voucher good for future travel on JetBlue in the amount paid by the Customer for the one way trip (or USD 50, whichever is greater).

3. Customers who experience an Onboard Ground Delay on Departure for five hours or more after scheduled arrival time are entitled to a voucher good for future travel on JetBlue in the amount paid by the Customer for the round trip (or the one way trip, doubled).

In-flight entertainment:

JetBlue offers 36 channels of DIRECTV® service on its flights in the Continental US. If our Live TV™ system is inoperable on flights in the Continental US, Customers are entitled to a USD 15 voucher good for future travel on JetBlue.

This document is representative of what is reflected in JetBlue's Contract of Carriage, the legally binding document between JetBlue and its Customers, and its terms are incorporated herein.

CANCELLATIONS

All Customers whose flight is cancelled by JetBlue will, at the Customer's option, receive a full refund or accommodation on the next available JetBlue flight at no additional charge or fare. If JetBlue cancels a flight within four hours of scheduled departure and the cancellation is due to a Controllable Irregularity, JetBlue will also issue the Customer a USD 50 voucher good for future travel on JetBlue.

DEPARTURE DELAYS

1. Customers whose flight is delayed for 1–1: 59 hours after scheduled departure time due to a *Controllable Irregularity* are entitled to a USD 25 voucher good for future travel on JetBlue.

(*Box 5.1 continued*)

(*Box 5.1 continued*)

2. Customers whose flight is delayed for 2–4: 59 hours after scheduled departure time due to a *Controllable Irregularity* are entitled to a USD 50 voucher good for future travel on JetBlue.

3. Customers whose flight is delayed for 5–5: 59 hours after scheduled departure time due to a *Controllable Irregularity* are entitled to a voucher good for future travel on JetBlue in the amount paid by the Customer for the one-way trip (or USD 50, which ever is greater).

4. Customers whose flight is delayed for six or more hours after scheduled departure time due to a *Controllable Irregularity* are entitled to a voucher good for future travel on JetBlue in the amount paid by the Customer for the round trip (or the one-way trip, doubled).

JetBlue Airways

118–29 Queens Blvd

Forest Hills, NY 11375

These Rights are subject to JetBlue's Contract of Carriage and, as applicable, the operational control of the flight crew, and apply to only JetBlue-operated flights.

*Available only on flights in the Continental US.

Source   www.jetblue.com/p/about/ourcompany/promise/Bill_Of_ Rights.pdf (accessed on 21 June 2010).

BOX 5.2
Seattle City's Citizens Bill of Rights

When doing business with the City of Seattle, Customers *are entitled to prompt, efficient and easily accessible services — from water and power to roads and public safety.* Customers *who contact any office or employee of the City of Seattle can expect excellent service. The Customer Bill of Rights is guided by four standards.*

Customer Bill of Rights

1. *Easy and understandable – City products and services should be easy to locate and access.*

   • The City should reach out to its Customers to inform them about City products and services.

(*Box 5.2 continued*)

(*Box 5.2 continued*)

- A Customer should be able to locate any City service and initiate a request with a single phone call, visit to seattle.gov, trip to a service centre or a letter.
- When a Customer's request involves multiple City offices or departments, the City will co-ordinate the work.
- A Customer should receive clear and accurate information.
- A Customer should be treated with courtesy and respect.

2. *Responsive – City employees should be helpful, connecting* Customers *with others who can help if they cannot.*

- The City should provide service hours and locations that are convenient to Customers.
- The City should provide estimates of how long, and if applicable, how much it will cost to fulfill a Customer's request.
- The City should both keep the Customer informed of progress and readily answer questions about the status of pending requests.

3. *Fair – There should be no economic, social or cultural barriers to accessing City products and services.*

- The City should collaborate with its Customers to ensure City services are designed and managed to meet Customers' needs.
- The City should provide interpretation services when necessary to fulfill a Customer's request.

4. *Results oriented –* Customers *should get results, not just process.*

- The City should, in a timely manner, follow up with the Customer after the request has been completed.
- The City should regularly evaluate and report on overall performance in addressing o. resolving Customers' requests.

For more information, contact the Customer Service Bureau at **www.seattle.gov/Customerservice or by calling (206)684-CITY(2489)**

Source http://www.seattle.gov/customerservice/translations/ FINALposter_aug08_English.pdf (accessed on 21 June 2010).

BOX 5.3
Travelocity Customer's Bill of Rights

(1) **You have the right to book with a travel company that looks out for you, all trip long.**

Neither overbooked hotel, nor pool renovation, nor missing rental car, nor lost reservation should stand in the way of you and a smooth trip. That's why Travelocity Guarantees that everything about your booking will be right, or we'll work with our partners to make it right, right away. And that's why this guarantee means that we look out for you from the very moment you book with Travelocity.

(2) **You have the right to the best overall value in travel.**

Travel enriches your life when it's done right. We understand that on top of a guaranteed low price, travellers need useful, insider information, the security of reliable Customer support and control over the details that make a trip smooth, efficient and truly great.

(3) **You have the right to unbiased information upfront.**

That's why Travelocity was the first to offer objective travel ratings – not inflated ratings to sell you – and independent reviews where travellers share their experiences, both good and bad. It's also why we give you the full price of your rental car, including the taxes upfront with car TotalPriceSM.

(4) **You have the right to a straightforward presentation of your options.**

We want you to choose the options that best suit you. If a hotel has rooms available, we won't lead you to believe that the hotel is sold out. We also won't subject you to impossible terms and conditions that make an offer hollow.

(5) **You have the right to find what you're looking for quickly and easily.**

That's why we redesigned our site for complete ease-of-use – so you can find that great last minute deal to Paris, or the best brunch in Salt Lake City (served in a 75-year-old trolley car diner tucked in the hills of Emigration Canyon).

(Box 5.3 continued)

(*Box 5.3 continued*)

> (6) **You have the right to speak with someone and get help anytime.**
>
> Call one of our knowledgeable representatives for help anytime at 888-872-8356 or 210-521-5871 (for international callers). We're here to help you 24/7.
>
> (7) **You have the right to be inspired by your travel company.**
> Like a well-travelled friend just back from a wine tour of Tuscany, we want to inspire you to see the world.
>
> **These are your rights. Take advantage of them. Let nothing stand between you and them — except maybe a pair of nice sunglasses.**

Source   http://www.travelocity.com/about/main/0,,%7CABOUT,00.
html (accessed on 21 June 2010).

Doug, who walked in a few minutes ago, suggests: "Our Customer Circles should examine how these Bill of Rights can also have a Circle of Promises built. Who would have to promise what, as an example? What kind of Customer Circles should we set up?"

Gyani says: "Travelocity is known as a discount web-based travel agency. Look how they use their Bill of Rights as an ad for themselves and to get Customers' trust!

"Here's a bus service (Box 5.4) that touches millions of consumers:

"You will note that various Bills of Rights exist. They range from public transportation to airlines. The question is, how many of these Bills of Rights are adhered to by the staff of these organizations, and how many are truly real. Our methodology of the Circle of Promises can bring these closer to being realistic and felt by the Customer."

Doug ponders over what he has learnt and the different Bills of Rights Krish has shown him. Should Glacier have one?

He feels that Customers must feel comfortable with what they are buying and the Company they buy from. They have to feel protected and taken care off. They need to be

BOX 5.4
Massachusets Bay Transport Bill of Rights

Customer Bill of Rights

In an effort to provide you with premier public transportation and customer service excellence, we pledge to honor these rights:

Your right to on-time service
If your service is delayed more than thirty minutes, your ride is on us. We guarantee it.[1]

Your right to safe service
Your safety is our top priority. If we're not performing to your standards, please "Write to the Top." Top level management will respond.

Your right to courteous, clean, accessible, and dependable service
Simply put – you deserve the best. If you find our service less than adequate, please "Write to the Top." Top level management will respond.

Your right to be notified of significant service delays
If your bus, subway, or commuter rail train is more than 15 minutes late, updated service information will be made available at the following locations: www.mbta.com, SmarTraveler – 617-374-1234 or •1 (for cell phone users), P.A. announcements on all subway platforms, and electronic message boards on all commuter rail platforms.

Your right to be heard
We promise to make your issues count. Convenient and prominently located bus, train, and station posters will get you the information you need to "Write to the Top." Top level management will respond to your concerns.

[1] The MBTA Customer Service Guarantee is based on the following terms and conditions: If any portion of your trip is delayed over 30 minutes, you are eligible for a complimentary fare. To redeem your complimentary fare, you must submit a claim within 10 days of the delay occurrence by filing an online claim form at www.mbta.com/contact_us/onlinereply.asp or by mailing an On Time Service Guarantee Claim Card. Claim Cards are available on buses, at subway stations, and at the following station schedule areas: North Station, South Station, Route 128, and Back Bay Stations.

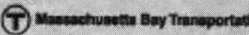 **Massachusetts Bay Transportation Authority**

Source http://www.mbta.com/customer support/customer_bill_of_ rights/ (accessed on 21 June 2010).

sure that the quality of the product, and in Glacier's case, the food products are safe and made from quality produce, and they are relatively fresh and so forth. A Bill of Rights would spell this out and would bring a comfort factor to the Customer. Yet Customers believe these Bills of Rights are often not worth the paper they are written on (shows their lack of trust in companies!). A Circle of Promises makes the Bill a reality. And when individuals tell the Customer that they have promised to uphold the rights, the Customer starts to feel good about and trust the company.

Yes! This makes sense, Doug thinks, from all points of view, including upholding the Bill of Rights, the involvement of the employees, the alignment of the top managers, the interconnection between internal and external Customers and a true commitment to the Customer.

A Call to Pam

Pam is a psychologist and is at work. Unlike most days, Pam is busy. Doug has finished reviewing the Bill of Rights and is walking to his office. He decides to say hello to Pam and calls her. Pam is surprised to hear from Doug. She thinks he manages to pick the wrong time. Doug starts by saying, "For a change I can talk to you. How about we talk about plans for the evening." Pam says that she cannot talk much.

Doug is so glad to hear her say this. He is the one who normally does not have the time. "You are becoming like my executives," he exults.

Pam says, "You're saying this because, for a change, I am busy, and so you compare me with your executives. Unlike them, I have learnt to focus on the real important things. That gives me time to think. Your executives have to learn to focus and not work on too many initiatives."

"Let me figure out how I introduce them to this concept. First, I have to get them going on another initiative, Total CVM." He says bye. He chews on his pencil as he thinks about what Pam has said about focus. He has to get the Bill of Rights going too. He has to get his executives to think about what they could do for the Customer in all departments.

CHAPTER SYNOPSIS

Advantages of the Customer Bill of Rights

This chapter builds on existing Customer's Bills of Rights, which are essentially excellent documents. For these really to work, you must have the commitment and the right attitude from the employees. Total CVM builds these attitudes.
It includes:

- Aligning of Top Managers
- Building the Interaction between Internal and External Customers
- Building Promises versus Contracts

Broken Promises and Monitoring of Promises

In addition, Total CVM builds individual promises to the Customer, backed up by promises to the frontline people by the supporting staff promising that they will give all necessary assistance for the frontline people to be able to keep their promises.

The chapter ends with examples of commercial Bills of Rights from JetBlue Airways, Seattle City's Citizens Bill of Rights, Travelocity and Massachusetts Bay Transport.

6

Strategic and Operational Managers and Total CVM

THE CEO AND THE CUSTOMER

Krish, Doug and Pam are having lunch. Pam says she has heard of the Bill of Rights, and the Circle of Promises. She bemoans the fact that executives promise their wives many things, such as they will take time off for a vacation, and then these never happen. She believes that for every promise made, there should be a matching promise made by the wife, so that if one promise is not kept, the other's promise might not be kept. Krish shifts uneasily. Doug squirms. Krish says this is way past his depth and expertise. Pam promises to discuss this later with Doug, as she has to go.

Krish, the Customer Guru, remarks: *"Pam is right. Promises must be backed up. We will talk about this in this session. Let's start.*

"The CEO has to provide a Customer Vision and provide leadership for the Customer programme. The Disney organization stresses this. Leaders have to share their vision, which means shared purpose, inspiration of passion, self-direction and convey values. They have to organize, commit and engage. The CEO has to build a Customer culture, well defined, clear to all and goal oriented.

"One of India's leading industrialists and CEOs, and proponents of TQM (Total Quality Management), gives talks on the importance of Quality. He is not interested in Customer Value or discussions.

He says he does not need to learn anything on the Customer. Quality has taught him all there is to know about the Customer. This epitomizes what some CEOs think. (Some want to learn and innovate; others either think they know it all or are too busy to learn about the value of a Customer; for some quality has become the be all and end all of their Customer thinking. They believe that the way to look at the Customer is through quality, and they do not realize this is not enough, and that processes cannot replace the human touch.) Other CEOs believe they are doing everything for Customers. Often the CEO is detrimental to the Customer becoming the real driver of the business. Doug, you are different!

"Believe me, in spite of my remarks on CEOs, there are many others like you out there.

"B. Muthuraman, MD of Tata Steel (including Corus), is really Customer conscious. But while the message goes down the organization that he is trying to change the organization, Total CVM is being practised only partly as he says the systems in place to run and control a large organization are not always in sync with Customer needs.[1] It requires a massive change in thinking.

"What is the major priority in the organization: profits or Customer loyalty? Are they mutually exclusive? In fact, they are related and Customer loyalty leads to growth, growth in market share, ROI (profits) and Shareholder Value.

"Having a great product is not enough. Having great processes are not enough. Having a great brand is not enough. Take GE. We worked with one of their major divisions in the US. They had great processes. They practised Six Sigma, and had all kinds of black belts floating around in their offices. However, their market share was not improving. Why? We were asked to help. We introduced the CVA concept, measured Customer Value Added, found the areas of weakness versus the competition, and suggested relatively simple steps to improve market perception and market share. CVA is used by them as the Voice of the Customer. They use the data and convert it into NPS or Net Promoter Score from the 'Will you recommend'

---

[1] Quoted in review of Gautam Mahajan, *Customer Value Investment: Formula for Sustained Business Success* (New Delhi: Response Books, 2008).

question. NPS is a measure of loyalty. Now Six Sigma is meant to be Customer-driven and to some extent, it is. But generally, it is driven by the company's (its employees') perception of what the Customer is thinking. The company's insight of what the Customer needs, may not be the same as the Customer's perception. That is why you have to measure Customer Value (and not through satisfaction studies). Thus having a great Customer focus and Customer view is important to create Customer Value.

"Unfortunately, some managers think processes are the be all and end all of management practices. Soft Customer related skills are losing out to impersonal IT/system driven processes, whether it is CRM or it is Customer Information Management (CIM). As I mentioned earlier, companies that try to get closer to the Customer, like American Express, are finding processes are not the entire solution.

"The shareholders want to know about your Customers, the rate of growth of Customers and their lifetime value, also called Return on Customers (ROC).

"One last thought. CEOs have to spend time with the Customer. CEOs of most successful companies tend to spend one day a week with Customers. Do you?

"Doug, can you fill this CEO Scorecard (Table 6.1)?"

Doug starts to fill this out. What he gives the Customer Guru shows many 'No's in it.

"Pretty good," remarks the Customer Guru. *"You got 14 'Yes'-es. This is, about 50 per cent 'Yes'-es...I think you're on your way."*

Krish continues, *"Most CEOs will get only a few 'Yes'-es! This is not meant to belittle them but to make them think about what they could be doing and what they are not doing. This is meant to educate them. The intelligent CEO will start to introspect and think about change."*

Doug interrupts, "I must say in defence of CEOs, they want to be Customer-driven, and they do everything they know about Customer focus. The problem is the same as you explained to me about the Quality movement 25 years ago. People thought they were doing everything by just meeting

TABLE 6.1
The CEO Scorecard

CEO Scorecard	Yes	No
1. Are you the Chief Value Creator?		
2.. Do you balance value creation for the shareholder and value creation for the Customer?		
3. Do you balance long-term with short-term profits?		
4. Do you know that Return on Customer (ROC) is increased through Total CVM?		
5. Do you know ROC=TSV (Total Shareholder Value)?		
6. Do you act as the Chief Customer Officer, or have you appointed one?		
7. Is the Customer truly numero uno in your organization or are you?		
8.. Do you measure Customer Value Added (Voice of Customer and Voice of Competitor)? Do you measure Voice of the Employee?		
9. Do you price using Customer Value Added and Value Maps?		
10. Do you have a Customer Value Added and a Customer reporting system that you receive at the same time as your financial and other reports?		
11. Do your executives have a well thought-out Customer role in addition to their functional goals?		
12. Do your executives have one or two customer-related goals in their key performance goals?		
13. Are you building Customer Conduits?		
14. Are bonuses driven from Customer results?		
15. Do you have a Customer strategy (that drives a corporate strategy)?		
16. Do you promote the concept of farming and hunting? Of Customer delight?		
17. Is the Customer DNA (Do Not Annoy) an employee mantra?		
18. Do you measure Customer assets? Are these growing?		
19. Do you measure Customer Lifetime Value?		
20. Who are your most valuable Customers? Are you pruning unprofitable Customers? Do you know how many Customers you have?		
21. Do you measure your share of the Customer wallet?		
22. Are you setting up Customer-Centric-Circles?		
23. Are you easily contactable by the Customer?		
24. Do you have an Employee Value added programme?		

(*Table 6.1 continued*)

(*Table 6.1 continued*)

CEO Scorecard	Yes	No
25. Do you think the purpose of a call centre is to self-destruct (that is not exist if there are no problems or in effect you are solving the Customers problems systemically, so that there is no need for the Customer to call) as opposed to using call centres as a way to touch the Customer?		
26. Do you get a Customer complaint sheet and action taken list?		
27. Do you receive Customer complaints calls personally at least once or twice a week?		
28. Do you spend time listening to Customers at a call centre?		
29. Do you typically try to spend one day a week with Customers?		
30. Do you stand behind the Customer's Bill of Rights?		
31. Are you prepared for the Customers to certify your company?		

Source Author.

quality standards using acceptable quality levels or AQLs. No one knew that this was just the tip of the iceberg of quality. In addition, no one knew about all the things we now know about quality, ISO[2] certifications and TQM.

"I think there is the same parallel on Customers. Knowledge on what companies and CEOs can do for the Customer is limited. CEOs have to be educated on all the steps and about Customers that go into Total CVM!"

Krish nods his head in agreement. *"I agree we need an education programme. But CEOs have to be ready to learn. This is one of the necessary steps in the Total CVM movement. Let us move forward."*

"Before that," Doug interrupts, "I've learnt that I cannot be a CEO god! I never thought that way, though I knew I was the Boss. But now, I am a Boss with two bosses, the Customers and the owners."

Krish remarks, *"Great thinking. Going forward, we had pointed out the CEO is the Chief Value Creator balancing and managing the value creation for the owners and the Customers.*

---

[2] International Standards Organization certifies companies for quality.

A smart CEO maximizes both. He realizes creating value for Customers creates value for the owner, and therefore he focuses on driving his business through the Customer. Are products being designed for the Customer? What will the product look like? Are the features Customer-required? What will the Customer want in the future and how will the product provide for the future, and how can we bring it out earlier and at a price point that makes it interesting for the Customer? How can we customize it? This goes for pricing from a Customer Value Added perspective to all aspects of the business. How can the entire company support the Customer through purchase and ownership and re-purchase, and build loyalty? How do we get employees to build their brand equity, thereby increasing corporate brand equity?

"The CEO asks: Is my staff Customer-oriented, are my people Customer-certified and is my company Customer-certified. If not, what do I need to do to get it the highest order of Customer appreciation and certification? How will it affect my price, brand and image?"

Who's more Important: The Shareholder or the Customer?

Krish continues, *"The CEO is part of the debate of whether shareholders are more important than Customers, and how he manages the relative importance of these two stakeholders. By law, the Company Board of Directors is accountable to shareholders, not to Customers or other stakeholders. This is Milton Friedman's view (to maximize shareholder returns). Peter Drucker on the other hand has argued that the purpose of the firm is to create Customer Value. Sumantra Ghoshal has stated that the other stakeholders, including Customers are just as important as the shareholders.[3] Just as significantly, the CEO has to ensure that delivering too*

---

[3] John Zinkin, "Strategic Marketing: Balancing Customer Value with Shareholder Value," *The Marketing Review*, 6, No. 2 (Summer 2006): 163–181.

much Customer Value does not diminish Shareholder Value. An example is not pricing high enough.

"In any event, maximizing Shareholder Value is measured by EVA (Economic Value Added), which is more impacted by marketing than financial manoeuvering! Which means it is influenced by Customer focus."

Doug says that while he agrees, he has to institutionalize this. To do this, he will ask for Customer-related tasks in the key performance areas and a reporting system to get Customer focus. He also wishes to maintain his shareholder focus.

The Customer Guru continues, *"Doug, we need to meet Jack Griswold, the COO, and outline his role."*

Doug asks, "Should I come or would you like to meet Jack separately?"

Krish says, *"Let me talk to him first. I do not want him to be defensive. He has to be receptive to thinking differently. Maybe later all of us could meet together. However, let us continue to discuss the COO's role."*

CHIEF CUSTOMER VALUE CREATOR
OR CHIEF OPERATING OFFICER

Doug says, "I would assume the Chief Customer Value Creator is akin to the Chief Operating Officer. He has the Chief Employee Value Creator or the HRD head reporting to him."

"You're right," says the Customer Guru. *"The Chief Customer Value Creator has all departments focused on maximizing value to Customers, whether it is products, logistics, service or marketing. Working through the Chief Employee Value Creator, the Chief Customer Value Creator ensures all functions are Customer-centric and Customer-sensitized."*

Doug adds, "The Chief Operating Officer through his marketing department measures Customer Value Added, and uses it to create more value for the Customer, predict market share, and uses value maps for pricing. He checks if the company is increasing its share of a Customer's wallet."

"And," says Krish, "*he looks at product introduction through CVA analysis. He looks at customization and co-creating Customer Value. He looks at Customer churn. He ensures various functions, such as manufacturing and information and IT, are customer-focused. He works with the Chief Value Creator (the CEO) and the Chief Shareholder Value Creator (the CFO) in balancing Customer Value and Shareholder Value.*

"*I'll set up a meeting with Jack Griswold, our COO, soon.*"

Meeting the COO

Jack is expecting Krish, the Customer Guru. Jack starts, "Krish, you know our products and our company. Doug has told me that all our people should focus on the Customer. We have virtually no contact with the end Customer and hence I can't see a need to involve everyone. We ought to find a way to have direct contact and access to the Customer. I think that is well nigh impossible."

Krish smiles, "*You are absolutely right. Let me give you the example of a top officer in a heavily regulated power industry, Tata Power. He said there is no way to influence price or the Customer (the price was fixed, and the Customer had no choice of power company or power provider). He stated that the Customer Relations Department is the repository of the Customer. However, we found numerous other contact points, such as service people, billing department, environment and safety departments, and there was also a Customer contact programme by the senior executives of the company.*

"*I had met this company's Customer Relations people. They had become complaint takers, and there was little they were doing to really add value and improve Customer conditions.*

"*The most cogent impact of Total CVM here will be an improvement in the power company's brand equity and in the Customer's price perception. In addition, the number of complaints will decrease as Customers started to like the company more. Costs will also come down.*

"At Tata Power, complaints came down from 9 per thousand to 2.7 per thousand Customers, in the quarter after the Total CVM programme was initiated.

"And in your industry the contact is also indirect. So what can you do?

"In Glacier's case, the grocery chains are your Customers, their retailers, and, of course, their people are all your Customers. You should have a contact programme with the grocery chain and their retail outlets. Most Customer-focused top executives spend 15 per cent of their time with Customers. And they ensure that they find the time for this. You must also install a Customer Value Chain Management system where you add value to the chain constituents, and members of the chain add value to each other.

"In addition, you are the repository of the Customer. You are the Chief Customer Value Creator. Almost everything you do impacts the Customer: for example, what you produce, he buys; what you price, he pays; your marketing people supposedly impact him; your service persons service him; in fact all your departments, in one way or other have direct or indirect contact with the Customer. And, you are therefore the main champion of the Customer in your company. You are the end (or start if you like) of the Customer Conduit in the company. You can be the Chief Customer Officer or appoint someone to play that role reporting to the CEO, so that he can hold your executives' hands in teaching them about their Customer roles and establishing Customer-related tasks.

"And what will this do for you? At the very least, this increased interaction will:

1. *Make the*

    a. *Customers happy and want to use your product.*
    b. *Customers more forgiving.*
    c. *Customers trust you.*
    d. *Customers want to buy from you.*

2. *Give you a better idea of your Customers' needs.*

   a. *Help you in Customer's preferred product development.*
   b. *Improve your offerings (packaging, size, freshness, inventory, mode of delivery, etc.) to the Customers. Remember the Quick pick-up counters you put up in Newark, Ohio?[4]*
   c. *Customize your logistics to suit your Customers.*

3. *Increase Customer contact and understanding at all levels of the organization.*

   a. *Improve relations with Customers' people, and increase value to them.*
   b. *Get your team aligned towards the Customer, resulting in newer, better and more Customer-related initiatives. Tell them their brand equity builds corporate.*
   c. *Install a Customer Value Chain Management system.*
   d. *Have everyone think of the Customer DNA (Do Not Annoy) and delight factors.*
   e. *Help you build a Customers' Bill of Rights and a Circle of Promises.*

4. *Impact your Customer's perception on your prices. Be able to charge him for increased benefits such as service, faster delivery, etc.*
5. *Get Customers to talk more about you and your products to others.*
6. *All this will improve your brand value. Your business results will improve, because everyone in your organization is focused on those who buy, or can buy more of your products and also on those who sell them for you."*

Jack smiles. "That's a long list of positives, and I am sure, worth a try. Let me figure out how to handle this."

Krish interjects, "*Note there are no downsides to this, except for the effort to change the attitude of people from being a 'Company*

---

[4] See Gautam Mahajan, *Customer Value Investment.*

Person' to a 'Customer Person'. And from boss-driven to Customer-driven. This will require wholehearted leadership from you, not luke-warm approval. And every now and again, you will forget because you will have other pressing priorities. Keep saying to yourself: 'What priority can be greater than Customer priority?'"

Jack is still smiling. "It sounds simple and seems easy to do. But I can imagine it won't happen easily."

"Well, for this to happen, you have to change yourself, and explain to the people under you that you are no longer the boss. You work for the Customer, and they (all your people) do too!

"It's a matter of understanding and practising Customer Value and it will become a way of business thinking! I am here to help you steer the organization in the right fashion."

Jack says he will start a Customer-focused meeting once a week with his direct reports, and then ask them to report on the customer once a month along with the financial and other reporting parameters. "Maybe I will ask them to put two customer-related goals in their key performance areas."

Krish hands a chart to Jack: *"This is a COO scorecard that I request you to fill up, when you get a chance (Table 6.2)."*

Jack agrees, and requests Krish to meet Shirley Madison, the CFO. He says he will set up the meeting for the next day.

Krish leaves. He calls Doug. He tells Doug about his meeting with Jack and says he is going to meet the CFO, Shirley Madison, the next day. Doug says he might sit through the meeting.

CHIEF SHAREHOLDER VALUE CREATOR OR CHIEF FINANCIAL OFFICER

Doug and Krish are sitting in Shirley Madison's office. Shirley is the CFO. Shirley knows that Doug is trying to make Glacier more Customer-focussed. She cannot think of her role beyond traditional billing, collections and credit ratings, balance

TABLE 6.2
The COO Scorecard

The COO Scorecard	Yes	No
1. Are you the Chief Customer Value Creator?		
2. Do you act as the Chief Customer Officer, or do you have one?		
3. Do you have a true Customer focus in your department?		
4. Do you spend time with Customers		
5. Do you have Customer related Key Result Area (KRAs)?		
6. Do your reports in all functions have Customer-related KRAs?		
7. Do you measure Customer Value Added (Voice of Customer and Voice of Competition)? Do you measure Voice of the Employee?		
8. Do you have bonuses linked to CVA or other Customer parameters?		
9. Do you price using Customer Value Added and Value Maps? Do you know a 1% reduction in price could reduce profits by 11%?		
10. Do you report Customer Value Added and have a Customer reporting system that you receive at the same time as your financial and other reports?		
11. Do your reports discuss Customer complaints and look at systemic improvements to remove Customer value impediments?		
12. Are you building Customer Conduits?		
13. Do you have Customer-Centric-Circles in your various departments?		
11. Do you promote the concept of farming and hunting? Of Customer delight?		
12. Is the Customer DNA (Do Not Annoy) an employee mantra?		
13. Who are your most valuable Customers? Are you pruning unprofitable Customers? Do you know how many Customers you have?		
14. Are you easily contactable by the Customer?		
15. Do you have an Employee Value added programme? Do you build employee brand equity?		
16. Do you think the purpose of a call centre is to self-destruct (that is, not to exist if there are no problems or in effect you are solving the Customers problems systemically, so that there is no need for the Customer to call) or do you think this is a way to touch the Customer? Is your call centre an action centre?		
17. Do you get a Customer complaint sheet and action taken list?		

(Table 6.2 continued)

(Table 6.2 continued)

The COO Scorecard	Yes	No
18. Do you receive Customer complaints calls personally at least once or twice a week?		
19. Do you contact the Chief Shareholder Value Creator to balance total Business Value creation and to discuss Customer value creation		
20. Do you know Customer Value equates with Business Value (CV = BV)?		

Source Author.

sheets and typical financial reporting, treasury functions, mergers and acquisitions, etc. Her role includes financial strategy and planning. She has welcomed an interaction with Krish. Krish explains the new organization chart. Krish addresses Shirley:

"Actually, Shirley, you are the Chief Shareholder Value Creator."

"How can I be that? That is the role of Doug or the CEO," says Shirley.

"Doug's role is just not looking at the Shareholder's Value but also at Customer Value and balancing these two. Of course, they are in a sense synonymous, but we differentiate them. We often try to look at the short term, where we short-change Customer Value. Your role is to be the champion of the shareholder, just as Jack Griswold, the COO, has to be the champion of the Customer. But you cannot be this without understanding Customer Value and your role in building it. You should be focused on the future, new businesses, new products/creations for Customers and the finances and Shareholder value. You are more than just a Chief Financial Officer. You have to look at future strategy, mergers and acquisitions and growth. You have to look at your scarcest resources: Customers, capital and investors. Today, you measure return on capital and return on investment, but not Return on Customers. The importance of price (the easiest item to reduce !) in profit creation makes it imperative you understand value pricing and ensure others follow it.

Return on Customer

"Return on Customers (ROC) is the cash flow from Customers plus change in Customer equity in a given period, divided by the beginning Customer equity, or:

$$\text{Return on Customers (ROC)} = \frac{\text{Cash flow from Customers in a period plus the change of Customer equity}}{\text{Customer equity at the start of the period}}$$

"Customer equity is another measure of value of the Customer."

Value of Customer

Shirley says: "The Value of the Customer or Customer Asset is what most companies are after (Box 6.1). Most consultants help companies to develop this. Eventually Customer Value increases the Value of the Customer. Total Customer Value Management focuses on adding value to the Customer and to the company, by measuring Customer Lifetime Value or Customer capital. The consultants pushing Value of the Customer have a distinctly different approach while focusing on developing processes."

BOX 6.1
Value of Customer

- The value of your relationship with your Customers
- Average value of each relationship can be measured by
  - revenue per Customer
  - average length of Customer relationship
  - total number of referrals that became Customers divided by total number of Customers plus 1 (the original Customer). Can be referred to as R
  - average spent per Customer per annum multiplied by relationship length with R (a measure of referrals)

Customer Equity or Customer Capital

"In addition, Shirley, you need to measure Customer Equity and Customer Capital." Krish hands Shirley a definition (Box 6.2):

BOX 6.2
Customer Equity or Customer Capital

- Asset value of current Customers
- Value of existing relationships (number of relationships times the average value of each relationship
    + Value of potential future earnings from existing Customers
    + Value of referral power
    − Cost of retention

"Shirley, as CFO, you could measure Customer assets, Customer capital and Customer Value Added. You should look at the Customer segmentation and authenticate marketing's thinking using financial and value indicators, including the value of these Customers to the organization.

"Are Customer Assets increasing? Or are they not increasing as fast as you would like them to increase? What is needed to increase the Customer Assets? Whom should you address? The COO or the Chief Marketing Officer, or many other officers?

"You should view the future from the point of view of the Customer because, as a wise CFO, you know this is what will create value for the shareholders.

"You should correlate Customer Value and its increase to ROI, and Shareholder Value and, indeed, share price or company book value and look at the investment in Customers and their return on investment (ROC) and to the company."

ROI Across the Board; ROI of Marketing

Shirley says, "You are right. We've looked at other Customer returns like ROC, Customer Assets, etc. We need to add this to our ROI measurements but also look at

- Returns on other investment
- Return on marketing investment
- Return on Customer Value investment

"I remember, Krish, your saying CVI equals increased ROI. That is, investment in Customer Value leads to increased ROI. Or measure return on Customer investment (generally CVI is very small).

"What about return on marketing investment?" asks Shirley.

Krish remarks, "*Very few marketing departments have a quantitative measure of their performance other than increase in sales and brand awareness. Most CEOs cannot gauge the business impact of marketing and its expenses. The ability to do so increases the effectiveness of the marketing department.*

"*An obvious way to get the ROI is to measure the increase in sales due to a marketing activity, be it selling, exhibitions, ad campaigns, brand building, etc. Increasingly, Customer measures such as Value of Customer, loyalty, CVA, satisfaction, better price perception and value creation are measures that influence ROI of Marketing.*

"*First, short-term ROI of marketing is also used as a simple index measuring the dollars of revenue (or market share, contribution margin or other desired outputs) for every dollar of marketing spend.*

"*Nicholas C. Watkis[5] advocates the Optimum Marketing Performance (OMP) as the particular indicator which encompasses the overall marketing. However, Customer measures may be just as good, along with ROI of various marketing activities.*"

---

[5] Nicholas C. Watkis, "How Good is Your Marketing Organization?" http://www.businessperformancemaximized.com/how_good_your_marketing.htm (accessed on 29 June 2010).

Customer Value and Share Prices

Krish asks, *"Shirley, did you know that a 1 per cent change in Customer satisfaction results in a 4.6 per cent change in market value?[6] That is why you have to work on improving value and satisfaction to the Customer, and broadcast its financial importance to the company.*

"In fact, return on Customer is equivalent to Total Shareholder Value. ROC = TSR,[7] where TSR is Total Shareholder Return, which is the total cash flow from dividends and change in shares.

TSR is computed as:

$$TSR = (Price_{end} - Price_{begin} + Dividends)/Price_{begin}$$

Where $Price_{begin}$ = share price at beginning of period, $Price_{end}$ = share price at end of period, Dividends = dividends paid

---

"Operating discounted cash flows are created by a Customer. ROC reflects this and is therefore tantamount to TSR."

Putting Customer Assets on Balance Sheets

Shirley Madison says, "Very often, the physical assets are not as large as the Customer assets. Take a pizza company like Dominos. Their physical assets are ovens; but their true assets are the Customer. If they were to be bought, their sales price would be based on their Customer assets, not on their physical assets. And the price would depend on the rate of new Customer induction, the per Customer sales or profit-ability, and the rate of increase of this less the attrition of the

---

[6] Claes Fornell, Sunil Mithas, Forrest V. Morgeson III and M.S. Krishnan, "Customer Satisfaction and Stock Prices: High Returns, Low Risk", *Journal of Marketing* 70 (January 2006): 3–14.

[7] Don Peppers and Martha Rogers, *Return on Customer: Creating Maximum Value from Your Scarcest Resource* (Broadway Business, 2005).

Customers (Customer Capital), and the potential geographical expansion.

"The Security and Exchange Commission (SEC) of USA is mooting such data be put on balance sheets."

Channel Partners

Shirley continues. "Let's talk channel partners. I do receive bills from the warehouses, and get payments from our chain partners, and we work on discounts. However, I have very little contact with them."

Krish gives an example of this, *"At a fertilizer company,[8] the dealers have to pay by bank draft for the fertilizer which they then send to dealers. A sales executive would call on a Friday and say we are ready to make a shipment. But first send us a bank draft. Now a draft means going to the bank, etc. In our CVA study, we had found these were causing difficulties. You know I always say we have to balance the convenience of the Customer with the convenience of the company. When the CVM implementation team understood the cause for the poor rating was drafts, they talked to the CFO, who agreed that a 30-year-long relationship meant they could accept a cheque, even though it might take a little longer to clear. The value scores have grown."*

Shirley says she likes this. "Maybe a better idea for the dealers to have accounts at the fertilizer company's bank and just do a direct transfer.

"I think that perhaps my staff or I should meet some of the channel partners, thank them for their prompt payments, and ask for their suggestions on billing and payments."

Krish is smiling and comments, *"Very nice. They will be surprised and delighted when this happens."*

"I remember when Whirlpool bought Kelvinator in India, I went to meet Kelvinator's marketing company (they had a separate

---

[8] From a Customer Value Foundation proprietary study.

company for marketing). The CEO told me that earlier in the day the new Managing Director of Whirlpool, Garrick DaSilva, had come, and now I had come. We never had anyone from Kelvinator visit us before. We always had to go see them."

Shirley nods and says that this is a good change, and it would be the start of a Customer-focus programme. She would get her people to think about Customers rather than processes.

Finance and Customer Contact

Shirley continues that it is important for her and her people to have Customer contact. At the very least, she should meet the CFOs of Glacier's Customers and should send letters thanking other CFOs for their support and timely payment. "My people should look at billing from the point of view of the Customer and better payment methods and options. We can think of seamless systems. We can think of letting the Customer view his statements, etc., and ask for modifications online, and make bill correction simple.

Co-control with the Customer

"Here we need to look at putting the Customer in control of his ordering and logistics and payment systems." Shirley thinks the Customer should be able to track shipments, even view manufacturing schedules, and log in their requirements into a manufacturing schedule, much like a meeting schedule template. They could also look at their account status and when credit notes could be expected.

"Eventually the Customer should be able to order into a flexible manufacturing system. In the retail trade, topping up on the shelf is a daily routine, but flexible manufacturing is not in place at Glacier."

Krish, who has been listening, turns to Shirley, *"You are raising so many issues that are worth considering. Note how your mind starts to work, and focuses on innovative thinking, because the Customer field is wide open to innovation. But let us move on to pricing."*

Pricing Using Value[9]

"You can teach marketing and other people how to price products taking into account Customer Value. There are two aspects to this:

"Aspect 1 is the pricing itself. An example is the way Dell priced its computers based on the Customers' needs, and what attributes they wanted and were willing to pay for.[10]

"Aspect 2 is how to turn price negotiations into value negotiations!

"It is not surprising that we find that Customers do not wish to pay for something they do not want, but will pay a price for something they truly want. This goes for product features too. Take cell phones. If you do not want a camera, and your cell phone comes bundled with one, the camera is worth zero to you and you do not want to pay for it, even though you are forced to. On the other hand, if you want a camera in your cell phone, you may search for a really good camera phone and be happy to pay for it.

"Smart CFOs realize this, and try to get the company and all people to think about pricing from a Customer's viewpoint. He urges executives to spend more time on Customer Value than on pricing. Pricing and good pricing will emerge automatically. Books have been written on using Customer value for pricing.[11] Leading consulting companies have written monograms on this and call it the recent and better way of pricing.

---

[9] Gautam Mahajan, "Adding Customer Value and Getting a Price for it", *The Economic Times*, March 16, 2008.

[10] For more information, please see Gautam Mahajan, *Customer Value Investment.*

[11] James C. Anderson, Nirmalya Kumar, James A. Narus, *Value Merchants: Demonstrating and Documenting Superior Value in Business Markets* (Harvard Business School Press, 2007).

"More importantly, pricing people have to understand the importance of price in the value matrix. Often, price is only 30 per cent and quality is 70 per cent of value (100 per cent). Why waste time on looking at pricing? Conventionally every one will focus on price, but if you understand the concept of Customer Value, price should be given its rightful importance/non-importance. If the importance per the Customer is 30 per cent, the company should not give price more importance than that."

Shirley smiles, "But in many products price has a relative importance of 70 per cent and quality 30 per cent. Shouldn't you worry about price here?"

"True," admits Krish. *"But if that is the case, then you are in a commodity market. And here you have a choice of playing the price game (which most people do), or seeing how you can improve quality and value, thereby reducing the importance of price. You have to decommoditize your product by making price less important. To do this you have to add value. This was best enunciated by Jeff Immelt[12] of GE who said that the only way to climb out of the commodity hell was to add Customer Value. Indian fertilizer companies have done this by building brand association and service to differentiate the product which is not a differentiator."*

Just then, Doug walks in and joins Krish and Shirley in the meeting. Doug asks Shirley, "Has Krish told you about using CVA for pricing? I just noticed that one of the recommendations for financial services companies is to use a Customer-centric approach which uses cost/value trade-offs by Customer segment to price in the future."

Krish says that he'll explain this to Shirley (Box 6.3).

Using Value Maps for Pricing

Doug tells Shirley, "Price is the easiest to give away, and a USD 1 price reduction means a USD 11 reduction in

---

[12] Jeff Immelt is Chairman of GE.

BOX 6.3
Example of Using CVA for Pricing

"Bradley Gale[13] studied pricing versus CVA for desktop computers. He took data from published reports on their rating of various computer features, and the price of each of the desktops reviewed. He then calculated the average rating of each feature, and their relative importance (or weight). Based on this, he was able to define the 'average' computer with the 'average' features and the 'average' price.

"Next, using the actual scores for each feature for each desktop model and the importance weight for that feature, he was able to gauge the value the feature was creating for Customers, and what it was worth to them. To do so, he used the data to define an 'average' computer, and how average features should be priced. Better than average features were worth more (if the Customer truly wanted them, they were worth even more!), and below average features meant a deterioration in price. Finally, using this, he could figure out which computer was worth more or less to the Customer compared to its price."

"This is an exciting way to look at a company's products and their features, and understanding what value they're actually adding to the Customer," remarks Doug. "Thus, if you have a feature that a Customer does not want, the Customer does not want to pay for it and thinks it is worthless or worth zero dollars! You recall the old Video Cassette Recorders (VCRs). They had a feature allowing 30 day recording. Most users found it useless and therefore would pay no extra for it! Had these VCR companies known about this, they would have designed the features differently."

Krish continues, "This shows the versatility of Customer Value. It is analytical, it is focused and it is strategic. It helps in improving processes, service and pricing. It is also makes all of these decisions more Customer-driven. Above all, it brings a passion for the Customer.

(Box 6.3 continued)

---

[13] Bradley Gale, white paper quoted in Gautam Mahajan, *Customer Value Investment.*

(Box 6.3 continued)

Price–Performance Profile for Desktop Computers

Benefit Attributes	Dell	PowerMac	Compaq	H-P	Sony	IBM	iMac	Micron	Gateway Essential	NEC	Gateway Profile	eMachines	Weights %
Speed	8.0	10.0	10.0	8.0	8.0	6.0	8.0	6.0	6.0	8.0	4.0	6.0	16.0
Multimedia Images	10.0	8.0	10.0	8.0	8.0	8.0	8.0	8.0	6.0	6.0	4.0	6.0	16.0
Multimedia Sound	10.0	8.0	10.0	8.0	8.0	8.0	6.0	8.0	8.0	8.0	8.0	6.0	8.0
Multimedia Features	8.0	8.0	8.0	10.0	10.0	10.0	8.0	10.0	8.0	8.0	10.0	6.0	8.0
Other Features	8.0	10.0	8.0	10.0	8.0	8.0	10.0	10.0	10.0	6.0	10.0	6.0	8.0
Expansion	10.0	8.0	8.0	8.0	6.0	8.0	4.0	6.0	6.0	8.0	6.0	6.0	8.0
System Restore	8.0	10.0	6.0	10.0	10.0	10.0	10.0	6.0	6.0	10.0	10.0	10.0	8.0
Manuals	8.0	8.0	6.0	6.0	6.0	6.0	8.0	6.0	6.0	4.0	8.0	6.0	4.0
Power	8.0	10.0	6.0	8.0	10.0	10.0	6.0	8.0	8.0	8.0	10.0	8.0	2.4
Display	8.0	8.0	10.0	8.0	8.0	8.0	6.0	6.0	6.0	8.0	10.0	8.0	1.6
Technical Support	7.6	6.7	5.9	6.4	6.7	6.5	6.7	7.2	7.0	5.6	7.0	6.7	10.0
Reliability	9.0	8.7	8.1	7.9	7.9	8.2	8.7	6.7	7.3	6.9	7.3	7.9	10.0
													100
Selling Price ($) Δ Market Share	1,921 (++)	2,858	2,410	2,548	2,500	2,348	1,199	1,518	1,528	2,020	2,359	899	

(Box 6.3 continued)

(Box 6.3 continued)

Value Scorecard for Desktop Computers

Differential Worth of each
Model versus the average
model($)

Benefit Attributes	Dell	PowerMac	Compaq	H-P	Sony	IBM	iMac	Micron	Gateway Essential	NEC	Gateway Profile	eMachines	Average
Speed	85	341	341	85	85	-171	85	-171	-171	85	-427	-171	0
Multimedia Images	320	64	320	64	64	64	64	64	-192	-192	-448	-192	0
Multimedia Sound	128	0	128	0	0	0	-128	0	0	0	0	-128	0
Multimedia Features	-43	-43	-43	85	85	85	-43	85	-43	-43	85	-171	0
Other Features	-43	85	-43	85	-43	-43	85	85	85	-171	85	-171	0
Expansion	192	64	64	64	-64	64	-192	-64	64	-64	-64	-64	0
System Restore	-75	53	-203	53	53	53	53	-203	53	53	53	53	0
Manuals	48	48	-16	-16	-16	-16	48	-16	-16	-80	48	-16	0
Power	-6	32	-45	-6	32	32	-45	-6	-6	-6	32	-6	0
Display	2	2	28	2	2	2	-23	-23	-23	2	28	2	0
Technical Support	75	3	-61	-21	0	-13	3	43	27	-85	27	0	0
Reliability	88	64	16	4	0	28	64	-92	-44	-80	-44	0	0
Differential Worth	772	714	487	400	199	86	-28	-298	-394	-452	-624	-863	0
Price Advantage	88	-849	-401	-539	-491	-339	810	491	481	-11	-350	1,110	0
Total Value Advantage	860	-135	86	-139	-292	-253	782	193	87	-463	-974	247	0
Fair-Value Price	2,781	2,723	2,496	2,409	2,208	2,095	1,981	1,711	1,615	1,557	1,385	1,146	2,009
Selling Price ($)	1,921	2,858	2,410	2,548	2,500	2,348	1,199	1,518	1,528	2,020	2,359	899	2,009
Total Value Advantage	860	-135	86	-139	-292	-253	782	193	87	-463	-974	247	0

Source Gautam Mahajan, *Customer Value Investment*, 128, 130.

profit, generally. You know you can also use Value Maps to decide a pricing policy. If you are adding excess value, and your price is low, you can increase price and decrease Value to the Customer. Or you can reduce the quality. You will notice there is a fair value line. If the value you deliver to the Customer is on this line, it means the Customer perceives he is paying a fair price. The benefits he gets match the cost of the product in his thinking. Thus, in Value Map 1 (Figure 6.1), you are giving away value. You could reduce value. You do this by using the Value Map where you would bring your company closer to the fair value line and reduce the value you add. You would do this by moving quality to the left and reducing value, while keeping price fixed.

FIGURE 6.1
Value Map 1

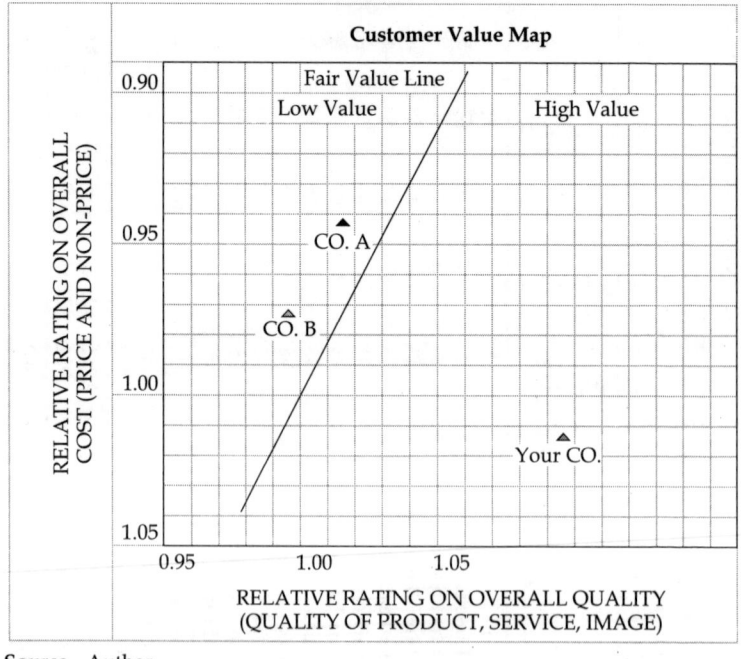

Source Author.

"On the other hand, you can increase the price, and you will be moving upwards towards the fair price line. Remember, price is a mixture of price terms (including price itself, discounts, credit and payment terms) and non-price terms such as price justification, just in time delivery, warranties, etc.

"Value Map 2 (Figure 6.2) shows that you can increase value by moving towards the fair value line. That is, you reduce price, and this brings you closer to the Fair Price Line.

"Thus, you adjust quality or price or both to increase or decrease value. Price is then based on the perception of the Customer and on the benefits you provide him: in short, the value your offering adds to him."

FIGURE 6.2
Value Map 2

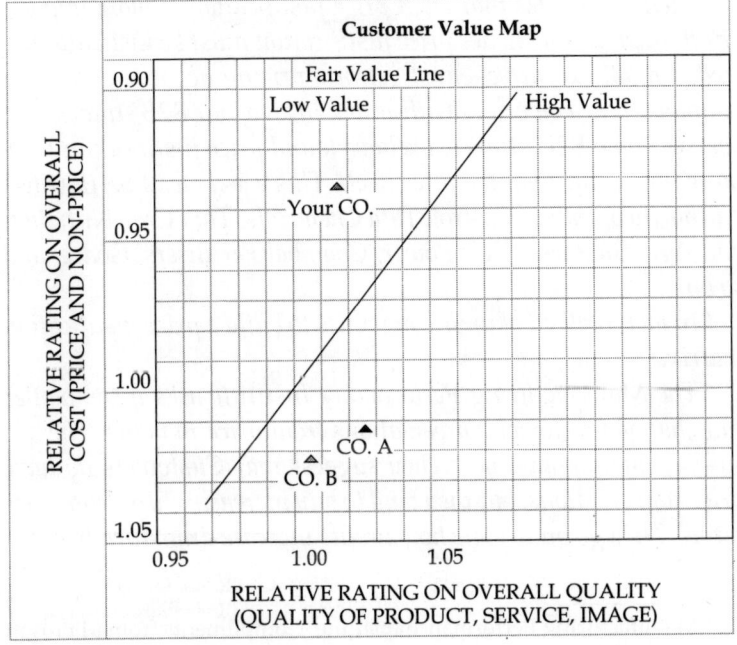

Turning Price Negotiation to a Value Negotiation[14]

Krish added: *"I am of the opinion that one should never go into a price negotiation to discuss price. That is what the purchasing manager wants to do: focus on and beat you down on price. Your job is to focus on the value you are creating for him. Cite the various advantages of your product and service. Remind him of all the things you have done for him, whether it is always being on time, working with him on Just in Time (JIT) and reducing inventory, better financial terms, superior quality, customization, great service, no complaints: whatever you have achieved for the Customer. It will become more difficult for him to hit you with the price stick, and you will get a better price. I met a DuPont executive on a plane who told me he was on the way to a price negotiation, and I advised him to convert it into a value discussion. He called me after the meeting that this strategy had worked well for him.*

"I tell companies that often price justification is more important than price, and hence price justification must be institutionalized, and all executives must get into pricing negotiations using templates based on price justification. In all of our B2B studies, and even in some B2C studies, we have found price justification to be more important than the price itself. This was true at SAIL (Steel Authority of India), Castrol, Tata Chemicals, Tata Crop Nutrition and Agri-Business, Tata Power, Chambal Fertilisers, Godrej and so on.

"In fact, I tell all of these companies to build a price justification matrix.

"The Manufacturing Performance Institute asks if companies can change Customer conversations from price to value. The answer is an emphatic yes. They suggest that Customers do have price conversations, but they tend to buy increasingly on non-price terms. They go on to state how profits increase dramatically when

---

[14] Manufacturing Performance Institute. Compliments from Microsoft Business Solution.

a product is sold on value, because the investment and expense do not increase proportional to the Customer Value (remember we say CVI = ROI!). Value increases also from the relationship, which Customers increasingly value.

"*Examples of value increase include:*

- *Better quality, reliability and timely delivery and service*
- *Reduced total cost of ownership*
- *Transparent access to information and service*
- *Providing business information even if unrelated to the product or service.*"

"This is what I would have said too," says Doug. "I couldn't agree more."

Krish adds: "*One of the most hotly debated issues in CRM circles, according to the Boeing Centre for Technology, in recent times is the issue of traditional accounting versus Customer accounting. The very objective of CRM, that is, to retain and grow the Customer Value indicates that that the measurement of any CRM effort should be based on its contribution to the growth in future Customer Value. The first step in the reconciliation of these two accounting methods is the generation of a Customer accounting report, designed to track the value of new and current Customers over time. At a macro level, these reports can take the form of an overall view of Customer Value status report; and at a micro or operational level, these reports can take the form of a campaign or project specific view report.*[15]

CO-CREATING PROFITS

"*Too often, companies think about win-win, and often the name of the game is to win twice. But if the CFO and the company looks at co-creating experiences with the Customer, then they can think of*

---

[15] Copyright 2000, The Boeing Centre for Technology, Information & Manufacturing.

ways and means to reduce costs together or grow markets together and co-create profits. Earlier, I had given examples of Fedex. Other examples are Just in Time manufacturing, reducing inventory and increasing profits; in the fruits and vegetable markets, intermediaries ripen and pack produce as per the supermarkets' requirements, mark the price and put them on the shelf, reducing handling and other costs."

Shirley says, "Hmm, that's worth a thought. I should also discuss with the delivery and marketing people on how we can co-create profits."

Krish hands Shirley the CFO Customer scorecard (Table 6.3) to fill out.

TABLE 6.3
The CFO Scorecard

The CFO Scorecard	Yes	No
1. Are you the Chief Shareholder Value Creator?		
2. Do you balance value creation for the shareholder and value creation for the Customer?		
3. Do you balance long-term with short-term profits?		
4. Do you know that ROC is increased through Total CVM?		
5 Do you know ROC=TSV?		
6. Do you think only profits and returns make up shareholder value. Are there other factors?		
7. Have you ever studied shareholders view on whether you add more value to them vs. competitors for their investment?		
8. Do you know what is important to shareholders other than returns and on what relative scale? Do you measure Total Shareholder Value?		
9. Do you measure Customer Value Added (Voice of Customer) Do you measure Voice of the Employee and Voice of the Competitor?		
10. Do you price using Customer Value Added and Value Maps?		
11. Do you measure Customer Assets and Customer capital?		
12. Do you measure ROC?		
13. Do you measure Customer Lifetime Value?		
14. Do you have a Customer Value Added and a Customer reporting system that you send same time as your financial and other reports?		
15. Do your executives have a well thought out Customer role in addition to their functional goals?		

(Table 6.3 continued)

(*Table 6.3 continued*)

The CFO Scorecard	Yes	No
16. Do your executives have one or two Customer related goals in their key performance goals?		
17. Do you help executives look at pricing from a Customers attribute point of view?		
18. Who are your most valuable Customers? Are you pruning unprofitable Customers?		
19. Is the Customer DNA (Do Not Annoy) an employee mantra?		
20. Do you measure your share of the Customer wallet?		
21. Are you setting up Customer-Centric-Circles in your functional departments?		
22. Are you easily contactable by the Customer?		
23. Do you get a Customer complaint sheet and action taken list?		
24. Do you receive Customer complaints calls personally at least once or twice a week?		
25. Do you co-create profits with Customers?		
26. Do you have a well thought-out Customer strategy? Is the corporate strategy in sync with the Customer strategy?		
27. Do you rationalize pricing decisions by using Customer Value based pricing? Do you teach this and price justification?		

Source Author.

Doug asks if he can summarize:

"The Chief Shareholder Value Creator:

- Understands and quantifies the increase of Shareholder Value with Customer Value and satisfaction increase
- Segments Customers by profitability, co-creates profits
- Measures Customer Lifetime Value
- Recommends how to grow Customer Lifetime Value
- Measures and finds ways to increase Customer assets
- Ensures Customer-focus and Customer-tasks are part of his department
- Institutes Customer-friendly billing, financial terms and payment receipts
- Establishes simple enquiry systems on bills, payments, etc.
- Ensures executive understand that Customer Value impacts pricing and urges them to grow Customer Value

- Teaches executives on how to do price negotiations
- Helps companies institutionalize price justification
- Keeps in contact with the Customers
- Balances convenience of company with convenience of Customer."

THE CHIEF CUSTOMER OFFICER

Doug has requested a meeting the following week with his two senior officers, Jack Griswold, COO, and Shirley Madison, CFO, along with Jimmy Vaidya, Head of Manufacturing, Rita Timko, Chief Marketing Officer and JoJo Mohindra, CIO. He has asked Krish Kumar, the Customer Guru to attend the meeting.

Doug clears his throat and says, "You've had discussions with Krish on Total Customer Value Management. I am keen we make our company a Customer-led company. What do you think?"

Jack speaks up: "You are right. I did not realize how little I did for the Customers. I always knew they were important but my other important priorities gave me less time to think of or do things for the Customer. Now I am convinced that the Customer should move up in my thinking; in fact, in all of our thoughts and actions. Krish has convinced me of positive results that the company will see from a Total CVM effort."

Doug says, "The first step is for you, Jack, to become the Chief Customer Value Creator. I do not want to make you the Chief Customer Officer (who will report to me). The CCO will help you. Shirley should become the Chief Shareholder Value Creator."

Krish, who has been nodding silently, says: *"Doug, this is a good move. We all know every company has a CXO for important functions. What can be more important than the Customer and a Chief Customer Officer? Yet companies do not have one. Somehow, a CCO does not find a role in a traditional organizational hierarchy. But having a CCO is imperative for a company entering Total CVM and becoming truly Customer-centric.*

"*Ideally, the CEO should be the Chief Customer Officer. In any event, one is needed to act as the representative of the Customer in the company. The CCO also ensures that the Chief Shareholder Value Creator is focusing on the Customer as much as the Chief Customer Value Creator is. The CCO ensures that the Chief Shareholder Value Creator understands Customer Value and what Customer Value creates for the company and for the shareholder (It creates TSV or Total Shareholder Value).*

"*Why do CEOs normally not play this role? It is a matter of time required to coach the different parts of the organization, and to ensure the Customer programme is moving on stream. The CEO can use an executive assistant to monitor the Customer programme, but the assistant cannot run it. He needs the assistance of a senior officer.*

"*The CEO, if he takes the mantle of the CCO, should use both the head of marketing and one officer who is traditionally not front-facing to assist him with rolling out and monitoring Customer programmes.*

"*If the CEO decides to add the CCO role to an existing officer, he should appoint a non-Customer facing officer, like the strategy officer, or the HRD head. (The HRD head has to be the Chief Employee Value Creator, and may not be an ideal choice.) The CCO role should go to someone who has company-wide tasks.*

"*The Chief Marketing Officer or a front facing officer has, anyway, to focus on Customers. If he takes the role of the CCO, it is likely that the non-Customer facing officers will not align to the Customer as readily, as they see the marketing person as really the Customer interface and in-charge!*

"*Ideally, of course, if the CEO decides to appoint a CCO, he should not be clubbed with some other function. It should be a new full time role.*

"*Preferably, the CCO should sit on the Board, and remind the Board of the importance of the Customer, while putting into place programmes to promote Customer delight and Customer-centricity and to implement Total CVM.*"

Doug agrees, "Yes, the CCO should be on the Board, and we have to find someone to do this job. We will all have to think of a candidate. However, Jack is on our Board, and so the new CCO may not need to be a Board member. Jack can speak for him."

Krish adds: *"The CCO has to ensure the Customer gets Board priority and attention."*

"But, more than that, having a CCO is a call for action. It sends a powerful message of the importance of the Customer, and the company means business for the Customer. The CCO pinpoints Customer-centricity as being the critical aspect of the business. Institutionalizing the function requires a strong person who builds a business case for the importance of the Customer, creating corporate and Customer Value.

"And the CCO brings in the Voice of the Customer and the Voice of the Competitor. He insists on the Voice of the Employee, Customer certification of employees and company certification from the point of view of the Customer. He connects employees, Customers and the company and its Customer offerings. He works with various functions and helps them convert to being Customer advocates, the first step to Customer-centricity.

"Moreover, the CCO must ensure that there is an environment where every complaint is handled to the Customer's satisfaction and that the Customer has no need to go to a third party to address his complaint or unhappiness. If necessary, the CCO should have an Ombudsman instituted by the company. The CCO has to facilitate all corporate functions to focus on the Customer, to facilitate Customer-centric processes, to ensure no Customer complaints happen, and if they happen, they are amicably resolved by instituting systems including Ombudsmen if necessary. In effect to make Customers happy and loyal. Of course, a Customer includes shareholders, channel partners and internal Customers.

"The CCO manages and improves the overall Customer experience.

"He makes sure Customer-Centric-Circles, Customer-centric training and certification is taking place. He maintains cross-functional contact with all departments and helps them with Customer focus. Please look at this sheet of paper." He passes it on.

The paper says:

CCOs have to:

- Build Customer strategy
- Provide an enabling environment for Customer-related work:
  - Be able to manage various tasks and agendas
  - Interact at all levels of the corporation
  - Provide priority and focus on the important Customer-related issues
  - Look for future initiatives
  - Be patient
- Cause long-term change of habits and attitudes and behaviour: get the executives to think of the Customer first, and not sales or profits
  - Ensure corporate enthusiasm, and longevity of the Customer-centric culture he is building
  - Build and monitor Customer Circles and the Circle of Promises
- Promote Customer advocacy
  - Decide what kind of Customers to keep
  - Reduce churn
  - Ensure people understand that at the end of the day each person in the organization has to be held accountable to the Customers
- Measure value
  - Bring in the Voice of the Customer into the organization
  - Ensure Customer action, including converting call centres into Action Centres
  - Give feed back to employees on how positive Customer action impacts positively on the company
  - Measure Return on Customer

- Institute rewards, bonus systems triggered by Customer satisfaction and Value
- Co-create Customer experience and customization, including co-creation of profits
- Enunciate the purpose of the organization. (Note, profit is not the purpose of the organization. Profit is necessary for the organization to survive, but the purpose is to create Customer value and Customer delight.)

The CCO implements and monitors:

- The Customer-in-Centre©
- The Customer-in-Control
- Customer customization
- Co-creation of Customer experience and profits
- Return on Customer measurements
- A Customer Uniqueness Programme (Recognizing each Customer as unique), and
- Builds a Customer strategy and a Customer-sensitive organization
- Customer roles for all departments
- Customer Performance Management System, including in KRAs and balance Scorecard
- Continuous Customer Improvement Programme
- Build corporate brand by building employee brand equity

Krish continues: *"In conclusion, the CCO should not become the Chief complaint officer or the Ombudsman. He should not become a Customer Service Manager or run a CRM function. Doug, as the CEO, you have to ensure that the CCO is institutionalized and a real function not a figurehead, or an add-on to another assignment.*

"Moreover, the CEO has to make sure that the CCO is not seen as the Customer contact, and, therefore, others in the company do not have to bother about the Customer.

"The CEO needs to assess the CCO on Customer Value Addition, on his ability to spot and eliminate processes that prevent delivery of value to the Customer, and how much the company culture is becoming accountable to the Customer.

"The CCO finds and builds Customer Champions to act as catalysts and leaders in change, and engender teamwork. Teamwork and team learning requires such people as facilitators or as catalysts, and requires people to suspend their beliefs to listen to others and to regard each other and colleagues who are present to help us.

"The Customer Champions also run the Customer Circles which should become a self-learning system. With Customer Circles, the organization is bound to become creative and innovative. People want to be part of such an organization, and participate in the innovation.

"The principle has to be that no one should be too proud to learn. And not too proud to learn from anyone. Continuous learning and participation will lead to Customer excellence. Teamwork and team learning requires a facilitator or a catalyst, and requires people to suspend their beliefs to listen to others and to regard each other and colleagues who are present to help us.

"Some will debate that CCOs are signs of immature Customer action and should self-extinct as the Customer culture comes in. I do not subscribe to this view.

"The CCO is a powerful message to the Customer that they have their advocate in the company sitting in the boardroom, and their voice will be heard! This message has to be communicated. The CCO should be closely associated with Corporate communications."

Doug tells Krish that he knows of maybe twenty companies himself that have a CCO. He had read that the son of the Chairman of Samsung had been made CCO of Samsung, as an important job on his way up. Krish says he knows of one Indian company that has appointed a CCO very recently, and that is Godrej Properties.

He continues, "To ensure we have the right person as the CCO, we can look at a CCO scorecard (Table 6.4)", which he hands out.

TABLE 6.4
The CCO Scorecard

The CCO Scorecard	Yes	No
1. Do you help build a Customer Strategy?		
2. Do you try to make different departments understand the value to the company from Total CVM?		
3. Do you discuss balancing long-term profits vs. short-term goals and how to increase long-term profits?		
4. Do you teach that ROC is increased through Total CVM?		
5. Do you teach ROC = TSV?		
6. Is the chief complaint taker different from you?		
5. Do you have an Ombudsman?		
6. Do you measure Customer Value Added (Voice of Customer)?		
7. Do you measure Voice of the Employee and Voice of the Competitor?		
8. Do you teach pricing using Customer Value		
9. Do you encourage a Customer Value Added and a Customer reporting system that the CEO receives at the same time as the financial and other reports?		
10. Do you help executives have a well thought out Customer role in addition to their functional goals?		
11. Do you measure Customer assets. Are these growing?		
12. Do you measure Customer lifetime value?		
13. Do you design bonus systems based on Customer Value Customer metrics and a Customer Performance Management system?		
14. Are you helping the CEO build Customer Conduits?		
15. Do you promote the concept of farming and hunting?		
16. Do you promote Customer delight?		
17. Is the Customer DNA (Do Not Annoy) an employee mantra?		
18. Do you build an enabling environment or do you think empowerment is enough?		
19. Do you promote Customer-Centric-Circles?		
20. Do you know how many Customers you have?		
21. Do employees know who your most valuable Customers are? Are you pruning unprofitable Customers?		
22. Do you help increase share of the Customer wallet?		
23. Are you easily contactable by the Customer?		
24. Do you have an Employee Value Added programme? Do you build employee brand equity?		
25. Do you promote Customer uniqueness: Treating different Customers differently? Co-create experience and profits?		
26. Do you receive Customer complaints calls personally at least once or twice a week?		

(Table 6.4 continued)

(*Table 6.4 continued*)

The CCO Scorecard	Yes	No
27. Do you correlate CVA with TSV?		
28. Do you treat employees, internal Customers, chain partners, shareholders as Customers?		
29. Do you have a Customer Uniqueness programme?		
30. Do you build the Customers' Bill of Rights and the Customer Circle of Promises?		
31. Is Total CVM in the Balanced Scorecard?		

Source Author.

CHAPTER SYNOPSIS

This Chapter starts the process of alignment and Customer-centric education of the top managers, which includes the CEO (the Chief Value Creator), the COO (the Chief Customer Value Creator), the CFO (the Chief Shareholder Value Creator), and the Chief Customer Officer. There are Customer-based scorecards to gauge the understanding of these officers on the Customer. These officers start to realize what their Customer roles could be.

The CEO and the Customer

The role of the CEO is discussed in detail. How he has to put the Customer first and how he has to align the company towards the Customer. In addition, the CEO Scorecard is developed.

Chief Customer Value Creator or Chief Operating Officer

The COO is the Chief Value Creator and has a very big Customer role, and what he has to do is discussed. Included is the COO Scorecard.

The Chief Customer Value Creator has all departments focused on maximizing value to Customers, whether it is products, logistics, service or marketing. Working through the Chief Employee Value Creator, the Chief Customer Value Creator ensures all functions are Customer-centric and Customer-sensitized.

Chief Shareholder Value Creator or Chief Financial Officer

Allied topics like Return on Customer, Value of Customer, Customer equity, ROI, and ROI of marketing are discussed with the CFO. In addition, the relationship between share prices and Customer Value is shown. Customer data reporting on balance sheets, the value of channel partners and Customer contact are all discussed. The CFO is told about co-controlling business and business processes with the Customer. The use of Value to price products is explained with examples.

The Chief Customer Officer

This is a pivotal role because the CCO coordinates between the Board and the employees at all levels, ensuring Customer Value Management is being installed. Selection, role and duties of the CCO are detailed.

7

Total CVM and Sales and Marketing: Chief Marketing Officer

A few days later, Doug and Krish are meeting with Rita Timko, Head of Sales and Marketing. Doug thinks of his stint in marketing and how he learnt from Krish about the importance of the Customer. Rita has had some exposure to the CVM ideas in the past.

Krish says, *"Chief Marketing Officers are often thought of as the custodian of the Customer. They balance hunting of new Customers with farming or taking care of existing Customers and making them into loyal Customers. They have to work with the Chief Customer Officer in catalyzing all functions to make the Customer happy, and indeed provide Customer delight and imbibe the Customers' DNA (Do Not Annoy). With Total CVM, Rita will not be the lone custodian of the Customer. Everyone in the organization will have a Customer role.*

"Rita has to convert her team to think about Customer assets, Customer momentum and Customer franchise."

- **Customer Franchise:** *Value of present and future Customer relationships or Customer Capital plus Customer Momentum.*
- **Customer Momentum:** *Is the ability to attract and sustain new Customers, and increase share of wallet for existing Customers.*

Doug adds that these factors along with Customer Value are important. "The importance of Customer Value in marketing is aptly described by Anderson and Narus.[1]

"We had talked about return on marketing before and said that CVA and loyalty and other Customer metrics best describe the returns.

"Narus says companies must pinpoint what their offerings are worth to Customers. Field measurements (Customer Value Added or CVA), he says are the best way to measure the marketing offering. He goes on to say how value measurements can be used to customize and create competitive advantage, which is what we have been saying about Customer Value Added, CVA.

"Following what I've said the Chief Marketing Officer devises strategy to increase Customer Value, Customer loyalty and market share," says Doug.

Rita agrees, "She has to teach her team the merit of improving Customer Lifetime Value and wallet share. She has to introduce Customer share marketing. She has to instill the value of cultivating Customers, the phone or in person, answering and returning calls and indeed making the Customer want to come back to the company."

"She has to devise a bonus system based on Customer feedback."

"She has to revamp the satisfaction studies and make them focused on the important needs of the Customer. These important needs will be assessed through a value study. She has to carry out a Customer Value Added study. She has to measure the Voice of the Customer and Voice of Competitor."

Doug agrees, "Krish, Rita is a converted person and is practising much of what she is saying."

---

[1] J.C. Anderson, J.A. Narus, "Business Marketing: Understand What Customers Value," *Harvard Business Review.* 76, no. 6 (1998 Nov–Dec): 53–55, 58–65. Northwestern University, J.L. Kellogg Graduate School of Management, Evanston, IL, USA.

Rita continues, "She has to understand the value her product/employees company/brand is creating for the Customer and how to increase it and get a price for it. She has to correlate Customer Value with market share."

"She has to use CVA data and value maps to optimize pricing, and to understand the fulfilled/unfulfilled needs of the Customer and design product and service offerings and options accordingly."

Krish is smiling: *"You have taken the words out of my mouth. I could not have said this better. Doug, we may be able to do more things in your company on Total CVM when we have people like Rita heading sales and marketing.*

CO-CREATING CUSTOMER VALUE

"But let's also talk about Co-creating Customer Value. Here you collaborate with the Customer in co-creating value for him and for your company (and for yourself). One has to work with Customers on what would provide value to them and work on creating this value. This is a win-win situation for all.

"In fact, you need to customize, and think of each Customer as an individual and design your offering to him.

"At first, it appears that this is a tall order because it is not what we are used to doing. We are used to conventional wisdom (and that's the way we do things) and we dare not innovate. But when you start to focus in on an audience of one, you will come up with solutions. An example is the Hong Kong tailor who takes your measurements over the net, and supplies you perfectly fitting suits, while the logistics chain readies to deliver.

"The days of selling to and manipulating the market and the Customer are over. Now we have to help him buy. We have to put the Customer in control and into a collaborative effort with the company and that will create winning companies and winning Customers."

Doug says, "This sounds a lot like prosumers where Customers are producers and consumers of products.

"The CMO must, as Krish said, keep the Customer happy, and indeed provide Customer delight and imbibe the Customers' DNA (Do Not Annoy). With Total CVM, you will share everyone in the organization all having a Customer role.

"The Chief Marketing Officer has to categorize/segment Customers. He should know how many Customers he has, how to make them less anonymous, how to touch them, how to service them with the products the Customer wants and how to put the Customer in control in his buying and product decisions (what he wants to buy and in the sizes and quantities he wants, and how he wants delivery)."

Doug continues, "I deal with one of the four big accounting firms. They helped my friend with an M&A transaction. During a second transaction, one of their managers sent a mail to my friend and Chairman of a multibillion dollar company asking for his mailing address. The client was flabbergasted.

"This is the **goldfish principle** where we keep asking the Customer for information we already have. The goldfish principle is the opposite of a learning relationship. Instead of learning from what we have experienced, or what the Customer has told us (in the example I gave, the company has the Customer's address!), we go back asking for information already with us or told or experience the same thing again!

"In ending, the CMO correlates CVA and market share, CVA and profit, and CVA and stock price.

"Co-creation can mean co-creation of experiences, of products, of manufacturing, of profits and technologies and systems. Readers have their own examples of co-creation."

CUSTOMER GROUP OF ONE: TREATING DIFFERENT CUSTOMERS DIFFERENTLY

"Treating different Customers differently creates Value for them and increases Return on Customer or (ROC). You increase the value of the Customer and ROC by not overspending on him, by giving him products and services he wants or is willing to pay for."

Krish adds, *"In India, Suresh Mohindra, a marketing executive, tells me about telemarketing; people calling him and telling him what their company can do for him. No one wants to hear what he wants them (the company) to do. So, they destroy value. However, what is worse, by not listening to him, and not looking at him as an individual Customer and taking into account his needs, they are losing an opportunity to create immense value. The value of the relationship built with an individual Customer is generally worth more than the cost of building it. Such Customers are always ready to fight for you, to meet you, and be understanding and to forgive you or favour you.*

"Generally, the cost of adding value is nil or low because it generally means companies are doing things right for the Customer. Being polite, attentive or willing to help costs nothing. Remember, CVI equals increased ROI. The Customer Value Investment (CVI) is generally very low, because it is just doing the right things from the Customers' viewpoint.[2]

"Recall that a brand does not interact with a Customer. A relationship does. Relationship builds trust which we know increases Customer Value and ROC (Return on Customer)."

Rita gives an example. Malcom Gladwell,[3] in his book *Blink*, studied doctors who were being sued, and who were likely to be sued. There was no correlation between skill and experience, and the tendency to be sued. It had little to do with the medical mistakes doctors made. The major factor is how patients were treated by the doctor. People just do not sue doctors they like or implicitly trust. And liking and trust has to do with being rushed, or given less time, or being treated poorly. The relationship is formed by giving time, courteous treatment and patient hearing and explanations.

"This, I suppose, is true in any business. Building a relationship is paramount."

---

[2] Gautam Mahajan, *Customer Value Investment*.
[3] Malcolm Gladwel, *Blink* (Back Bay Books, 2007).

"A great example, Rita," continues Krish. *"Knowing the worth of a Customer and building a relationship is particularly important when a recessionary environment exists.*

"ICICI Bank in India has built a flexible insurance programme for diabetic Customers in India which understands individual Customer's needs, their risk profile and their lifestyle. If the lifestyle promotes diabetes (excessive sugar intake and no exercise), versus one that reduces sugar (careful diet and exercise), the risk is different for each of these two Customers and the insurance premium is different. In addition, it gives the Customer an economic incentive to be healthy."

INCREASING VALUE FROM A CUSTOMER

Rita Timko, the Chief Marketing Officer, remarks: "We have also to look at value from a Customer or value of the Customer.

- Wallet share. How much business goes to competition?
- How to get that business while increasing price through demonstrated value increase, and price justification.
- Additional business by adding value, or customizing, and understanding unknown needs.
- Reducing costs of transaction.
- Other products/services to sell?
- Value from preventing defection.
- Value from referrals."

Krish adds, *"We should also measure Value of Customer (a measure of profits) and get rid of poor value Customers unless we perceive they will be of value in the future."*

VALUE SELLING

Rita says that value selling is also necessary. She continues:
"The CMO teaches her people about value selling. Not only selling on monetary value of the offering but all the

other value parameters, such as promptness, availability, quality, relationship, etc. They all have a price factor that the Customer should be willing to pay should he want the service or availability or no product blackout."

Krish says: *"The CMO has to teach his people to be able to tell the Customer about the value of the offering to the Customer's Customer and how it will help the Customer add value to his Customer. Now you are doing value creation selling."*

"Price comes last. Work on how not to take a NO. To do so we have to build a price justification template. Many studies on B2B businesses have shown very often the price justification is much more important than the price. Yet, very few companies build price justification templates. Individual sales people wing their way through price justification. You need to first understand what creates value to the Customer and how much that value is worth to him, and what he will pay for it.

"The price justification note should reflect these and carry the purchasing manager's name on it so that he can show it to his superiors on why he selected a more 'expensive' vendor.

"Therefore, to do value selling you have to know your Customer's business, help him improve his business, and to do so you need to get to know your Customer's Customers and their needs. The reward system must reflect value selling and value creation."

VALUE ADDITION IN THE CHAIN

Krish moves onto the selling chain: *"By and large, our studies in companies using channel partners or delivery-chain partners shows often there is a deterioration of value as you go from the company to the dealer/distributor to the retailer to the end Customer, particularly in India. There are some exceptions: a neighbourhood mom and pop store may add more value than a product a Customer buys. However, generally the reverse is often the case.*

"We find that we have to concentrate on the channel partners to add value. This becomes difficult when the delivery chain partner sells competitive products. Your channel partner will add value to

your Customers if you add more value to him than the competitors add to him.

"The best way to look at a chain is to think of the company as the Navy, the aircraft carrier as the distributor and the jet planes as the retailers. They all have speed, a mission, and want to deliver what the company desires and with speed and efficiency.

"Nevertheless, most channel partners view themselves as subservient to the parent company. They do not build their own brand equity. We asked the dealers of one company (let's call them ABC, and let's assume ABC has very high brand equity), suppose 50 per cent of your business comes from ABC, and 50 per cent from its competitors, and ABC left you. How much business would you be left with? The answer from many dealers was 20–30 per cent because ABC was such a respected brand. This realization made the dealers think of themselves, and their own brand equity or lack of it! They called me back, suggesting things they could do to improve their brand equity and seeking my advice.

"In fact the loyalty of the dealers to ABC was 50 per cent; the loyalty of the retailers to ABC (and retailers have limited contact with ABC) was 50 per cent, but to the dealer was 20 per cent. (This shows the dealers were not adding value downwards.) The loyalty of the end Customer to ABC was 60 per cent, but to the retailer was 10 per cent, another disconnect.

"Tata is working with its delivery chain to add value to the end Customer and to build the individual channel partners' own brand equity. This in turn will help them increase and deliver Customer Value."

THE ROLE OF MARKETING IN TOTAL CVM

Rita says the role of marketing in Total CVM includes:

1. Farming and Hunting
   a. Hunting or acquiring new Customers
   b. Farming or nurturing existing Customers

    c. Treating Customers as Assets and maintaining the Customer asset

    d. Partnering the Customer and co-creating value

    e. Putting the Customer in Control

    f. Providing easy access to the company for Customers, and making it easy for Customers to buy

    g. Providing a quick solution to Customer's queries and problems and systemically reducing these

    h. Ensuring call centres are Customer-centric and paying attention to them (not thinking we have out-sourced to a call centre and we have no Customer responsibility). Converting them to action centres

2. Improve value in the delivery chain

    a. Outline and systemize Customers' DNA

    b. Look at Customer delight factors

    c. Measure Customer Value (Voice of the Customer) and Voice of the Competitor

    d. Increase Customer Value

    e. Build Customer trust

    f. Help channel partners build their brand equity and Customer Value creation

3. Understand competitive strategy through Voice of the Competitor

4. Look at pricing from a Customer's perspective

    a. De-commoditize and sell on value, not price

    b. Understand price negotiations and convert into value negotiations

    c. Have a price justification model/template

    d. Value selling

    e. Get a price increase for every value, benefit or service you provide, using a Customer Value pricing methodology

5. Understand and use CVA

    a. CVA versus Market share

    b. Correlate CVA versus wallet share

    c. Measure CVA versus profitability and share price

    d. Understand competition better and to create a competitive strategy. Pre-empt competitive strategy and tactics

6. Working with other departments in improving Customer Value and build a company Customer strategy. Co-create experience and profit.

MARKETING AND OTHER FUNCTIONS

Normally, marketing people are more Customer sensitive than people from non-Customer facing departments. But in the quest of Customer Value creation, marketing has to get other departments to understand Customer Value. The tools to use include getting people from diverse departments into Customer Circles. Another tool is the Customer Bill of Rights and the Circle of Promises, where the Customer-facing people promise Customers certain rights, which are supported by back-to-back promises from supporting functions in order to keep the promises to the Customer. (See Chapter 10 for Customer Circles and Chapter 5 for the Customer Bill of Rights.)

CONVERT CALL CENTRES TO ACTION CENTRES

Krish attributes this to a Customer Value Foundation consultant, as he talks about call centres. One of the most irritating aspects of dealing with a company is often the call centre. All of us have horror stories to tell. Sixty-seven per cent of Americans sometimes have to make a fuss to get problems resolved, according to Emily Yellin,[4] and nearly all (94 per cent) find it irksome to deal with a recording rather than with

---

[4] Emily Yellin, *Your Call is (Not that) Important to Us* (Free Press, 2009).

a human being. GetHuman.com shows waiting times on calls for many companies. AT&T has a waiting time of 17.7 minutes and Comcast 13.3 minutes! According to a recent Customer Rage Study, 68 per cent were very upset by their problems. Fifty-seven per cent of all those who had serious complaints decided not to deal with the company again.

Call centres are impersonal. The concept of a personal account manager does not exist, though companies such as Verizon have tried this. Call centre people are faceless and never come in true contact with the Customers. They hear Customers' problems but are often not authorized to or responsible to solve problems. Call centres are viewed from interaction matrixes, not from relationship building. They are treated as cost centres, not as strategic advantage centres. Call centre associates must have requisite information, and have the authority and the empathy to solve Customer problems.

Krish paraphrases what he was told by Customer Value Foundation:

> The Customer Value Foundation consultant visited a call centre (name withheld) and was amazed at the responses of the call centre employees. When Customers called with a question, where is your serviceman, the call centre first asked 10 questions (including who are you, your address, the type of plan, the last time you paid a bill, the last service call, etc.) A few seconds' response became a few minutes' interaction and the Customer often did not get his answer. The call centre was outsourced. The consultant met the VP of the call centre, who emphasized how good they were, and showed the consultant a 50-slide report sent on a monthly basis, which showed remarkable progress. The young VP could not understand the Customer Value Foundation's consultant's questions about the Customers getting what they wanted.
>
> The consultant went back to the company, who had out-sourced to the call centre. He asked them what they thought of the call centre. They showed him the same reports and said the call centre was good and was improving based on the reports. When the consultant asked them how many

slides in the report were relevant, they were embarrassed. They had only glanced at the report. When he asked them about the impact of the call centre on the Customer, no one had really looked at it (even though there was some feedback from Customers). When he gave them examples of what was happening, they were quite shocked. These irritations to Customers were never captured.

The consultant then had the call centre supervisors visit ABC's office. He asked them their problem with the company and the Customers, and what the real problems of Customers were. The company was in for a bigger shock when the call centre executives said that when they called the company at the appropriate centre to report a problem, some of the company's offices were difficult to contact, and others had very rude, non-cooperative employees and asked the call centre people who the hell they thought they were (and you work for us). Moreover, many Customers were irked at the lack of correct responses from the call centre as they were not equipped to handle the Customers' problems.

This is when we started a programme to convert the call centre to an action centre.

The reports were changed to reflect Customer needs, not call centre parameters. The reports were shortened so that people read them and took action.

The co-ordination between the company and the call centre led to more co-operation, greater empowerment for the call centre, and the call centre is well on its route to become an action centre.

Another company, in white goods, has a small call centre in their office. The employees are outsourced, including the supervisor.

The Customer Value Foundation consultant listened to the calls from the Customers. One lady called and said a remote controller had not been delivered with her TV. The call officer went to the supervisor's desk. The supervisor called the dealer and asked about the remote controller. The dealer answered, "All Customers say they have not received the remote control." The supervisor reminded him that on the delivery report, there was a missing remote controller. She insisted the dealer replace it by the next day. The call centre executive went back to his desk, but the Customer had hung up. No one called her back, though hopefully her problem was solved. No one checked with the Customer or the dealer the next day if the controller was delivered.

Another Customer called and she said that her air conditioner's swing motor was to be replaced and it was 10 days since the promised date. The call officer asks the Customer if he could put her on hold, and goes to the supervisor who calls the dealer, who says the part is not in stock. The supervisor insists on a conference call with the company's parts centre. After figuring out the part number of the motor, it turns out it is in stock and can be sent to the dealer the same day. The dealer promises to install it the next day. The call centre executives finds the Customer has hung up—and no one calls the Customer back and there is no feedback on whether the part was delivered and installed. A few days later, someone will call and ask about the satisfaction of the transaction, and may be shocked to find that the motor was not installed!

The supervisor's actions are the start of an action centre. The company needs to close the loop, and have a call back and results oriented feedback (not satisfaction) when the job was supposed to be done.

The conversion of call centres to action centres will improve Customer Value and a sense of achievement.

In another example, the consultant had made company call centre employees participate in the Customer Circles. Six weeks later, they reported that the referrals had increased by 30 per cent. What had they done? They had used what they had learnt and postulated in the Customer Circles on what the frontline people should do. This include the Customers' DNA, delight factors and being more patient, listening better and proactiveness. The results were startling and were high motivators for the success of Customer focus.

Krish ends by saying: "*Company officials responsible for call centres should ensure that they (themselves and the call centres) are really Customer-friendly and effective, and the call centres are action centres. They must visit and understand how the call centres work. They should assess, like any other endeavour in the company, whether the call centres are being useful to the company and to the Customer. This is the Total CVM approach.*"

CUSTOMER LOYALTY VERSUS
CUSTOMER RETENTION

Rita tells Krish, "Many marketers confuse Customer retention with loyalty. Many companies measure Customer retention and talk about means to improve retention. While this works, companies forget that retention of Customers happens often because Customers have little choice, or they have inertia (or are too lazy to move). To retain Customers longer, you need to increase Customer Value and thereby get more permanence in retention of Customers."

"*I agree,*" says Krish. "*Jeremy Otte[5] writes about Customer retention versus Customer loyalty. He says most companies have Customer retention programmes such as direct mailings or telephone services that keep the company in the front of Customer's minds and offer them the new products or service. In addition, the Customer needs service for problems and for Customer retention. This is usually handled with a Customer service desk, phone number or website that consumers or intermediaries can go through to initiate the resolution. Many times, these avenues can create additional stress for the consumer due to waiting periods, acknowledgeable associates or rules and regulations. Customer retention focusses on impersonal contact and is handled as a numbers game. The more Customers a company contacts with retention propaganda, the better chance of keeping those people as Customers. Problems are dealt with in a reactive manner.*

"*Now, talking about Customer loyalty, Otte says that very few companies have Customer loyalty programmes, compared to Customer retention programmes. However, this, he says, is changing and more companies are looking at Customer loyalty. The word loyalty itself, according to Otte, implies a deeper connection between business and consumer. With this connection with a*

---

[5] http://www.helium.com/items/653441-Customer-retention-versus-Customer-loyalty?page=2 (accessed on 21 July 2010).

product or service, Customers will fight for your company even if you wrong them.

"Customer loyalty engenders Customer trust of their Customer base. This is achieved by a more personal marketing campaign to the consumer. People want to genuinely feel like the company has an interest in them, not just their money. Thus, telemarketing, instead of relying on a script, has professionals talking to the Customer, not part-time students.

"The second part of Customer loyalty is giving the Customer a sense of belonging. And they need to know you will be there to help with every aspect along the way, and you could gain Customers for life.

"As you can see, Customer loyalty and Customer retention have some very important differences. Retention has a reactive nature, while loyalty has proactive one. If a company is adept enough to focus more on loyalty than retention, only the sky is the limit.

"Murphy Spoyles has an interesting analogy.[6] He states that when you drive your business, Customer loyalty is the windshield, and Customer retention is the rear-view mirror. His suggestion is not to focus on retention too much or too long because you will drive off the road. Rather, you should focus on, and measure Customer loyalty and thereby steer your business in a completely new direction!"

TOTAL CVM AND OTHER
BUSINESS PROCESSES

If we accept that all business is there because of Customers, then all business processes should be Customer-driven. People designing business processes and systems under Total CVM will learn to drive processes by focusing on the Customer.

---

[6] http://www.helium.com/items/657711-Customer-retention- versus-Customer-loyalty3/29 (accessed on 21 July 2010).

Krish is discussing business processes with Doug, Rita and JoJo:

"How do you integrate Customer Value into business processes? There is a reason for processes: to take away human interaction, mistakes and judgement. This means planning requires companies to modify processes for different Customer and business partner interaction. And it is important for marketing to examine these processes as many impact Customers.

"An example is Enterprise Resource Planning (ERP) systems such as SAP: ERP becomes more supreme than the people who use it. These people are affected by it and so are their Customers (including suppliers). An example is a power company who is used to giving large construction and engineering contracts. When they wanted to give me a consulting contract, their ERP process demanded income tax statement, workman's compensation proof, past contracts, reports, etc. These are (by their own admission) not necessary for my type of engagement) but the ERP system held-up the contract for a month because a purchase order could not be cut. While I applaud the discipline, the ERP and financial people had failed in their design. But what is more important is that no one did anything, and so the ERP system is blamed. Value is being destroyed. And, I am sure their next Customer will have the same problem, because no one tackles systemic issues!

"Therefore, Doug, I suggest first the team looks at value creation, and insists on End-user/Customer-friendly process design. You have to handle the "I don't care" syndrome. The CIO has to be Customer driven, and not company driven alone."

Doug says, "Too often, lack of time is considered an issue. People are doing so many things that they lose focus. I think your task matrix is crucial and we have to relieve people of irrelevant and unnecessary tasks.

"We also have to ensure that there is an awareness and desire to suggest and make systemic changes, and that processes are designed from the viewpoint of the Customers, keeping in mind the need to control and manage the company efficiently. We have to manage control (and inflexibility) with flexible mechanisms and designs."

Krish says, *"Let me leave you a few worksheets on Total Performance Optimization as practised by many companies, with a Customer Value twist in it."*

CORRELATING CVA WITH MARKET SHARE AND BUSINESS RESULTS

These correlations (Figures 7.1, 7.2 and 7.3) were shown earlier in Chapter 2.

The CVA results correlate with price, loyalty, market share, wallet share and ROI.

Creating Competitive Advantage

Increasing CVA increases competitive advantage. Moreover, the CVA scores also show what the competition's strategy

FIGURE 7.1
Market Share versus Value

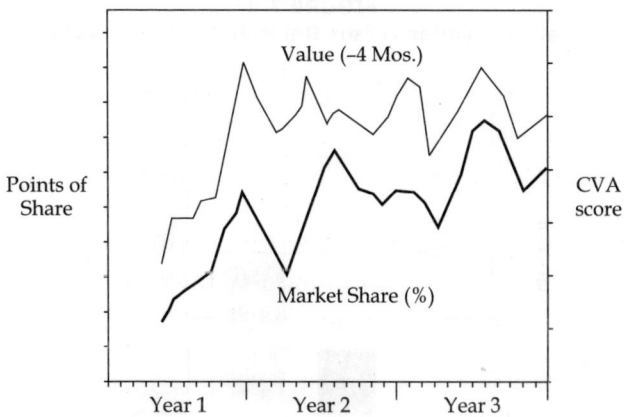

Source   Ray Kordupleski, *Mastering Customer Value Management*, shown in Gautam Mahajan, *Customer Value Investment*.
Note   Example from telecom percentage installs.

FIGURE 7.2
ROI versus Relative Customer Value

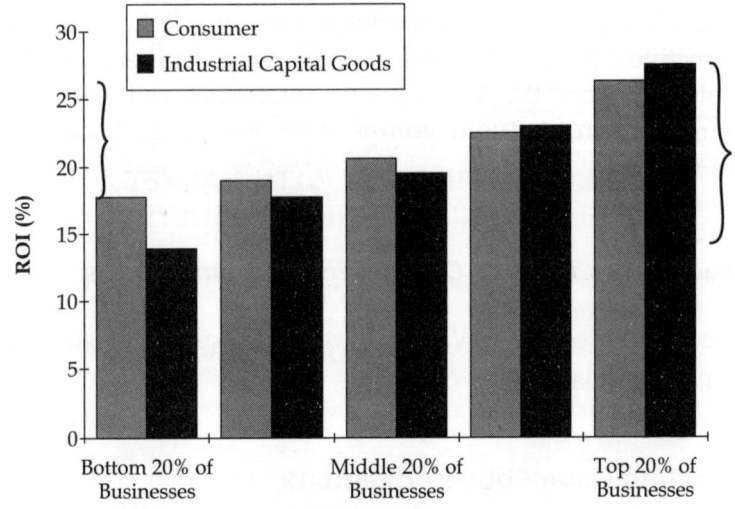

Source Ray Kordupleski, *Mastering Customer Value Management*, shown in Gautam Mahajan, *Customer Value Investment*.
Note PIMS data of over 1, 000 companies.

FIGURE 7.3
Share of Wallet versus Relative Customer Value

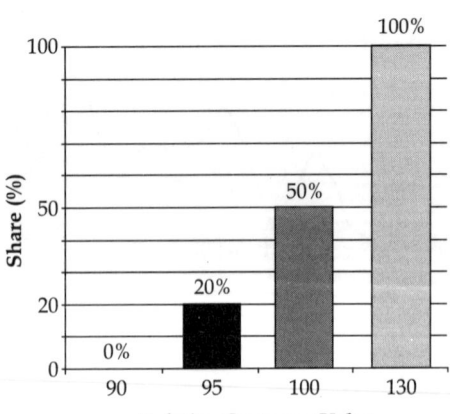

Source Ray Kordupleski, *Mastering Customer Value Management*, shown in Gautam Mahajan, *Customer Value Investment*.

could be, and allows your company to pre-empt competitive action. Lastly, since CVA is a measure of how well your Total CVM programme is working, the scores tell you about corrective action and therefore increasing competitive advantage. Beyond this, because CVA relates to loyalty, market share and profits, your competitive advantage becomes self-evident.

Predicting Churn of Customers and Employees

Once you know your CVA score, you can create a correlation between total number of Customers (and market share) and the loss (churn) and gain of Customers. Stickiness comes from loyalty gains.

With Employee Value Added (EVA) scores, you can predict employee churn. When EVA scores are high, employees tend to stick to you, else they leave.

DRIVING PROCESS OPTIMIZATION WITH CUSTOMER VALUE

Krish is having a cup of coffee with Rita Timko, the Chief Marketing Officer, and JoJo Mohindra, the Chief Information Officer. Rita comments, "Remember Total CVM or Total Customer Value Management is managing value to the company and to the Customer and showing they are two sides of the same coin. Processes can be used to determine what Customers want. Processes include:

- Customer Contact Management
- Customer Feedback (or Voice of the Customer) Management
- Customer Interaction Management
- Business Processes

"Business processes include Operations Management, People Management, Organizational Effectiveness, Process Optimization, Systems and Technology Management, Quality Management and many others.

"The idea is to integrate these so that the processes capture and are driven not only by Customer information but also Customer Value, and each process is tested for Customer usefulness, Customer friendliness and Customer Value. The idea is to drive processes from not only business efficiencies and optimization issues, but to synergize Customer needs by understanding them, and use all people and other resources to increase Customer Value throughout the company in an integrated, efficient way. This, of course, means the attitude is focused on business and Customer Value seamlessly and, in an ideal situation, effortlessly.

"So what information should processes pick up or answer?

- Are these processes obtaining usable information?

    - Is the information being used?
    - Does the information provide courses of action, and alternative methods of solutions?

- Are there Customer metrics such as cost of ownership?

    - Customer Lifetime Value?
    - Customer assets and its growth
    - Customer Value Added

- Is there a process to ensure Customer promises are being kept, that Customer response is timely?

    - Is Customer Interaction Management working?
    - What is Customer expectation and what is being delivered? How are Customer retention, repurchase and profitability being impacted? It should

lead to touchpoint optimization (optimal usage and effectiveness of touchpoints, cost and cost effectiveness and Customer Value impact). This covers service optimization.

- Are there processes that integrate into business processes to ensure Customer needs?

  - Are processes designed or capable of modification for each segment of Customer?
  - Do they reflect best practices?
  - What is falling into the crack?

"Processes should then lead to Customer Value Optimization, integrating CVA and other loyalty creators. Remember CVA also gives you the critical and most important loyalty creators and loyalty destroyers. What we want is to end up with using resources to get loyalty."

JoJo says, Figure 7.4 shows such a process and value optimization programme.

Customer Interaction

"Companies need to look at Customer Interaction as a means to Total CVM. Intervox Customer Interaction Management (CIM) includes looking at employees, touchpoints, Customer Value and processes.

"If done and handled properly, this will lead to customer-centric processes, leading to better support to the touchpoints and the people to deliver better Customer Value.

"What we want is to end up with using resources to get loyalty.

FIGURE 7.4
Four Key Programmes to Drive Value

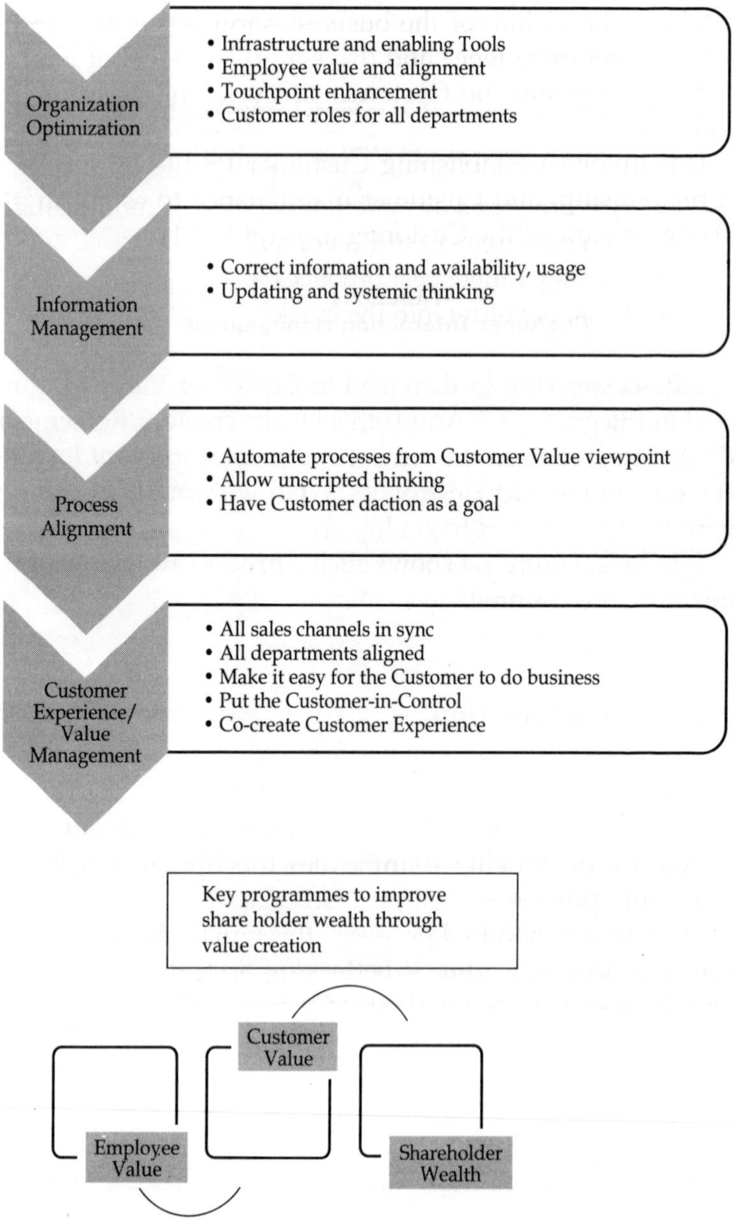

Organization Optimization	• Infrastructure and enabling Tools • Employee value and alignment • Touchpoint enhancement • Customer roles for all departments
Information Management	• Correct information and availability, usage • Updating and systemic thinking
Process Alignment	• Automate processes from Customer Value viewpoint • Allow unscripted thinking • Have Customer daction as a goal
Customer Experience/ Value Management	• All sales channels in sync • All departments aligned • Make it easy for the Customer to do business • Put the Customer-in-Control • Co-create Customer Experience

Key programmes to improve share holder wealth through value creation

Customer Value

Employee Value

Shareholder Wealth

Source Author.

Business Services

"Establish the vision for the business services, understand the Customer experience and drive a greater level of intelligence throughout the Customer lifecycle and associated processes.

"This involves establishing Customer Profile, including the relationship, and Customer maintenance to establish a 360 degree view of the Customer (see Table 7.1).

TABLE 7.1
Customer Interaction Management

		Assess	Design	Implement	Optimize
Customer Needs	CVA and Voice of Customer Study				
Customer Performance Management System	Metrics, KRAs				
Employee Value	Employee awareness and Value creators				
Employee Tools	Enablers				
Touch Points	If adequate, back-end and front-end				
Other departments	Finance, HRD, IT, logistics				
Customer Circles	Continuous Customer Improvement Programme, Courtesy System, Bill of Rights, teamwork				
Processes	Customer driven, Convenience of Customer				
Value creation	Loyalty, Market share				

Source Author.

"These help companies with building Customer-centricity.

"Why I give these examples is because companies are making Customer-centric a way of business success and increasing business and Shareholder Value. They have imbibed aspects of Total CVM into their programmes."

The Customer and Social Media

Today's Customer is more aware, and wants to lead his buying and vendor experience. He is more net savvy and uses various social networks. The company's marketing department must use this tendency of the Customer to co-create advantage and Customer experience for both the Customer and the company. Customer Collaboration Management (CCM) is a system suggested for this. In a recent survey, over 90 per cent of Customers thought that companys should engage in Social Media sites, and about 56 per cent felt that a company provides them better service by doing so (see Figure 7.5). Often they move from a basic discussion to what is called Crowd Service, harnessing the wisdom of the crowd for better service and interaction. Costs of Customer service reduces over the long run, as more and more self-service happens.

FIGURE 7.5
Consumer Usage of Social Media
(US Consumers, Daily or Weekly)

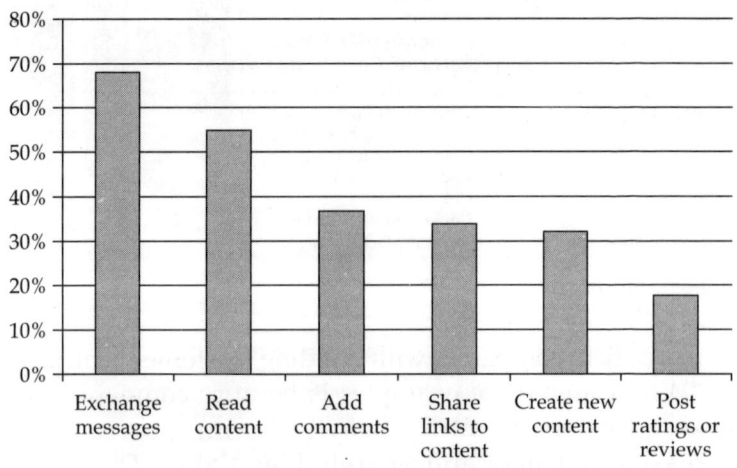

Source   Customer Think, June 2009, available at http://www.customer think.com/article/crowdservice_clear_and_present_roi_for_social_crm (accessed on 29 June 2010).

But, before embarking on social media programmes, ensure that the company is delivering value and on its promise, otherwise the social media will backfire.

Understanding Customer Emotions

At the end, dealing with Customers is all about their emotions, and building their trust. When you get their emotional involvement and trust, you get their loyalty. Thus, understanding emotional drivers leading to a purchase decision are important. Ad makers have always used this. Marketing people must recognize this as much as the Customer service people. In fact product innovators must understand Customer emotions. One way is to make the Customer feel the company and their representatives are allies, not on the other side or adversaries. Finally, emotions and trust come from a feeling of being a partner of the company or that the company is your partner. This leads to Customer experience. Smart business people take this further and co-create Customer experience (see Figure 7.6).

FIGURE 7.6
Hierarchy of Emotional Value

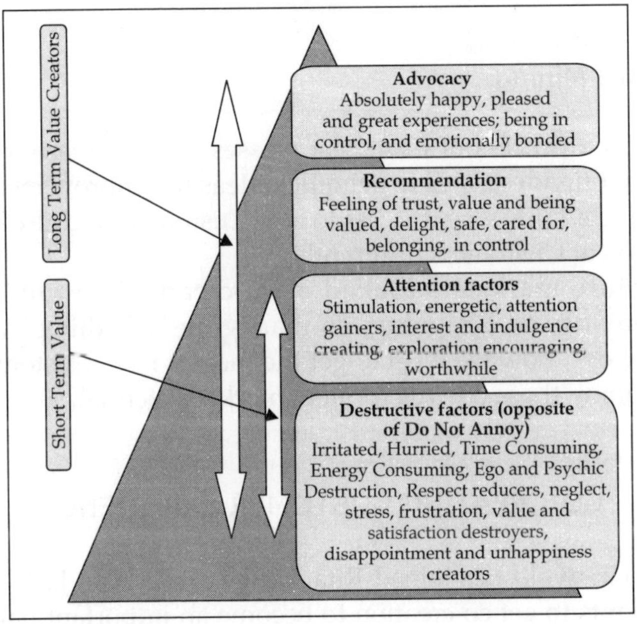

Advocacy
Absolutely happy, pleased and great experiences; being in control, and emotionally bonded

Recommendation
Feeling of trust, value and being valued, delight, safe, cared for, belonging, in control

Attention factors
Stimulation, energetic, attention gainers, interest and indulgence creating, exploration encouraging, worthwhile

Destructive factors (opposite of Do Not Annoy)
Irritated, Hurried, Time Consuming, Energy Consuming, Ego and Psychic Destruction, Respect reducers, neglect, stress, frustration, value and satisfaction destroyers, disappointment and unhappiness creators

Long Term Value Creators

Short Term Value

Source Author.

Neuromarketing: Attitude is a Customer Strategy

Neuromarketing is another form of understanding Customer emotions and attitudes. Companies try to get into the head of the Customer to figure out what they want and what they like and dislike, and what creates trust in the Customer's mind.

Frito-Lay, as reported in *The New York Times*, used its neuromarketing research to design chips and the packaging for "guilty women to make them feel less guilty when buying fattening food". Snack brands such as Sun Chips is put into new brown packages, and websites are being designed around the women's needs.

Neuromarketing also has potential to improve the Customer experience in contact centres as well. Agents till now have been trained to use key phrases such as "Well Mr Smith, you know we work very hard here to look out for your best interest." This upset Customers. Now they are trained to use words that can placate angry Customers.

Crowd Mining

This is a process of using the masses as a database to get marketing ideas, and to get quick ideas for improvement of products. One can get access to new Customers and also start to look at Customers differently.

Before marketers looked at co-creating, co-funding, co-buying, co-designing, co-managing "anything" with "crowds", now we wish to get the masses in as Customers, to mining those crowds for new market potential.

CO-CREATING CUSTOMER EXPERIENCE

Jack Griswold has joined Rita Timko and Krish. Jack says he wants to get co-creation to become an important part of Glacier's Customer Value initiatives.

He recalls that as a result of their previous Customer Value intervention with Grocery World in Newark, Ohio, they had listened to Customer suggestions, some saying the food was too bland, and the others wanting different flavours. Glacier's response to this was to give packets of different flavourings to the Customer along with his purchase of the canned foods, or the ready-to-eat foods. The homemaker was able to customize the offering to her friends or family, by adding the flavourings while heating, and thereby customizing the food to their liking.

"That is really a form of co-creating Customer experience," says Krish.

Rita says that at a very basic level, co-creation requires marketing and company people to think of so many obvious things. "You know more than the Customer, and so it is not easy to bring things down to their level (in Customer Value, talking down to a Customer is a major negative and a value destruction factor). Next, our selling methodology should be to help the Customer buy the items, not just to sell them. Here you look out for the Customer interactions, and capturing the Voice of the Customer.

"Lastly, the company organization should not drive the Customer, the Customer should drive the organization."

Jack adds, "When you go to a Disney park, you just don't go for a ride, you go for an experience. And in many places, the experience is co-created, whether in the sing-along or in the rides where you are part of it. And many of these rides are co-created with the help of the riders or the Customers.

And Disney recognizes the experience and co-creating it is all about people. To quote them, "You can design and create, and build the most wonderful place in the world. But it takes people to make the dream a reality."

Jack continues saying that Disney is an obvious example where the expressed view is co-creation. "Elsewhere it can be implied or explicit (as in Disney). In its ultimate analysis, co-creating is all about innovation as much as it is of experience. You innovate by having interested employees wanting to collaborate with willing Customers, or sometimes even by listening to disgruntled Customers.

"Co-creation also means interaction, which implies two sides working together (Customer and company). This also means there are people involved, and therefore there are personal reactions and feelings. One has to overcome self-centred behaviour to seek customer familiarity, which builds alignment. To do so, our employees must be engaged before they will engage with Customers. They work better when measured, incentivized and recognized."

"Customer Experience requires marketing people to understand how Customers use, enjoy (or not) and view the product or services they get. We have to provide the environment for this experience not to be just positive but also a great experience. As companies get smarter, they work together with the Customer in co-creating the Customer experience, whether product, service or both.

"In the very simplistic sense, the experience helps us build the hierarchy of Customer's needs in the order shown in Figure 7.7.

FIGURE 7.7
Hierarchy of Customer's Needs

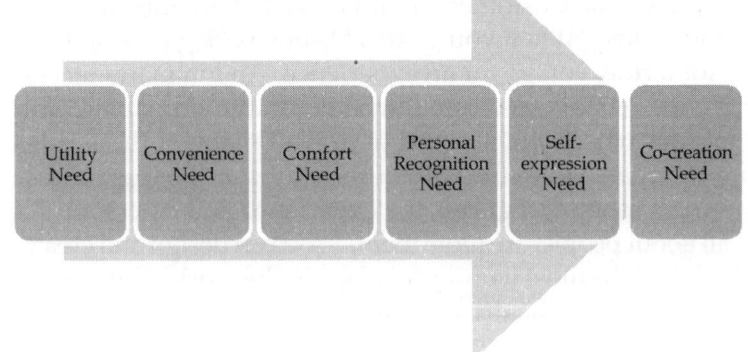

Utility Need | Convenience Need | Comfort Need | Personal Recognition Need | Self-expression Need | Co-creation Need

Source   Author.

"Can the Customer suggest the products or service to us? Can we understand his real need? Peter Drucker reminds us, the purpose of buying a drill is not to acquire a drill but to make holes! That is the utility need. And we need to make the hole conveniently. How do we create these ideas for us, such as being able to do so comfortably? So we may think of a cordless drill.

"Another example of fulfilling a need is replacing purchase of software products by a service that really focuses on the needs of the Customer. The Customer does not really want software products, he wants the computer to do something for him, and this could be done through a service. Google Apps and Google Docs are examples of services built around products.

"Next, Customers want to be noticed and recognized. Loyalty clubs are example of this. Other examples are being picked for answering questions. Self-expression needs are best described through blogs, making suggestions for improvements, getting involved with the company on their customization efforts.

"Co-creation is the culmination of all these needs leading to a partnership between the Customer and the company, implicit or explicit.

"To get these ideas from the Customer, we must seem to want Customers to do so or invite them to send information, post information blog ideas in an easy way?

"Co-creation leads to co-operative innovation (see Figure 7.8). Not only is it co-operative but it is also customer-led, sponsored or partnered.

"Co-creation has been looked at as just a marketing tool (meaning customization), but is more than that. It is the building of a partnership.

"In hospitals, instead of white and clinical, efficient and forbidding ambience, one can co-create Customer experience. If there is a collaborative effort between the medical practitioners, the hospital administrators, the family and patient, we may build a family-centric hospital concept, improving the care, and creating a better patient experience. Dr John I. Todor of The Whetstone Edge, LLC, tells of his visit the new Alberta Children's Hospital in Calgary, Canada

FIGURE 7.8
Customer Partnership: Involving Customers as Co-innovators

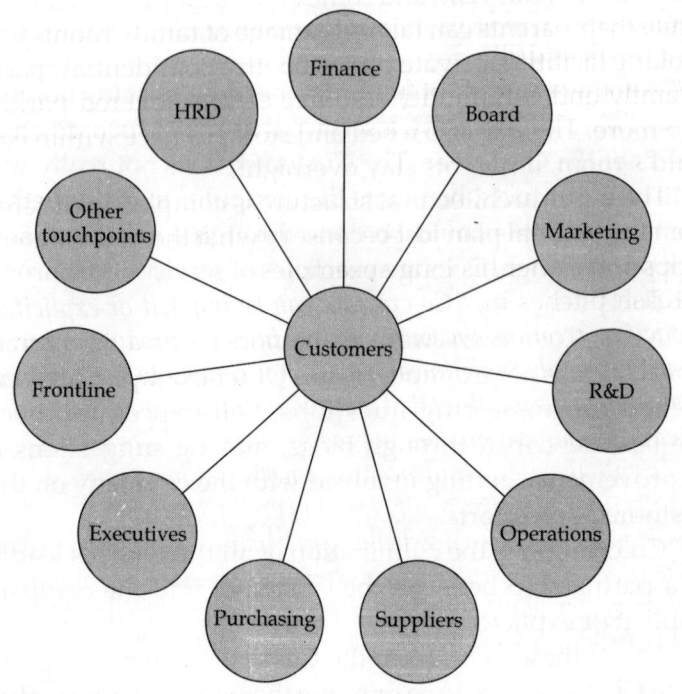

Source Author.

where the family-centred care concept is in place. Net result, treatment is more effective: patients are less stressed, recovery times are improved and caregivers experience higher job satisfaction, due in part to more efficient use of professional time and resources.

"The hospital took the help of children and parents to suggest design and other suggestions to apply this family-centred care approach. They wanted it to be colourful and cheerful atmosphere in a low-rise building, they got a brightly coloured building that looks like it is made out of Lego blocks.

"Steve Hoscheit, CEO of the Alberta Children's Hospital Foundation, summarizes the design features and the experience it enables: 'Children staying at the hospital will have access to play areas, Healing Gardens, a pet room (where their own pet can visit) and some of the best views in the city, while their parents can take advantage of family rooms with cooking facilities, private phone booths, confidential spaces, a family and community resource centre, covered parking and more. There is also a bed and storage space within each child's room, if parents stay overnight.'

"The entire architectural structure is completely different from the original plan just because of what the kids wanted." Jack pauses after his long speech.

Krish pitches in, *"Co-creation can be implicit or explicit. In implicit co-creation, the Customer modifies the product or service to suit his need. Sometimes they cannot convey to the company, because there is a mind-set that the product must be used as intended. Often the modification does not get to the manufacturer.*

"Explicit co-creation occurs when Customer openly seeks manufacturer's help to modify existing product or create something new. This can range from something as trivial as changing the colour of the product to very complex engineering – such as building a nuclear power plant. Apple and I-pod is a classic example." He hands Jack and Rita the following note (see Box 7.1):

Types of Explicit Co-creation

Explicit co-creation can further be classified into eight types, based on the level of involvement of the manufacture and the Customer.

Levels of Customer relationships and Co-creation[7]

Co-creation is all about customizing the offerings to meet Customer needs. The extent to which a company is willing

---

[7] Posted by Arun Kottolli Labels: *Innovation Management, Leadership, Marketing* http://arunkottolli.blogspot.com/2008/08/CustomerCustomer-co-creation-and-innovation.html (accessed on 21 July 2010).

BOX 7.1
Types of Explicit Co-creation

Type-1: *Mass Customization*, like Dell does, where the computer is customized through example. The Customer is basically only selecting or giving basic inputs.

Type-2: *Product Finishing*, where only certain add-ons like colour, trim, etc. can be chosen. Auto companies do this.

Type-3: *Product Adaptation*, where the basic design is then customized to the Customers needs. For example, SAP and ERP software are customized as per the Customers needs, engineered and designed goods such as electric generators.

Type-4: *Customized Experience*. Consultants are a classic example of customizing to the Customer's unique need, or in leasing individual leases can be designed, for example at GE Aviation.

Type-5: *Real time Customization*, where companies like Fedex allow Customers to change delivery times on the Internet.

Type-6: *Open Community Product Design and Development*, such as Harley Davidson clubs, open office suites, blogging, etc.

Type-7: *New Service Design*, where Customers can log-on and get feedback on availability of parts, or where software companies get ideas for new design, or updates.

Type-8: *New Product Design and Development*, where Customers engage suppliers to develop products for them. Continental Can developed the half litre PET bottle for Coca-Cola years ago.

Source   Author.

to customize/modify a product or a service is based on the quality of relationship it enjoys with the Customer: higher the level of relationship, greater the levels of co-creation. This implies that co-creation at the highest level—that is, new product development or new service development is reserved only for select few Customers.

The Table 7.2 maps the types of co-creation with the levels of Customer relationships. This mapping is not absolute—it is only indicative. The mapping between types of co-creation and levels of Customer relationships varies with industry and economic outlook.

TABLE 7.2
Types of Co-creation

Type of Co-creation	Levels of Customer Relationships
Mass Customization	Level-1: Utility Need Level-2: Convenience Need Level-3: Comfort Need
Product Finishing	Level-1: Utility Need Level-2: Convenience Need Level-3: Comfort Need Level-4: Personal Recognition Need Level-5: Self-expression Need
Product Adaptation	Level-3: Comfort Need Level-4: Personal Recognition Need Level-5: Self-expression Need
Customized Experience	Level-4: Personal Recognition Need Level-5: Self-expression Need
Real Time Customization	Level-4: Personal Recognition Need Level-5: Self-expression Need
Open Community Product Design and Development	Level-4: Personal Recognition Need Level-5: Self-expression Need
New Service Design	Level-6: Co-creation Need
New Product Design and Development	Level-6: Co-creation Need

Source   http://3.bp.blogspot.com/_aHVs3aKh49Q/SKrIYccZ7eI/AAAAAAAAA
VY/BRyw0J5HiOY/s1600-h/Co-creation.jpg (accessed on 29 June 2010).

Krish adds, *"Today co-creation is a great strategy for innovation. Thus, understanding how to engage a Customer, and different ways of co-creation is an important step.*

"As managers learn to deliver more to the Customer, if companies are aware, they will utilize and create opportunities for co-creation. At the very least, we can gather knowledge.

"No wonder, Bruce Temkin[8] says his manifesto is: 'Great Customer Experience Is Free'. In fact, I have been saying Customer Value is for free and can get more by co-creation of profits!"

---

[8] Bruce Temkin, in his blog *Customer Experience Matters*, available at http://experiencematters.wordpress.com.

CHAPTER SYNOPSIS

This Chapter focuses on the Chief Marketing Officer, because they tend to have the maximum contact with Customers. After walking them through value concepts, and customization of offerings, we discuss how to increase value of the Customer for the benefit of the company, value selling and adding value to the chain and to the Customer through the chain. We also discuss how marketing can use other functions in the company to add value and how to solve vexing problems of the call centres by converting them to action centres.

The Marketing people are urged not to mistake Customer retention for their loyalty. They are advised to make business processes Customer-friendly.

They are asked to measure Customer metrics, including CVA, and told how CVA correlates with market share, wallet share and with ROI. Further, how Customer data and information can be used to create competitive advantage and in pre-empting competitive moves. CVA and Employee Value added can be used to predict Customer and employee churn.

The chapter goes on to discuss the value of Customer interaction and business services. Marketing personnel must also learn about Customer's emotion and forming an emotional bond with the Customer, and co-creating, co-innovating with the Customer, and on concepts of crowd and neuromarketing, and social media.

8

Total CVM: Support, Staff and Operational Managers

Doug suggest Krish should talk to Glacier's other senior colleagues in the support and manufacturing functions. Doug wants all the senior managers to be aligned to Total CVM. He wants Krish to develop a Customer role for each of these functions.

CHIEF MANUFACTURING OFFICER

Krish then meets Jimmy Vaidya, Glacier's Chief Manufacturing Officer. Krish starts by saying, *"There are so many examples of manufacturing (one size fits all, or you can have any colour as long as it is black), or marketing (let's add more and upgrade our Customer to spend more with us), ignoring the Customer's needs and forcing him to select (or worse still, just get) what is available or is closest to his need."*

Jimmy Vaidya says that at the end of the day, the Customer gets what he wants when he wants!

Krish remarks, *"Good you say that, but it does not always happen.*

"It is important that manufacturing has a Customer focus, beyond quality products at competitive prices. Manufacturing has to be in close touch with the Customer to understand problems in the product, in packaging and in delivery. Does the Customer need to get impressions of the manufacturing process? In your case, health and safety and environmental issues. Does he want to feel that

Manufacturing cares for him, and will modify possible production plans to suit him."

Jimmy says he recalls two stories told by Vivek Talwar, VP of Business Excellence at Tata Power.

The first is about a catalyst manufacturer in America. Catalysts last for a finite time and if not replaced on time by the Customer in his plant (normally they can be changed on line), the downtime can be long. On a Friday evening, the Customer's plant engineer discovered he did not have a specific catalyst. So he calls his account executive at the catalyst supplier. The executive is out of town. So is his boss. The plant engineer calls the plant and gets the security guard. The key managers have left for the weekend. The plant engineer insists he has to talk to someone. "Oh", says the guard, "the shipping clerk is in." He can connect to him. The plant engineer tells the shipping clerk of his need, and if he does not get the catalyst over the weekend, the shut down will be disastrous. The shipping clerk says he knows the Customer company and checks if he has catalyst in stock. Yes, he does. He needs a purchase order. The plant engineer says he can only send that on Monday and that will be too late. He can send an e-mail confirming that they will place the formal order by Monday but wants immediate delivery. The shipping clerk scratches his head, and says he'll take a chance of getting his bosses teed off and will send the catalysts. Saturday evening the catalysts are delivered. The Customer's need has been fulfilled.

It turns out that the bosses are in Europe for a company meeting. They get back on Monday evening to USA. The plant manager calls the supplier's sales manager and says thanks for helping us in a crisis. You guys were super. The sales manager does not know what transpired that weekend, and he has to be told of how their Customer's crisis was defused.

On Tuesday, the President of the chemical company calls the President of their supplier catalyst company. The chemical company wants to thank the supplier President for doing something unusual in supplying the catalyst over the weekend without a purchase order. Now, this is a no-no. Nothing is to be shipped without a purchase order. In India, the shipping clerk would be fired or charge-sheeted. In the USA, he was commended and also reprimanded, and asked not to ship without a purchase order unless there were extraordinary circumstances.

Krish says, *"What a way to add Customer Value and delight. The Customer will think hard before he changes suppliers. By the way, the lowly shipping clerk is the face of the company, because the first thing a Customer sees is the shipment, the mode of shipping, the packaging and the paper work, all in the control of the shipping clerk. If the truck is not loaded right, pallets will fall over, to the Customer's disgust!"*

Jimmy continues, "I have a better example from Talwar. A small single pilot plane over Boston calls in and says he has engine trouble. Boston tells him to land in Hartford. On the way, Hartford diverts him to Manchester, NH. Before he reaches there, the engine is spluttering. He places one final call to the engine manufacturer, and tells the plant manager of his problem. The plant manager, who has a non-cooperative unionized workforce, puts the call on the public address system, and now everyone is hearing the pilot asking for help. The engine sounds worse, and suddenly, they hear the sound of an explosion. The plane has crashed. There is absolute and stunned silence in the plant. The plant manager says, 'People die, because we don't do our job right.' The message gets through to the workers."

"I am with you," remarks Krish. *"That is why everyone in the company and everyone in manufacturing have to be responsible for and add value to the Customer. Let's talk about customization and a Customer size of one."*

The Individual Customer and Customization

Jimmy states: "I can relate to all of this. I can give you examples of the footwear industry and the furniture industry to customize for an audience of one. To do so, one has to combine the net, systems, manufacturing and logistics.

"Take, for example, C.K. Prahalad. He often talks about customization and looking at a Customer sample size of one. Instead of buying shoes that are available at a store, the company can measure your foot, and make the design of your shoe with a perfect, snug fit, instead of asking you to buy a shoe that might pinch and be told by the shoe salesperson that it would be OK when the shoe is broken in.

"Why would you go elsewhere if you could get perfect fitting shoes in a couple of days, without having to go to the shop and be told a particular shoe is not in stock? And will this not make you a captive Customer?

"The furniture industry can deliver Customer designed furniture in a couple of days using computer aided design, raw material inventory, flexible manufacturing and delivery logistics to the Customer's advantage."

Jimmy adds, "Flexible manufacturing has changed the way manufacturing people think. When I was growing up, scale and the economies of scale were the buzzwords. The longer the run, the better and more economical the production. Didn't matter what inventories you built up or how long the Customer might have to wait for a new run to get the goods. Today, flexible manufacturing allows the manufacturing people to produce custom-made items in lots, often of one! And the Customer does not have to wait, and the finished goods inventory is diminished, although raw material inventory in some cases increases, (though this can be economized with JIT or just-in-time purchases).

"Articles and research on agile manufacturing for Customer Value have been conducted in many places, including the University of Brighton.[1]

"Boehringer Ingelheim provides clients in the global biopharmaceutical manufacturing market with the highest

---

[1] Jeff Readman, Brian Square, John Bessant and Steve Brown, "The Application of Agile Manufacturing for Customer Value", *Journal of Financial Transformation*, 18 (2006): 133–141.

quality custom manufacturing, while staying competitively priced.

"The company's global R&D organization, strong bio-pharmaceutical pipeline portfolio, reputed infrastructure and trusted manufacturing capability and capacity are examples of Boehringer Ingelheim's determination to provide quality custom manufacturing to its Customers and at very competitive prices."[2]

Krish looks happy. *"This is how the Chief Manufacturing Officer should be thinking. He should be thinking of ways and means to get items to the end Customer, almost as fast as he can take a product home from a store. Blue-sky thinking, you say? Logistics are such in India where a single Customer gets individualized delivery. What does this mean? The distribution system from a retailer is so close to the Customer that all he has to do is hire a cycle rickshaw to deliver the product, and if there is an installation (often outsourced), it is right away. There is no huge truck that has a delivery route to follow, and if the sequence is broken, then the driver has to shift items from the back of the truck first before he can get the out-of-turn goods out of the truck.*

"The management thinker, C.K. Prahalad suggests such innovations are possible in India, partly because in many cases companies do not have to unlearn the economies of scale, and central warehouses.

"The point I am making is that the Chief Manufacturing Officer has to think of the Customer's convenience, and has to dovetail it into the manufacturing and delivery process as best he can. He has to think of ease of packaging, and disposal of packaging materials, of ease of installation, of ease of maintenance, and not to have the Customer wait for the product, etc.[3]

---

[2] From Boehringer Ingelheim, available at http://www.boehringer-ingelheim.com/corporate/asp/news/ndetail.asp?ID=2634 (accessed in 2009).

[3] Vibhu Kalyan, "Dynamic Customer Value Management in a Supply Chain: Asset Values under Demand Uncertainty Using Airline Yield Management Techniques", *Academia/Industry Working Conference on Research Challenges* (AIWORC, 2000), 147.

"In order to understand lean manufacturing, it is necessary to realise that lean focuses more on how we think about the manufacturing process than anything else. Lean manufacturing is the combined team work of sales, marketing, purchasing and manufacturing that work in harmony. By identifying both who the Customer is and how they define value, lean manufacturing allows companies and individuals to focus resources on adding value. By manufacturing to Customer demand, driving out waste and continuously improving, companies can satisfy Customers, employees and shareholders alike.

"In fact, they define waste as not physical waste, but what the Customer will not pay for![4]

"Lean manufacturing concepts enable institutions to expand existing cost reduction opportunities, while simultaneously creating Customer Value outside manufacturing in other business areas such as financial services. Thus, manufacturing people with the Chief Customer Officer can take this to all levels of operations."

Krish ends the meeting by saying, *"Jimmy, think of instituting Customer Circles in your department and participate in the Customers' Bill of Rights and the Circle of Promises. This will ensure focus on Customers and Continuous Customer Improvement Programmes."*

THE CHIEF EMPLOYEE VALUE CREATOR OR VP HUMAN RESOURCES DEVELOPMENT

Doug asks if Krish has met Cindy Pandit, Glacier's VP of HRD. Krish says he hasn't but will do so soon.

A few days later, Krish is meeting with Cindy Pandit. Krish starts by saying, *"Cindy, we have been working with HRD professionals to assign them their Customer role. By aligning to the Customer and Business strategy, their role is seen as a line function,*

---

[4] http://www.vorne.com/solutions/learning_center/lean_manufacturing. htm (accessed in 2009).

not a staff function. Glacier must design a Customer Culture that has top leadership belief, and entire team participation leading to:

- *Enunciating Customer strategy*
- *Building values*
- *Developing Customer-centric goals, metrics, KRAs*
- *Customer-related relevance*
- *Self-awareness and Customer awareness, Courtesy system*
- *Customer feedback*
- *Customer-focused actions*
- *Building Brand Equity of employees and thereby the company*
- *An attitude shift to do the right things for the Customer and be self-driven*
- *Increase employee engagement and Employee Value.*

"Remember the Customer could be your employee, internal Customer and external Customer, or your shareholders. Entire team participation includes a bottom-led approach (see Figure 8.1). One excellent tool to get this participation is through Customer Circles.

FIGURE 8.1

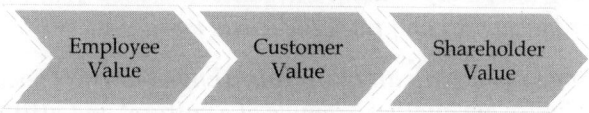

Employee Value → Customer Value → Shareholder Value

Source Author.

"The CCO has to work with the the HRD head and the team and convert the HRD head into the Chief Employee Value Creator (CEVC). Before embarking on the role of the CEVC, he should understand the Customer-related roles of various functions and department heads. In so understanding, the CEVC is able to select the right people for the right job and establish a cultural environment for the Customer to come first.

"HRD people know that ordinary people working with extraordinary systems and leadership produce extraordinary results.

Michael Basch,[5] formerly of Fedex, says: determined people make conditions. They are not the victims of them. Determined people, working together, can accomplish everything for a Customer!

"Examples of what the Customer-centric culture should imbibe are:

*"**Customer Partnerships:** A Customer partnership is more than "Putting Customers first", or finding mutually satisfactory solutions to shared problems, or a dedication to excellence in every sale or service encounter. It also requires commitment to forging long-term relationships that create synergies of knowledge, security and adaptability for both parties, including co-creation of Customer experience and co-controlling Customers' needs and processes or putting the Customer in control, (as an example, systems that must be co-designed from the point of view of the Customer). Robustness comes from the frontline and the people culture, and the front end of the system must be Customer-driven.*

"An illustration of putting the Customer in control is what Fedex did in letting the Customer track his shipped package himself. This made the Customer feel he was in control, because he could know anytime where the package was and this made him feel comfortable. By tracking the parcel himself, the Customer saved Fedex labour to answer his queries and track the parcel for him.

*"**Frontline Leadership and Employee Engagement:** Customer-Centric-Circles are another example of a cultural and attitudinal shift to be led by the CEVC (Chief Employee Value Creator). Customer Circles transfer some Customer leadership to frontline employees. Teamwork and engagement becomes another cultural framework in Customer Circles. Happier employees and a happier Customers are the results of these Circles.*

*"**Education and Certification of People:** From the point of view of the Customer. Putting a Customer certification programme together is important. Educating employees and bringing to the*

---

[5] Michael D. Basch, *Customer Culture: How FedEx and Other Great Companies Put the Customer First Every Day* (Financial Times Press, 2002).

forefront awareness, and self-esteem, and Customer focus is crucial. Certification is not just for technical skills but also for people and Customer skills.

*"**Employee Respect:** It is not only respecting employees, but also means that employees must develop awareness of what is right for them, and learn to have respect for, and to love themselves. (This is more important in developing countries where there is a strong hierarchical or feudal system, and the awareness and self-esteem of many employees is low. They live in conditions that does not engender awareness of what in the West are, simply put, hygiene factors. Moreover, conditions are such that they have to fight to get into a bus, get proper housing and medical treatment for themselves, or get their kids into school, or just have the ultimate put downer of poverty! Therefore, they cannot understand why Customers are not happy when they are better off than the employees are.)*

*"**Employee Awareness:** All employees have a sense of awareness of what is right or not. They also experience certain things and treatment that is meted out to them as Customers. Poor treatment or poor conditions are often accepted. Here we need to build awareness that such treatment by a supplier is not acceptable, and that we should learn from this and not do the same to our Customers. Employees are aware of the bad treatment they receive when they are Customers. These employees must resolve to ensure such conditions are eliminated in their interaction with Customers in their own companies. This is also employee self-education.*

*"**Employee Brand Equity and Value:** Employees carry a brand equity that their colleagues, bosses and customers perceive. Building Employee Value builds brand equity.*

Cindy says, "How many senior managers come to work after experiencing a problem with a call centre or a shop or a service? They are very upset. After letting out steam they get into their work and become operational managers. They become company people. They stop being Customeric. They never ask if their company gives the Customer similarly poor experiences, and what they can do about it.

"In fact, I have noticed, when I have a problem with a product or a service provider, often the problem is generic, and a change in the system is required. Once I called American Express on a long distance call and asked for their toll free number. This was in India. They said it was on the bill. I had a copy of the bill and there was no such number. The person insisted the number was on the bill. It turned out the number was on the tear-off portion, which we send with the cheque! I mentioned this to a senior manager, and told him to put the number elsewhere on the bill. Nothing was done until years later when the bill was revamped. I guess the attitude is, 'It ain't my job, or who cares, or even worse, Customer beware.'

"Worse still, my card was denied in Marseilles, France. I called American Express in Paris. The operator in Paris was not only unhelpful, but did not have the number to call in the States! I had to get the number through directory enquiry of AT&T, so that I could get my card re-instated."

Krish agrees with Cindy. He continues: "*What we miss, particularly in developing countries, is that the level of awareness of employees is low. Their expectations are low, and therefore often they cannot understand the demands of a Customer. Why is he asking for something that I do not think is important? The task of making the Customer happy becomes difficult.*

"*You will agree that very often employee awareness does not translate to Customer awareness. In fact as 'informed and aware Customers', the employees enter their offices to become 'Company people' and are often not determined to change the system in the Customers favour, based on what they have learnt from their own experiences as Customers.*

Courtesy System in the Company

"*The courtesy system is a starting point of employee respect and Customer respect. Some ingredients of a courtesy system are:*

- *Greet and Farewell*
- *Smile*
- *Speak very politely*
- *Apologize and make restitution*
- *Be positive when you*

  - *Talk about problems*
  - *Talk about people*
  - *Blame the system not people. Do not blame each other but find systemic reasons for problems and find solutions for them.*

- *Tell the truth*
- *Respect each other, and each others' contributions and problems*

"*The employee self-esteem, morale and Customer awareness has to be improved. If your company has incorporated these changes, you are ahead of the game.*

"*Godrej, the large Indian conglomerate we have mentioned before, noted an improvement in employee morale and in teamwork based on installing the courtesy system as a starting point of the Total CVM programme. Other steps were building employee self-esteem and awareness.*

"*Michael D. Basch[6] who was one of the founding executives of Federal Express suggests the EAGLE approach. You:*

- *Empower me as a Customer*
- *Accept full responsibility*
- *Give me what you promise*
- *Listen and Respond*
- *Enjoy what you are doing*

"*The employees are very special assets of the company. They have to take care of an even more important asset, the Customer. HRD professionals measure employee assets.*

---

[6] Michael D. Basch, *Customer Culture*.

"Assets are lost when the Customer or an employee leaves.

"The HRD chief looks at employee churn. He measures Employee Value Added. He understands that only value-added employees can add value to Customers. He looks at bonus and rating systems based on adding value to employees and to Customers.

"He correlates employee churn or its reduction to Employee Value Added. He correlates Customer Value Added to Employee Value Added. He sees the investment in Employee Value Added as a Customer investment as much as an employee investment.

"He ensures that the employee sees the value he is able to add to the Customer and essentially to the company thereby making him feel that his contribution is meaningful and that he is important to the company and to the Customer. In a sense, we help build the employees' brand equity (see Boxes 8.1 and 8.2)."

Cindy responds, "Wow! That is a lot to do and change. If I look at my classic function, it is to recruit and help keep good people and weed out poor performers, and design people development and compensation programmes, and ensure employees are happy. My job includes taking care of unions, team building, labour relations, etc."

BOX 8.1
Example of a Call Centre HRD Mission

What should the mission statement of an HRD head of a call centre be? Should it be:

> *My mission is to build the most efficient call centre team to complete a call fast, or*
>
> *My mission is to have the team give the Customer satisfaction, or*
>
> *My mission is to build a team of value-added-people, who can add value to the Customer irrespective of function, direct touchpoint, indirect, supervisory and back room people, including accounting and financial analysts, IT and marketing people. In addition, I will help educate and enable these people on creating value and lead them through a value creation certification process to change the attitude of the call centre.*

In short, my call centre will become a Customer Action Centre, where calls are not just answered, but results are achieved to the Customers' satisfaction.

Source Author.

BOX 8.2
An Example: Epson

*"As an example, look at Epson's HRD policy. It flows from a philosophy of **trust-based management** with integrity as a cornerstone to retain relationships, and to provide high value to Customers. Seiji Hanaoka, President and COO, Seiko Epson Corporation says their mission is to **surprise and delight**. In fact, Epson says, "**All services for the benefit of Customers**." (bold emphasis is mine).Thus they are converting call centres into action centres, and solving Customers' problems on the spot, or having a one day turn-around time for repairs.*

*"At Epson, they believe that **each employee is an asset on loan from society**."*

Source global.epson.com/community/sr/2007/pdf/2007_en_sr.pdf (accessed on 21 July 2010).

Krish agrees. He continues: *"What I suggest to companies and HRD chiefs is to start an awareness programme for the employees, where employees must build:*

1. *Respect for themselves, and pride in themselves*
2. *Respect for company*
3. *Respect for company's procedures (it does not mean you cannot question them) and thereby*
4. *Respect for Customer*

"This part of Total CVM is very important. What you teach an employee is awareness, and not to accept second-rate facilities at work. As an example, if you have diabetes why should you be forced to take tea with sugar in it? Many Indian companies have this kind of pre-sweetened tea sent around to the employees. And if an employee accepts this or has no choice, he cannot understand why a Customer may want something different or is finicky.

"At one major Indian company, we were able to get frontline people aligned to the Customer. Many frontline people were unionized, and management termed them 'unprofessional' or as 'having an attitude' problem. By introducing the Voice of the Employee, and working on the employees' self-esteem, we could understand the

pain of the employee. Typically, we learnt that some irate Customers would abuse an employee, and then complain to the employee's boss about the employee. The boss would pull up the employee for misbehaving with the Customer. So the employee got it from both ends! The end result was they became employees with poor attitude.

"At Godrej, not only were the frontline people more motivated, but also teamwork improved and the complaints reduced.

"Customer Circles also helped add Value to the employee in a Tata company by making him feel important and needed, a member of the team. This helped them to add value to themselves and value to the company by engendering a cohesive, cooperative team building, Customer-focused environment.

"But once the employees opened up and started to talk about their pain at work, and after we listened to the Voice of the Employee and Voice of the Customer, we installed the Courtesy System in the company which is a starting point of employee respect. These two actions opened up the employees to look at the Customer positively. So much so, they put together the Customer's DNA (Do Not Annoy) and delight creators. Their computer desktop showed Customer Value quotations. They instituted many positive Customer-centric tasks. This included a comfortable and Customer-friendly meeting room for Customers to visit or to register complaints, Customer reach out buses for bill payment convenience and Customer contact, a better Customer bill correction system, and a better listening system.

"This is the power of listening to the Voice of the Employee and thereby growing Customer respect."

Krish hands out a memo summarizing the Voice of the Employee that is shown below.

Voice of Employee

Very few companies spend time listening to the employee. The top officers generally hear the Voice of the Employee in a filtered way from their direct reports. The true Voice of the Employee does not reach the top brass unless too late.

More important, the Voice of the Employee also gives management a perspective of the Customer and what the Customer is saying as seen from the employee's vantage, and understanding the problems faced by them in dealing with the Customer.

One has to teach the employee or build:

- Employee Value
  - Employee self-respect and awareness
  - Increased employee value parameters
  - Respect for company and processes
  - Respect for Customer
  - Employee Value Added should be measured. It is the ratio of the value you add to your employees versus the value your competitors add to their employees

Employee Value can be measured by Employee Value Added, a technique similar to capturing the Customer Value Added. Employee Value Added is a better measure than employee satisfaction of how good a company is in the eyes of employees.

- Your importance
  - To yourself
  - To the Customer
  - To the company and your impact on it
  - Building your brand equity within and outside the company

- Importance of Customer
  - To business and owners
  - Customer Lifetime Value
  - Market share and wallet share and profits
  - Loyalty versus retention
  - Brand touching versus Customer touching

- Customer Value
  - Definition
  - Value and loyalty, market share, profits and share price
  - Customer Value and business
  - You and Customer Value
  - Customer Value Added and business metrics

Remember, EVA correlates with employee churn.

Krish leaves Cindy with the Chief Employee Value Creator scorecard (Table 8.1).

Total CVM and New Employee Induction

The Total CVM programme and what it means, and its importance to the company and the Customers should be taught to new employees during their induction programme. What does this mean to the employee and what is her expected role in the Total CVM programme? What is the Customer philosophy of the company?

These will start the employee on the right Customer footing and inculcate a Customer thought process in him.

Tata Power has considered doing this.

Krish pops into Doug's office and updates him on what is happening. Doug tells Krish he can see that someone's time is required to get the Company going on Total CVM, just as it did during a Total Quality programme. He is now sure a Chief Customer Officer is needed. Krish agrees, and says he has a meeting with Vikki Solomon, Head of Quality.

Krish hands Doug the following:

The HRD Customer Role

- Organizational Transformation: No CEO gods
- Become a line function by aligning to the Customer and business

Table 8.1: The Chief Employee Value Creator Scorecard

The Chief Employee Value Creator Scorecard	Yes	No
1. Do you promote value co-creation for employees?		
2. Do you measure Voice of Employee and Employee Value Added?		
3. Do you understand what creates employee self-respect and awareness?		
4. Do you work on employee engagement, and help them become pro-active and build their brand equity?		
5. Do you hear what the employee has to say about the competition, Customer and company?		
6. Do you promote respect for employee, company, its processes, and the Customer?		
7. Do you believe in employee education instead of training? Do you have a self-learning system?		
8. Do you build an enabling environment or do you think empowerment is enough?		
9. Do you balance value creation for the employee and the Customer?		
10. Do you teach Total CVM metrics?		
11. Do you act as the Chief Employee Value Creator?		
12. Is the Employee truly numero uno in your books?		
13. Do you give bonuses based on Customer Value, Customer delight and Customer relationship creation, in short a Customer Performance Management System?		
14. Do you have a Customer Value Added and a Customer reporting system that you receive at the same time as your financial and other reports?		
15. Do you have a Courtesy system in your company?		
16. Do your executives have one or two customer-related goals in their key performance goals?		
17. Are you building Customer employee conduits?		
18. Do you have employees participating in Customer Circles?		
19. Do you have an Employee–Customer strategy? Or an HRD Customer strategy?		
20. Is the Customer DNA (Do Not Annoy) an employee mantra?		
21. Do you measure Employee assets? Are these growing? Do you correlate with Customer assets?		
22. Do you measure Customer lifetime value?		
23. Do you correlate Employee Value with Customer Value?		
24. Do you get a Customer complaint sheet and action taken list?		
25. Do you receive Customer complaints calls personally at least once or twice a week?		

Source Author.

- Building a Customer-centric culture
- Designing a Customer and employee strategy from an HRD point of view: Chief Employee Value Creator
- Determining HRD tasks in Customer Excellence
- Building Employee Value, awareness, self-esteem and pro-activeness
- Measuring employee assets and Customer assets and correlating them
- Implementing a Courtesy System
- Improving teamwork and continuous Customer and employee improvement programmes
- Aligning the entire organization to the Customer
- Customer certification
- Bill of Rights and the Circle of Promises
- Building brand equity of employees and the company
- Customer Performance Management System
  - Key Result Area (KRA): Bonuses on Customer Performance
- Develop the role of a Chief Customer Officer
- From Best Practices to Next Practices

THE CHIEF QUALITY OFFICER

Krish is sitting with Vikki Solomon, Glacier's Chief Quality Officer. Vikki has long years of developing TQM programmes in companies, putting quality circles into place along with Continuous Improvement Programmes. After discussing Vikki's work, Krish starts on why he is helping Glacier's with Total CVM, and how TQM and Total CVM relate and co-exist. *"I will repeat what I told Doug about TQM."*

Krish continues: *"Claes Fornell in his article 'Customer Satisfaction and Stock Prices: High Returns, Low Risk'[7] makes a case*

---

[7] Claes Fornell, Sunil Mithas, Forrest V. Morgeson III and M.S. Krishnan, "Customer Satisfaction and Stock Prices: High Returns, Low Risk," *Journal of Marketing*, Vol. 70 (January 2006): 3–14.

*for satisfaction and value correlating to better prices, increased
shareholder value. A one per cent increase in Customer satisfaction
leads to a 4.6 per cent increase in share price.*

"*I certainly believe that the quality movement has provided
immense value to the Customer and thereby to the companies
through product improvement and quality, service, etc. However,
it may be that today TQM is becoming a hygiene factor and a
way of doing business. Those still catching up are disadvantaged.
I think this is true today where TQM is deeply ingrained in many
competing companies. I do not subscribe to the view that there is no
advantage. There will always be a continued benefit of practising
TQM. But TQM gains in one company have to be compared to
TQM gains of competition, and if there is no incremental gain,
then the advantage differentiation diminishes.*

"*However, the TQM and the quality people have set up outstanding processes and systems that allow the company to adhere to
TQM, and have brought in a sense of participation of and discipline
into the work force which is admirable.*"

Vikki states: "I think the Chief Quality Officer must build
on the TQM movement and help manage the Total CVM
processes, by embracing the Customer-Centric-Circles, and
other Total CVM concepts. His ability to train and reach
out to various functions can be used to make the company
Customer-centric. Customer Circles must include Customer
continuous improvement programmes. Customer Circles
have to be action-oriented"

Krish nods in agreement, "*So you, too, have a role in the
Total CVM movement that goes beyond just quality. You can
be the process implementation chief, using TQM procedures for
Total CVM.*

"*What I have to say to quality personnel is that if you do not
return phone calls or you come to meetings late then your quality
fundamentals are poor.*

"*The Chief Quality Officer expands his function to look at the
quality of the delivery of value to the Customer, and helps in the
Customer Circles.*"

CHIEF TECHNOLOGY OFFICER

Rohit Carson, Glacier's CTO, Doug Evert, President of Glacier Products and Krish Kumar, the Customer Guru, are having tea and discussing Total CVM. Krish says he wants to talk about the value the technology team can add. Rohit says he has an example of what not adding value can do. He quotes:

> Many years ago, Continental Can had a very innovative R&D group. They came up with brilliant packaging ideas that Continental spent money on developing, but they flopped in the market place. This is because there was no clear-cut Customer Value proposition. Either the product was too expensive for the perceived benefit, or the market was not ready for this. Products included the shaped can, the resealable can, the plastic formed can, the maxi can (1 and 2 litre beverage can) and the like. They were driven by technology and the Chief Technology Officer.
>
> Over and beyond these, they went into magic pills for curing alcoholism, a new type of storage battery, bed mattresses using levers and the like, which never took off! The programmes had no relationship with existing business or Customers.

Krish agrees. He then starts, *"The CTO is just as important as the marketing people in making product decisions based on Customer needs and desires (whether latent or otherwise). He has to do things the way Michelin did.*

Product Decisions Using CVM

"An example of using CVM for technology and product development is that of Michelin, a French company that was able to catapult to the number one position in the world over American, German and Japanese companies. This story is told by Bradley Gale (see Box 8.3)," continues Krish.

BOX 8.3
Using CVM at Michelin for
New Products and Technologies

"Tyres came with bias cord for strength and features. Bias technology was dominated by the Americans, Germans and Japanese companies where rayon, polyester or steel cord and fabric were laid layer by layer at a bias or diagonally, (and opposite in direction to the previous layer).

"The Americans were focusing on increasing market share, reducing costs and on becoming quality leaders. They felt price was the most important feature.

"Michelin figured the market was splitting into two, radials and bias. Radials were growing faster than the sluggish growth in bias tires. Michelin had close to 100 per cent in radials, but their total market share was (according to the Americans, a measly) 3 per cent, not important enough to worry.

"Margins in bias tyres were awful, but no one paid attention to or understood the margins in radials.

"CVA studies showed that radials were rated poor in price vs. bias tires, thereby getting a CVA score of 0.9."

Doug remarks, "It's understandable why the Americans thought price was important and would throttle the radial push. But I suppose, they did not look at the quality from a Customer Value point of view, as Michelin did."

"Yes. The ratings, however on safety, handling and durability were 1.29, 1.5, and 1.5. Ride was rated poor at 0.86.

"Using importance weight ratios, the CVA score was 1.0 for radials over bias tires; radials were no big deal.

"Michelin also discovered that for bias tires the price weight was 66 per cent (and quality was 34 per cent).

"However, Michelin figured that radials would first enter the premium segment. To their surprise, the price weight for tires in the premium segment was 50 per cent, because the product attributes were becoming more important. That meant overall value was (0.5*0.9, the CVA score for price) plus (0.5*1.2, the overall CVA score for quality). The overall value was therefore 1.05 versus bias tyres!"

"That's higher value than bias tyres," interjects Doug.

"You're absolutely right. Michelin plotted fair value maps for bias and for radials, and found they were adding more value!

"Eventually, Michelin introduced radials into the U.S. to find that their designs were not compatible with American cars, and rode rough. With Ford, they were able to develop a compatible suspension, so that the ride was smooth. The relative rating on ride went from 0.86 to 1.2, also increasing the overall value of radials versus bias tires to 1.1. This is shown in the following table.

(Box 8.3 continued)

(*Box 8.3 continued*)

	Profile: Radial versus Bias Tyres						
	Scores			*Importance Weights*		*Importance Weights*	
Attributes	*Radial*	*Bias*	*Ratio*	*(Pre Radial)*	*CVA*	*(Post Radial)*	*CVA*
Price	7.2	8.0	0.9	0.67		0.50	
Relative Price			1.11				1.05
Safety	9	7	1.29	40			
Ride	7	8	0.86	30			
			1.2		1.0		1.1
Handling	8	6	1.33	10			
Durability	9	6	1.50	10			
Overall Quality				0.33		0.50	

"The rest is history. By ignoring Customer Value and the Voice of the Customer, American tyre makers brought on their own downfall. A small Japanese company, Ishibashi (meaning stone bridge) bought Firestone and emulated Michelin in radials through their new company, Bridgestone!"

Source Adapted from Bradley T. Gale, *Managing Customer Value* (The Free Press, 1994), 178 and quoted in Mahajan, Customer Value Investment.

New Products

Rohit says, "More companies are now talking more about using Customer Value to decide on product development issues, which include:

"Customer Value techniques for introducing a new product and creating a valuable product portfolio, with strategy alignment and optimal investment intensity to deliver increased Customer Value. John Osarczuk, Product Manager, CNH, practices this approach and uses the Design-to-Cost methodology, which focuses early product development efforts by evaluating these opportunities and established Customer Value data:

- Using Customer Value as the portfolio criterion to decide how to exploit unfulfilled market niches

- Tackles tough questions about what products to launch, where to invest/divest, and how to avoid costly product failures
- Includes real case studies showing the merits of transforming the business drivers of your product portfolio to a Customer Value approach
- Provides strategic vision and a blueprint for measuring Customer Value and using it to reinvent your portfolio management process
- Offers free downloadable articles on collecting the voice of the Customer and creating a framework for measuring innovation — available from the Web — Added Value Download Resource Centre[8]

"Other books talk about CVA measurement, and using this for designing products.[9]

"To be successful requires:

- How to measure Customer Value accurately
- A quantitative view of strategic alignment
- Estimating the costs to develop a new product, both inside and outside of your company
- How to integrate financial projections later with Customer Value measurements to gauge the likelihood of product success."

Value to the Company versus Customer Value

Doug says: "I wanted to sit in this meeting because, when I go through what literature says about CTOs and Customer Value, I find the definition of Customer Value is one that of

---

[8] Sheila Mello, Wayne Mackey, Ronald Lasser, Richard Tait, *Value Innovation Portfolio Management: Achieving Double-digit Growth Through Customer Value* (J. Ross Publishing , 2006).

[9] Kai Yang, *Voice of the Customer Capture and Analysis*, (McGraw Hill, 2008).

adding value to the company and not of Customer Value. The CTO has to find the true Voice of the Customer, and react to it.

"Very often, the CTO thinks improved products are the be all and end all of CVM.

"An example of using technology for creating Customer Value is one enunciated by Rana Kapoor, CEO, YES Bank.

"Yes Bank's new CIO Aditya Menon, along with other business heads, is busy translating technology to provide the 'new, new experience' to the bank's Customers. Yes Bank's top management believes (that the) branch banking experience has scope for further enhancements. Menon, for instance, will be introducing a new facility for Customers standing in queues, wherein, most of their transactions and queries would be resolved through WiFi-enabled hand held devices carried by Customer service agents at the bank.

"Remember, ordinary people working with extraordinary systems and leadership produce extraordinary results.

"Systems must be designed from the point of view of the Customer. Robustness comes from the frontline and the people culture, and the front end of the system must be Customer-driven. I met a senior VP at Amex who lamented that their systems were not Customer-driven. She said that where they had scripts, things worked well until someone asked an unscripted question. Then things fell apart.

"She went further to talk about those enabled employees who were there to help on an unscripted fashion, platinum cardholders: how they managed to get life-saving drugs to members, how they retrieved someone's cell phone from one city (where the member had left it) and had it ferried to another city to a Customer's delight."

Krish says, "CTOs in a software company, for example, have to design systems for the convenience of the Customer and not just from the convenience of the designer or the designer's company. He has to learn what irks a Customer in installing, running and maintaining the system and avoid these. Very often, it requires a *strong relationship with various people in the client's organization, not just their engineering or manufacturing manager. The CTO's people should maintain contact with the client's engineers and end users through the life cycle of a process, a machine or a system, not just leaving it to the sales person, or the account manager to handle."*

Just then, JoJo Mohindra walks in. Krish starts to leave, but Doug insists he talks to JoJo. Rohit says he'll join them so that he can learn some more.

THE CHIEF INFORMATION OR IT OFFICER

JoJo Mohindra, CIO, and Krish are chatting about Total CVM. Rohit is listening. JoJo says that IT professionals are finding that Customer Value is important in their function. Some are building the Customer experience, others Customer trust and communication by building Customer requirements into performance, Customer information, putting the Customer in control, etc. Customers are asking for more contact/s rather than being given Customer specs by another department. The alignment with business results will make CIOs line managers, not staff functions as they are now. I have worked with a company in the U.S. building specialty software for the rental segment that seeks to maximize its value by Customer feedback. Where they need to improve is to understand true Customer Value and how to deliver it consistently.

The CIO has to devise systems to connect Customers to producers and the logistic chains in flexible manufacturing where the Customer gets custom-made products to suit his need. This helps the company focus on the Customer as an individual, rather than saying you can have any car as long as it is black.

Krish says, *"I have discussed customization with the Chief Marketing Officer and I will ask her to fill you in.*

"The CIO should not devise processes and systems from the company's viewpoint but from the viewpoint of increasing Customer Value. To do so they will necessarily design a system good for the Customers and the company.

"He measures and/or devises systems for:

- *Customer Value Added, Customer needs*
- *Customer metrics – Current Value, Long Term Value (LTV) and potential, performance metrics*
- *Incorporating "Customer needs" into segmentation and targeting*
- *Managing marketing, sales and service around Customer Value*
- *Distributing Customer intelligence to all Customer touchpoints for action*
- *Organizational alignment around Customer Value (KRA [Key Result Areas] and incentives)*
- *Looking at price justification modules and pricing from a Customer's need and what Customer Values*
- *Creating a learning organization for continuous improvement*
- *A 360 degree view of the company focusing on the Customer from all departments*

"To do so, structure IT around Customers and business processes, use CRM and other Customer-centric tools. CIO and IT should interact with Customers. Deloitte[10] *suggests using Customer Value as a measure of performance. The best way to enhance the probability that you are delivering value to your Customers is to ask them!*

"Primary market research can provide answers to key questions such as the following:

- *Does the value proposition of the IT offering match the value proposition as perceived by the Customer?*
  - *Is the Voice of the Customer reflected in the offering?*

---

[10] Deloitte Touche Tohmatsu, a consulting company.

- *Have new product concepts been tested in the market to validate acceptance, market digestion and market timing?*

- *Have newly launched websites and user interfaces been tested for usability and Customer usefulness and usability?*

  - *Does the website fully realize the business and offering objectives?*

- *Has the market been properly segmented and sized for the opportunity?*

  - *Is there clear competitive differentiation?*
  - *Have usability studies been performed to assess and refine the user experience on the product and the website?*

- *Does the company have a brand strategy that is sustainable and does the business model deliver on the brand promise?*

- *Have processes and systems been vetted for Customer friendliness?"*

"Armed with this type of information," comments JoJo, "technology companies can gain important advantage with current and prospective Customers—a leverage that can translate into increased business during a period of tightened IT spending and greater scepticism of the real ROI of technology investments.[11]

"AspenTech has a unique understanding of the special requirements of business optimization for the process industries. Its ability to address the challenges that its Customers face with solutions that deliver compelling value propositions give it a clear competitive advantage, says Frost & Sullivan team leader Sathyajit Rao."[12]

Krish thanks JoJo and Rohit and leaves.

---

[11] Gantry Group Newsletter, "Valuing Technology Companies: Shift to Customer Value," Issue No. 4, October 2001.

[12] Frost & Sullivan Honours Aspen Technology with 2004 Customer Value Enhancement Award.

Project Management and Portfolio Management

Krish and Jimmy Vaidya along with Jack Griswold are discussing other uses of Total CVM.

"Many people are looking at where to invest. For example," says Jimmy, "Product Development Consultants[13] discuss how project managers and portfolio managers are challenged to find an appropriate and *profitable* balance of projects in their project or product portfolio. The successful ones decide which products deserve more investment or which projects to abandon based on Customer Value. They find and invest in the innovations that will delight Customers and avoid costly product failures. The key to choosing products that contribute to sustainable profitability lies in changing the metrics you use to evaluate potential new products from financial measurements to assessments of Customer Value. Project Managers can add value to the Customer using Total CVM techniques."

CHIEF COMMUNICATION OFFICER

Homi Daruwala is the Chief Communication Officer. Doug is meeting him. Is he a functional officer or a strategic officer, Doug wonders? A functional officer thinks of promoting the company's image from the company's viewpoint. A strategic officer thinks beyond functional issues and looks at the Customer differently.

Doug had always liked Homi and had thought he did a good job. Was it really good enough? Armed with what he knew, it really was not. Did Homi look at the Customer, he mused. What is the Customer's viewpoint, what are his needs?

---

[13] Product Development Consultants: http://209.85.175.104/search ?q=cache:9n4cxFRVEqoJ:www.pdcinc.com/practice/portfolio.html+ Customer+value+and+functional+management&hl=en&ct=clnk&cd=6 (accessed in 2009).

The Customer wants to deal with a company with:

- Credibility

  - Reputation for truth
  - Accurate in its statements and interaction with Customers
  - Reputation for Fairness

- Reliability

  - Interactions rather than statements
  - Does what it is supposed to do
  - Does what it says
  - No ambiguity

- Intimacy

  - Safety, security and integrity (for example, keep important personal information secure)
  - Close to the Customer

- Not self-orientation or self-interested

  - Self-oriented companies get less trust
  - Seen as greedy, for themselves
  - Do not see Customer's point of view

Eventually you have to create trust and a relationship, give the Customer what he wants, which includes customization, convenience, ease of doing business.

Whose job is this? With Total CVM it becomes clear! Homi should also be looking at this. The closest he had come to the Customer was to look at shareholders and communicate with them.

Homi calls Rita Timko, and asks her to join in with Krish. Homi tells Rita of the conversation so far and on his role in creating Customer trust.

Rita says: "Homi, you are right. To become your Customer's trusted partner you have to build basic reputation, relationship and time build trust. You have to play on the Customers emotional needs. To do so we have to:

- Learn our Customer's business
- Help the Customers improve their business
- Know our Customer's Customers

"Our reward system must reflect all of this. It must recognize value creation"

As they start to discuss this, Homi nods. "You are right! I never looked at the Customer as *also* being my responsibility. But I can see why, and how I can do things. I can communicate to the world our Customer focus, and internally build a movement focused on the Customer. We can have a chat board for blogging on Customer ideas, complaints and how to resolve. We can build Customer interaction and get their trust."

AND FINALLY THE BOARD ROOM

Doug is telling Krish: "It is important that Customer Value is discussed in the Board room. I met an outside director of a publicly listed company who had made Customer Value a cornerstone of their business philosophy. The director was surprised as this had never been mentioned in the Board room! Such discussions get the support of the shareholders to Total CVM."

Krish agrees. He says that is one reason why the Chief Customer Officer should be a Board level person.

Doug says, "Now you need to tell me about frontline people."

CHAPTER SYNOPSIS

This chapter covers the Customer roles of the Manufacturing, HRD, Quality, Technology, New Products Officers and the

Chief Information or IT Officer and the Chief Communication Officers and how they can move from being staff functions to line functions, by aligning to the Customer.

Chief Manufacturing Officer

The Chief Manufacturing officer discusses how to add value to the customer through customization using lean and agile manufacturing systems, and how they impact the individual customer. The importance of packaging, logistics, delivery, etc., to the Customer is important for growing Customer Value.

The Employee Value Creator or VP HRD

The VP of HRD discusses the courtesy system to make employees friendlier with each other and to the Customer. The VP is asked to gather the value of the employee and increase value to the employee and become the Chief Employee Value Creator. He has to build self-esteem and awareness of employees. A scorecard measures his effectiveness with employees and Customers.

The Chief Quality Officer

The Chief Quality Officer expands his function to look at the quality of the delivery of value to the Customer, and helps in the Customer Circles, and uses quality type procedures for Customer Value.

Chief Technology Officer

He makes product decisions using CVM. An example of Using CVM at Michelin for new products and technologies is shown. He uses Customer Value for:

New products
Value to the Company versus Customer Value

The Chief Information or IT Officer

Project Management and Portfolio Management using CVM, and building Customer-led processes are among his tasks.

Chief Communication Officer

He has to look at increasing value to the Customer and the shareholders.

Finally, Total CVM has to be discussed in the Board of Directors meetings to make it effective and to get shareholder's support.

9

The Frontline People

CUSTOMER VALUE AND TOUCHPOINTS

Krish is in a discussion with Doug: *"There is no doubt that the employees are the most important part of the Customer Value creation cycle through their touching of the Customer directly and indirectly. These include Moment of Truth interactions (direct, call centre, etc.), communications, service, delivery, etc., presuming that the product, company and brand are adding adequate value. The differentiators are the touchpoints and the touching (in short, the human touch)."*

Doug interjects, "Therefore, it is important that employees and touchpoints are enabled, they know what to say, what not to say. In short, they should know and be governed by the Customer's DNA (Do Not Annoy), and the Customer's Delight Factors. They should become aware of potential Customer irritants. Frontline employees should be telling the company what not to do, and what to correct in its policies and in its systems and processes to become more Customer-friendly. In addition, a personal commitment and awareness has to be built up. This is done through the Customer Circles and the Circle of Promises emanating from the Customer's Bill of Rights.

"Krish, I can give you an example from a friend of mine in India. Corporate travellers on a particular airline can buy a booklet of 12 coupon tickets that can be used for travel within a six-month period. This is a super-saver scheme and saves money. My friend called the airline to make a reservation and after he was booked onto a flight he was told he had to go to the ticket office to validate the coupon for travel. What is the purpose of coupons if it requires the Customer to do unnecessary work? Where is the concern for the Customer, his convenience and his needs? And when pointed out to the supervisor and the duty manager, the answer is: this is company policy. No one thinks it is his business to question policy or to escalate the matter upwards to get a Customer-friendly resolution."

Krish answers, *"Great example and it always happens. Which brings me to some aspects of value creation? One has to have regard for the Customer's needs including his:*

- *Time*
- *Energy*
- *Psychic*
- *Respect*
- *Convenience*
- *Image*

"These are all costs that the Customer has to bear! Expanding this further:

- **Time:** *The cost of time is often considered to be higher than that of money, and Customers dislike having their time wasted.*
- **Energy:** *The effort made to acquire a product or service and the physical and mental effort is also a cost paid by Customers.*
- **Psychic Needs:** *Psychic factors include dealing with new people, waiting, filling up forms, the need to understand new procedures and the effort to adjust oneself to new things and situations.*
- **Respect:** *Respect is the dignified treatment people receive from business in terms of trust, courtesy, recognition and care. This is also related to the service given by companies to its Customers. Lack of respect can be a cost to the Customer.*

- *Convenience:* *Convenience is the ease with which one receives the product or service. Abundant availability, home delivery and proximity are some of the elements which can add on the convenience of Customers.*
- *Image:* *Professional people who deliver the service build the image for a product or service, and make the Customer feel important. Losing their image is a cost that the Customer has to bear."*

Doug stops him, "These are mantras for the company to remember. Larry Malarkar of Starwood Hotels and Resorts, the large global hotel chain often muses why hotels have the youngest, prettiest girls at the reception, rather than the experienced people who give continuity to and recognize Customers. After all, the concierges are allowed to be older people! This is an example of the Customer's psychic needs and image being impacted, because they have to deal with new people."

Krish continues, *"I agree. These must be a company's mantras.*

"But moving forward with our touchpoints and our frontline people. Why aren't the above Customer costs and irritants obvious to them?

"We have to start at the frontline level. In Customer Circles, members might say, 'Guests like to deal with the same people.' So then they search for solutions, and the solutions can be many. One is to note the persons who have interacted with Customers, and if that person is not available to say, Mr X, normally Sheila checks you in, but she is off duty. Do you mind if I do so? My name is…'

"To get the frontline people motivated, first, as we discussed earlier, there is an issue of self-respect and creating awareness of what is right to the frontline people. We use Voice of Employee techniques to help in this self-analysis of frontline people. Often, such people are not exposed to the needs of the Customer, the travails of the Customer and they forget about these when they deal with Customers. Value addition of an employee also means increasing his value to the company. It means building his self-respect and

his awareness of what is right, of what are his rights, and then it becomes easier for him to see the Customers' rights. We encourage employees to become aware of their transactional experiences with their suppliers. What irritates them in the interaction? What do they need to do to prevent such irritants annoying their own Customers? (How often do you notice poor treatment from your suppliers? This awareness is so important because you can use it to prevent similar problems happening to your Customers. Unfortunately, many a times, we do not change things in our company that we are aware of and find irksome to us when we are Customers, showing our awareness and concern is only surface in nature. We come into the office and become company people and forget we were Customers and the pain meted to us as Customers by our suppliers).

"Second and even more important is the culture of the organization, and the messages sent and received by the frontline people. Many frontline people become used to following orders, and they lose their creativity and drive, unless they have external motivation to be Ccustomer-centric.

"I also believe frontline people know more than many of us what a Customer really wants. If he does not do what the Customer wants, then either he doesn't care, or he doesn't think about this or he just decides to do what he has been told to do. No frontline person will ever tell you he should be rude to a Customer or make a Customer wait or ignore a Customer. He will tell you all the right things to do for the Customer. And to make this happen, we have to afford him the opportunity to tell us what he thinks he and the company could and should do.

"To increase his awareness in this exercise, it is also necessary to understand the pain he gets in his work, in his interaction with the Customer, and the delight he gets from the company and the Customers. When he is able to voice these, he also can articulate what causes pain or pleasure for a Customer and can think of the right and proper things to do.

"These are pre-requisite steps in what we call Customer Circles or Customer-Centric-Circles. I also refer to this as Bottom-up Total CVM."

CREATE CUSTOMER CHAMPIONS

Doug adds, "From my experience with Customer Circles at Grocery World in Newark, Ohio,[1] I find many employees would love to be Customer Champions. The successful members of the Customer Circles can be designated Customer Champions. Remember, you told me Godrej HiCare gave out Customer Champion buttons to frontline employees who were successful members of the Customer Circles. These Customer Champions wear these buttons proudly.

"Housewives ask the technicians what a Customer Champion means, and when technicians explain their role is to please the Customer and make them happy, the Customers get pre-destined to like the service.

"Other employees ask what Customer Champion buttons mean. The Customer Champions explain their role, their involvement with the Total CVM programme, and the advantage to the Customer, to the company and themselves. Other employees become eager to become Customer Champions, a sign of belonging and recognition from the company.

"Customer Champions mean:

Customeric, and Continuous Customer improvement ideas

Hot line to Customer Happiness

Advocacy for Customer within company with action

Manage and build Customer Circles

Pro-active to Customer and his needs, and processes

Ignite others with his Customer passion; Ideas for improvement

Openness to Customer's feedback, and to learning and educating by sharing

Next Customer practices creation

Share how they became Customeric, examples of mistakes they made and share good ideas

---

[1] The Grocery World store was where the Customer Circles experiment was tried by Glacier's. See Gautam Mahajan, *Customer Value Investment*.

"In fact, Fedex has a Customer Advocacy Team (CAT). This is a central team. Customer Champions should be dispersed in the company and co-ordinated by the Chief Customer Officer whose role is Customer advocacy.

"Given in the following section is who Customer Champions are and what is required from them.

Customer Champions

"These should ideally be the co-ordinators or leaders of Customer Circles. They should lead the Customer programme by example.

1. First, leaders must be champions of the Customer experience. By example and by emphasis, they must set high expectations for satisfying customers in their organizations. Second, employee empathy is what creates distinctive service. It's not enough to put on a happy face. Our champions of the Customer understand that their employees must know what it feels like to be on the other side of the counter.
2. Be prepared to work tirelessly for the Customer.
3. Customer Champions should promote Customer Championship (doing things right for the Customer).
4. Be facilitators and guides for Customer-centricity.
5. Be role models, and others should look up to them and respect them.
6. Be able to start and coach new Customer Circles.
7. Should have made good Customer Improvement suggestions.
8. Be able to deliver value to the Customer.
9. Best to have volunteers rather than appoint by mandate.

"Customer Champions have to be proactive to Customer needs. I just stayed at the Cecil Hotel in Shimla, the original Oberoi Group hotel. The staff was very courteous and looked out for Customer needs. The room service or the doormen did not hang around looking for tips, as all tips were centralized. Moreover, the staff multitasked. One evening, a group of 50 people were waiting in the lobby to be picked up for dinner outside the hotel. Transportation was delayed by half-an-hour. The host requested drinks be served and they only had half-an-hour. Suddenly, I saw may Hotel staff behind the bar. I recognized the housekeeper, and I asked her what she was doing. She said, 'My job!'

"I spoke to Srikant Peri, the General Manager, who said everyone pitched in. The concierge and the front office staff were the same, and it was not surprising that the person who checked you in today took your luggage down tomorrow. This reduces wait time and anxiety. Truly the sign of a great hotel and a great Customer attitude. This staff are true Customer Champions."

Touchpoint Mapping

Customers come into contact with companies at different points in time. Rather than look at specific touchpoints we will look at the interactions, and which touchpoints are involved. For someone selling white goods or automobiles, we recommend this touchpoint map (Table 9.1). The reader is encouraged to add to the map based on his or her experience.

Ray Kordupleski[2] calls this the Customer Waterfall of Needs, and expresses it graphically (Figure 9.1), using an auto dealership as an example. The Waterfall of Needs shows how the Customer's needs cascades from one level to the next. The touchpoint mapping depends on the Customer's waterfall of needs, and the various touchpoints meeting these needs. Thus you can use the Waterfall of Needs to create touchpoint maps.

The figure is called a waterfall, because onestep cascades to the next one.

---

[2] Ray Kordupleski is the father of CVM and author of *Mastering Customer Value Management*.

TABLE 9.1
Touchpoint Map

Stage	Type of Interaction	Touchpoints	Touchpoint Need	Department
Awareness leading to need	Social interaction	Friends, colleagues	Ambassador Loyal Customer	
	Store	Browsing/Retail clerk	Awareness Create desire Help in decision-making	Channel partner
	Ads	Media Flyers	Awareness Create desire Help in decision	Media partner Communications
	Call centres	Call centre executive	Pleasant, knowledgeable, persuasive Awareness Help in decision Make it easy to buy	Call Centre Marketing IT Processes/Scripts
	Net info	Browsing	Easy to read, user friendly, educative, informative Easy to buy	Marketing Updating IT Processes Communications

Information/Enquiry	Call company/ Call centre	Agents, employees		Marketing IT/Processes Channel partner Stores
	Browse	Browsing	Information Awareness	Web update and ease of browsing
	Ask friends, other users		Information Awareness	
	Go to store		Information Awareness	
Buying decision	Check options	Store clerk, expert	Information Awareness	Store Sales & Marketing
	Fits my needs	Store clerk, expert	Decision making	Store Sales & Marketing
	Fits my budget/ affordability	Store clerk, expert, credit department	Price Price justification Financing options	Store Sales & Marketing
	Best value	Store clerk	Decision	Store Sales & Marketing

(Table 9.1 continued).

(*Table 9.1 continued*)

Stage	Type of Interaction	Touchpoints	Touchpoint Need	Department
Buying	Call centre	Call centre executive	Speedy, helpful, friendly, knowledgeable	Call centre Marketing Processes/IT Credit
	Store	Sales person Check out clerk Check, credit card authorization	Speedy, helpful, friendly, knowledgeable	Channel partner Marketing Logistics Finance
	In-house	Salesperson	Speedy, helpful, friendly, knowledgeable	Marketing Customer centric certifier Logistics IT
	Net		Speedy, helpful, user friendly, adequate info Ease of buying	IT Marketing Processes Logistics
Delivery	Store/Net/Call Centre	Logistics person Delivery person	Speedy, helpful, user friendly, adequate info	Store/Warehouse/Logistics/Trucking Partner
Installation		Installer	Prompt, helpful, takes down correct address and directions and convenience for installation	Installation Partner/Call Centre Meeting setup

Service Contract		Store clerk, company executive, call centre officer	Friendly, quick, informative	Service department
Extended Payment		Credit officer	Friendly, speedy, helpful	Finance/Finance Partner
Billing		Billing clerk	Speedy, accurate, friendly	Billing Department IT Finance
Usage	Phone/net			
Service		Service department Service man	Easy to use Easy to reach Prompt Helpful	Call centre Web Service schedule Service address Service technician Billing Payment
Complaints	Letter/Phone call/net	Call centre Company executive Store clerk	Friendly Helpful empathetic Solution oriented	Web call centre Store Customer centre Manufacturing quality
Explanation	Net/manual	Company expert	Friendly Helpful Easy to understand Complete	Manuals Web Call centre Customer centre

(Table 9.1 continued)

(*Table 9.1 continued*)

Stage	Type of Interaction	Touchpoints	Touchpoint Need	Department
Follow-up by Selling chain	Call centre or executive		Friendly solicitous	
Customer experience	All	All touchpoints	Customer delight Customer DNA	Marketing Top Management Functional Heads
Value created	All	Product Price Customer experience Brand	Desire to create Value (understand Customer's needs)	Measurement Market Share Profits
More value added Products/Service		Store Company Service person	Value added Meets Customer needs	Sales/Marketing/Service people Store
Cancel service		Call centre executive	Easy to do Helpful Action oriented	Call centre Web
Become advocate/detractor			Based on experience	Service centre

Source Author.

FIGURE 9.1
Customer Waterfall of Needs

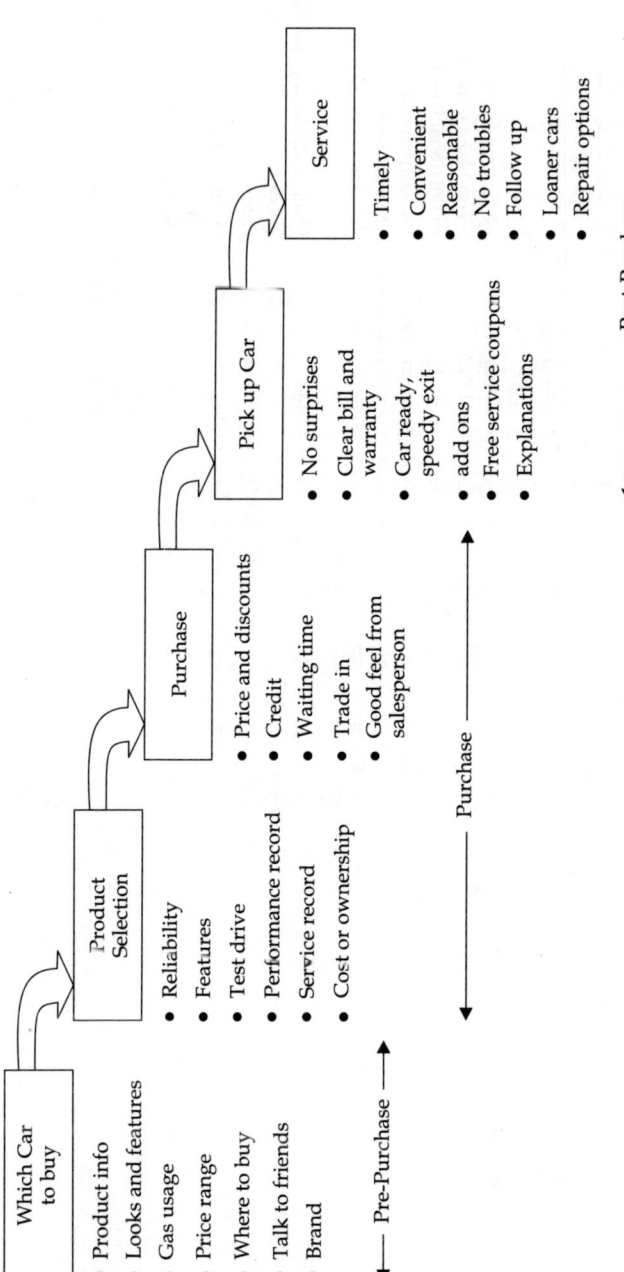

Source Author.

CHAPTER SYNOPSIS

The frontline people are most important to the company in adding Customer Value.

- The awareness and self-esteem of the frontline people has to be built to be able to get them to relate to the Customers.
- These people are the touchpoints and have to be sensitized to the Customer's needs.
- Touchpoint mapping is suggested, and creating Customer Champions of frontline people is encouraged. We discuss:

  - Customer Value and Touchpoints
  - The importance of the Customers time, energy, convenience, psychic and image needs (lack of these translate to a cost to the Customer)

Other topics that we address include:

- Create Customer Champions and Customer Circles
- Touchpoint Mapping
- We also show the Customers' Waterfall of Needs

10

Bottom-up Total CVM: Customer Circles

Doug is addressing his staff meeting. It has been expanded to include functional heads, such as the purchasing manager, who do not report directly to him. He has also invited the Customer Guru, Krish Kumar.

Doug addresses the group, "You all know Krish, whom you have interacted with. Krish helped us with increasing Customer Value in retail stores in Ohio when I was responsible for the area. Most of you know what Customer-Centric-Circles are. We have started a Customer alignment at all functions as part of our Total CVM objectives. We have started 'Customer Conduits', which is a top-down approach, driven by the CEO to make the organization Customer-centric.

"Customer-Centric-Circles or Customer Circles for short are a bottom-up approach. To recap:

"The term 'Customer-Centric-Circles' is really a misnomer, because it is a company-sponsored group of people (generally frontline employees, some managers and others from support functions) mostly having regular contact with Customers, and for a Total CVM programme people from communications, IT, business development, environmental affairs, manufacturing and product development among others. Customer Circles may not necessarily have Customers in it per se but this group of people will focus on the Customer."

The purchasing manager says she doesn't understand. What use is it to have Customer-Centric-Circles without Customers?

Doug responds, "Ideally we would like to have Customers in the Customer Circles. However, it is difficult to get the right type of analytical Customers who could commit the time to be in an ongoing initiative. In any event, the Customer Circle is a task force to run a Customer-focused project with targets, responsibilities and timetables. The first step is to raise the awareness of employees on Customers.

"They develop strategies for dealing with Customers at a local level. They devise ways and means to make it easier for the Customer to do business with them. They find ways to touch the Customer and to give the Customer a great experience. Customer data, information, inputs, complaints or plaudits, these should be made available to the Customer Circle, as and when it is available, or an effort should be made to collect such feedback.[1]

"The process starts by building an awareness of the importance of the Customer. What you'll find is that the group will come up with better ways to handle a Customer. Through this process, Customer awareness in the company and among the employees will invariably increase.

"But before all this, we must understand the Voice of the Employee, his pain points, and increase his awareness on the Customer. Along with this, we must capture the Voice of the Customer and the Voice of the Competitor."

Krish, who has been quiet adds, *"Basically, this is a bottom-up approach to energizing an organization to become Customer-centric.*

"Yes," says Doug excitedly, "and they must collect data on the Customer, plan on how to track every contact and experience, and chart out future touches and experience, keeping the retailer in the forefront. They must talk to the Customer, get feedback from the market place and learn what they can about the competition in both formal and informal ways."

---

[1] Customer Value Foundation study: Customer Value Management study in the fertilizer market, Producer-Dealer-Retailer-Farmer, 2005.

"I guess Customer-Centric-Circles are akin to level 3 empowerment described by Jan Carlzon,[2] where employees are self-managing and can make decisions. They will take ownership of the Customer and the Customer initiatives, because these are their own ideas."

"Well, here we are making the employees the owners for Customer focus," says Doug. "What the employees propose is common sense. What they suggest is what the company would have wanted them to do! For starters, you do not touch the consumers, they are remote to you, and anonymous and just touching them will be very useful to your sales."

What we find is that if we can show the frontline people the results of their actions through Customer feedback, and if this is positive, we find that the frontline people get a sense of pride and a sense of achievement. The motivation level on serving Customers better goes up."

Krish then hands the group notes on Customer Circles, and asks them to read these:

CUSTOMER CIRCLES AND SHARED VISIONS

Customer Circles engender shared vision and teamwork. They are a pillar of a learning organization, where people work together for shared goals and beliefs. They allow the building of promises, and working together to make things happen. They lead to creativity, and making people think about mastery, and in this case, mastery of habits, responses, approaches to the Customer, of building systems and methods for better Customer delight and Customer Value.

A shared vision is not necessarily an idea but a desire or a force in people's minds and hearts that drives them to achieve extraordinary goals; for example making Customers happy! Sharing of the vision means people work together. People have

---

[2] Jan Carlzon, *Moments of Truth* (Harper Perennial, 1987).

to be convinced that they want to do something good for the Customer, you cannot force them. No one can give someone his vision. You encourage them to have a personal vision and try to build it into a shared vision.

During Customer Circles, we have to ask people why Customers become happy with the frontline people and why they become unhappy. Often, they respond that the Customers' unhappiness is caused by their unreasonableness or high-unmet expectations. On introspection, the group often reaches the conclusion that it is their own actions or inactions that cause dissatisfaction in the Customer's mind. With this awareness, they search for solutions, including their own behaviour modification.

The group builds its own self-esteem and awareness and decides on action steps, including building the Customers' delight factors and Do Not Annoy (DNA) factors (see Box 10.1).

The problem with a top-down approach is that top management "dictates" a vision, and does not build it with buy-in of key players at all levels, nor is it built on personal and shared visions. Visions spread because of commitment, enrolment, clarity, enthusiasm, reinforcement and communication.

Understanding current reality and accepting it, without clouding it with perceptions and blame avoidance, are important to shared visions and Customer Circles.

Cynicism, being ordered or told to do things, of being taught rather than self-learning and organizational structure, all conspire against success of Customer Circles.

CUSTOMER CIRCLES AND TEAM LEARNING

Customer Circles are inter-disciplinary teams. The success of Customer Circles depends on individual excellence and learning, and how well the team members work together. It depends on managing individual skills and merit with team spirit. Unaligned teams waste energy. So teams have to learn to align themselves and develop the capacity of the

BOX 10.1
Examples of Customer Circles

1. The Tata Power Customer Circles led to the introduction of the courtesy system (smiling and greeting at work). The Customer Circles realized that the Customers were being inconvenienced when they visited the Tata Power office. The Circles designed special signs and put them up for the Customers to get to the Customer department. Soon thereafter, an existing office was converted into a comfortable Customer meeting room. The Customer did not have to search for the right Tata Power representative. They just picked up the intercom as they came off the elevator. The person who responded ensured the right person came to meet them in the meeting room.

Individual Customer facing employees started to put Customer-related quotes on their desktops. They made laminated cards they carry showing Customers' DNA (Do Not Annoy). On the reverse side of the card are the Customer delight factors.

An example of the card is given in Figures 10.1 and 10.2.

Service people who fix fuses have started to carry cards showing how to save energy, and leave these with Customers shown in Figure 10.3.

Sub-station managers invite important Customers to the sub-station to show the Customers they have dedicated control panels for them with the Customer's name on them.

Call Centres have better co-ordination on answering billing related enquiries.

Complaints fell from 9 per thousand to 2.7 per thousand in the quarter following the formation of Customer Circles.

2. Godrej frontline people are saying in the last three months after inception of Customer Circles, that they are feeling happy about work. The co-ordination has improved, the mistakes are reduced and bickering in the team has reduced. Addresses and telephone numbers are properly being given to the service technicians, appointments are confirmed. The service technicians are smiling and greeting the Customers better, and briefing them better, so much so that many Customers offer them tea and ask for them by name for future services.

Service Centre personnel setting up appointments are getting 30 per cent more referrals. The technicians are giving referrals they receive from Customers directly to the sales people who are able to convert these referrals into business. Previously, the referrals went into the system (and they still do), but by the time the salesperson got it and contacted the Customer the business had gone!

Salespeople tell me they are able to get better pricing for corporate clients because the service and follow up has improved.

(Box 10.1 continued)

(Box 10.1 continued)

Customer Circles suggested dress codes, and also insisted there be folders to put the Customer's service sheets, so that the Customer sees and signs nice and crisp sheets rather than folded sheets.

The Customer Circles have spread the message to others in their service centres, and these employees being exposed to this are performing better due to the example set by the Customer Circles people and the newer entrants into the Customer Circles are seeing on the results. The enthusiasm is stunning.

Better documentation and inspection reports are being made, and service technicians can use the inspection reports in a better way to solve the Customers' problems.

3. At Tata Chemicals Crop Nutrition and Agri-Business, Customer Circles have helped Dealers and Retailers focus on each other and the end Customer, the farmer, and to provide extraordinary service to them. Problems of delivery and supply chain, payments and billing between the dealers and the company were resolved once they started to talk together as equals and team members, listening to each other, accepting problems (and not saying, that's the way it is) and finding solutions.

Source Author.

team to deliver more than the individual can. Teams are dependent on the members, who need each other to achieve more and deliver. It requires listening and respect, such that you let your own opinions be overridden. It teaches you to overcome conflict and use dialog to work together, and it builds discipline of team learning. Dialogue makes people observe and improve their own ideas and thinking.

Teamwork and team learning requires a facilitator or a catalyst, and requires people to suspend their beliefs to listen to others and to regard each other and colleagues who are present to help us.

These Customer Circles can become a self-learning system. With Customer Circles, the organization is bound to become creative and innovative. People want to be part of such an organization, and participate in the innovation.

The principle has to be that no one should be too proud to learn. And not too proud to learn from anyone. Continuous learning and participation will lead to Customer excellence.

FIGURE 10.1
Customer's Delight Factors

TATA
TATA POWER

WHAT DELIGHTS CUSTOMER

- o Courteous behavior & presentation
- o Converse with customer while on service call.
- o Senior people making courtesy call once a while.
- o Easy bill payment facilities
- o Education on tariff & energy conservation measures.
- o Easy accessibility.
- o Quick problem resolution & timely feedback.
- o Keeping up promises & assurances.
- o Dealing with knowledgeable & confident people.
- o Giving him importance & treating with respect.
- o Advance information on power shutdowns
- o Visiting Customer facilities to understand their processes and giving valuable suggestions guidance in energy management.

Lighting up Lives!

Source   Tata Power.

For learning and innovation to happen, one must think like a small company and eliminate the "Not Invented Here" syndrome. Moreover, one must look at all ideas, look for ideal solutions and then modify them to make them practical. Too many great ideas do not see the light of day because someone shoots them down and says these can't be done, or the idea is too expensive. How many things that were expensive

FIGURE 10.2
Customer's Do Not Annoy (DNA) Factors

TATA
TATA POWER

WHAT ANNOYS CUSTOMER

o **Telling customer that we are busy & contact later.**

o **Not believing the customer.**

o **Disconnecting customer call during conversation.**

o **Addressing customer like friend rather than a customer.**

o **Making promises that can not be kept**

o **No timely feedback**

o **Not resolving the problem within reasonable time**

o **Dealing with unknowledgeable people.**

o **Not available for meeting the customer at agreed time.**

o **Telling him this is the way Tata Power works.**

Lighting up Lives!

Source   Tata Power.

when introduced are now much, much cheaper like TVs, cell phones, calculators. The list is endless.

One also has to stop people from being compulsive of ownership of ideas. They have to be shared. This also requires humility. With this listening becomes easier. People have to be large-hearted to share ideas and to celebrate someone else's idea.

FIGURE 10.3
Energy Conservation Tips

ENERGY CONSERVATION TIPS

- Minimize/Shift usage during the 10 am–8 pm peak time and avoid adding to the load.
- Switch on AC an hour after starting work and switch off an hour before closing.
- Run all ACs at 24° C.
- Switch off all electrical appliances from the plug point.
- Set computers to sleep and Hibernate mode.
- Replace incandescent bulbs with compact fluorescent lamps (CFLs) in your homes and premises to save upto 75% of electricity.

Source   Tata Power.

Discussing and learning from mistakes made by the group, by the company or outside the company is another important part of learning. Learn to drive change better and faster.

Move from best practices to next practices. Thus, build Customer excellence.

CUSTOMER CIRCLES AND CELEBRATION/RECOGNITION

Not only do we discuss what we can do in Customer Circles, we also have to talk about things we have done wrong. We must celebrate and recognize what we do for Customers, and build on this. With Corporate communications, we must record Customer stories, where we have done wonderful things for the Customer. These stories should adorn the office walls of the Chief Customer Officer and the Customer Champions.

We have to recognize the great stories, and the people behind these, and even build a recognition system.

We must recognize that people who have self-esteem and are aware, will feel good about themselves and will produce good results for Customers. And obviously those who produce good results will feel good about themselves.

Also achieving good results for oneself, and for others and for Customers, ends up being fun, and a culture of fun and teamwork occurs, where we celebrate and recognize success (see Box 10.1).

ROLLING OUT CUSTOMER CIRCLES

First and foremost, remember new Customer Circles are not set up to impart training or education. The idea is that the Circle members must decide what they should do with the older members acting as catalysts and facilitators, and not as teachers. Each new Customer Circle and its members must decide (with the help of people from the core Customer Circles) what they should do for the Customer. Not only should the learnings from previous Customer Circles be incorporated but also new ideas should emerge.

In addition, the Customer Bill of Rights and the Circle of Promises that have been developed by the older Customer Circles have to be ratified and the Circle of Promises started in the new Circles.

Customer Circles have to be self-propagating and self-learning. There has to be a continuous Customer improvement effort.

At Godrej, it was decided (Box 10.2):

BOX 10.2
Customer Circles at Godrej

- The Circle itself

  The core group should be 10–12 people (maximum 20 people).
  Customer Circle meetings should be done on a monthly basis.
  There should be a leader.
  Agenda for the Customer Circle should be pre-defined.
  The learning should be passed down voluntarily.
  Do not teach, coach instead.

(Box 10.2 continued)

(*Box 10.2 continued*)

> Share experiences.
> Do not be in a rush: this is a self-learning and self-realization programme.

- During the meeting

> Action steps after each agenda discussion.
> Previous agenda action steps reviews.
> Follow up steps, what, who and how should we do it?
> Customer Circles not to become a complaint centre for participants.
> Continuous Customer Improvement Programme (CCIP).
> Think of broken promises and kept promises, and what to do about them.
> Set up a date for the next meeting.

> Remember, the Customer Circles start with Employee Value, awareness and self-esteem building. This includes employee and team bonding.
> The hygiene factors or the Customer's DNA are built first, followed by the delight factors and the Bill of Rights. The problem in continuous improvement programmes are that there are two parts, the soft side or cultural and attitudinal changes, and the 'hard' side, or the tasks that have to be done. Typically, people prefer to work on processes and what they know and what generally are their tasks (we will reduce complaint resolution to 2 days from 2 and a half days). This task could have been done anyway, without Customer Circles. Watch out for these.
> Given below is a synopsis of Customer-Circles:

Customer Circles

The Customer Circles should have:

1. An agenda
2. A review of the tasks set out in the previous meeting, and of achievements
3. The Circles should develop Customer's DNA, Customer delight factors and courtesy systems
4. A reiview of the Customer Bill of Rights, and the Circle of Promises

(*Box 10.2 continued*)

(Box 10.2 continued)

> a. Promises kept: Reinforce them
> b. Promises broken: Ask if they can be kept. If not, discard. If yes, reinforce
>
> 5. Continuous Customer Improvement Programme
>
> a. Work related
> b. Soft or Customer related
>
> An example is the I CARE program from the Safety, Health and Environment (SHE) Department
>
> 6. Set up tasks for various people, including responsibilities for implementation and time lines, etc.
> 7. Establish date for tasks and next meeting
>
> The minutes of the meeting should be circulated within a day to show seriousness and importance of the Customer Circle. Minutes should go to the CCO also.
>
> The Customer Circles and their members (limited to 20 or less) should have a reward and recognition programme.
>
> There should be central co-ordinator (Chief Customer Officer) who should have a process to review progress of meeting, including:
>
> a. Frequency
> b. Attendance
> c. Tasks to be done including:
>
> Customer DNA, delight factors and courtesy systems.
> Customer continuous improvement programmes, key and immediate, secondary and long term.
> Customer Bill of Rights and Circle of Promises related.
>
> d. Participation
> e. New ideas
> f. Implementation steps
> g. Bills of Rights and Promises kept
> h. Follow-up action
> i. Minutes
> j. Next meeting

Source   Author.

CHAPTER SYNOPSIS

This chapter describes how

- the frontline people can be aligned to the Customer using Customer Circles, which have to be built in various departments and across the company.
- Continuous Customer Improvement Programmes along with monitoring of the Circle of Promises are part of the results.
- To roll out the circles, not through processes but through shared learnings. Team learning, shared visions are resultants.

Examples of how Customer Circles have worked are depicted.

Customer Circles and Shared Visions
Customer Circles and Team Learning
Examples of Customer Circles
Rolling Out Customer Circles

11

Total CVM and Certification

Doug, Jack, Shirley and Krish agree that they have enough on their plate, with all the new initiatives underway on Total CVM. Krish says he wants them to know of other Total CVM initiatives, which Glacier might wish to incorporate later. Glacier's top managers admit that while they should be aware of certification, they should look at it once they are more ready. Krish agrees, and adds, "I will just give you a hand out describing certification both of employees and the company. The first is accompanied by an education programme for the employees on Customer-centricity, behaviour and Customer treatment."

They all agree. Doug calls in Cindy, Head of HRD. After she joins them, Krish shares the following with them.

CUSTOMER EDUCATION AND
CERTIFICATION OF EMPLOYEES

"Since companies are generally driven by processes, efficiency and technology, it stands to reason that most employees are provided (or taught) the technical skills required to perform their tasks, and may even be certified for carrying out this task. Thus, a service technician may be trained on how to service an air-conditioner or a refrigerator. A retail sales clerk may be taught about the products he is to sell and even how to categorize Customers. None of these people is generally taught how to handle Customers, and indeed is not certified for Customer contact. Total CVM requires that a necessary step is certification of touchpoints from a Customer viewpoint."

Cindy nods her head. "You are right. The focus is on job-related skills, and often not on soft skills. Employees are certified for their technical competence, but rarely for their Customer-centricity. Krish, I am sure such a certification process not only involves training, job content, written examinations, covering not only Customer problem handling, and Customer delight improvement, Customers' DNA (Do Not Annoy), oral and play acting assessment."

Krish agrees: *"Moreover, the certification is an ongoing process, of learning, on the job assessment and ensuring that what is being said and what is really being done are in sync. On the job assessment is an essential part of the ongoing certification process.*

"Customer Value Foundation has such certification processes."

COMPANY CERTIFICATION

Krish hands Doug, Jack, Shirley and Cindy the following note on the Customer Value Foundation's Company Customer Certification programme. This proprietary Customer Certification by Customer Value Foundation can be used by Customers to assess companies from (but not limited to):

1. Management:
   - Are the top managers aligned to the Customer?
   - Is there a CEO god syndrome?
   - Is the Customer the Boss?
   - Is there a Chief Customer Officer?
   - Does the company have an Ombudsman?
   - Is there a good complaint resolution mechanism?

2. Strategic:
   - Is there an understanding that Customer Value and Shareholder Value are related?
   - Is there well thought-out Customer strategy with action steps?
   - Does Customer strategy drive business strategy?

- Are short-term profits a major driver of the company?
- Is there an understanding that the convenience of the company and the convenience of the Customer be in accord?
- Are Customer Value Added and satisfaction being measured?
- Is the company keeping ahead of competition on the Customer front?

3. Does the company have a Customers Bill of Rights with back-to-back promises from various individuals and departments?

- Is the Customer Bill of Rights backed up by employee promises?
- Does the company honour its guarantees, and stand behind its products and services?
- Is this company trustworthy?
- Is this company Customer-centric?
- Does the company have Customer-centric processes?
- If the product does not work within a given time (depends on what should be industry norms, will they take it back, or say go to our service centre?

4. Employees:

- Employee Value added, self-esteem and awareness programmes
- Are employees helped to build their brand equity?
- Are the employees Customer certified?
- Are there Customer Circles?
- Are there Customer Conduits? Functional alignment?
- Are there Customer Value tasks in each department
- Is its complaint handling procedures Customer-friendly? Are the company employees Customer-friendly?

5. Channel partners:

   - Are the company's channel partners certified and Customer-centric?
   - Are they adding or destroying value?
   - Are they building their Brand equity?
   - Are they strategically aligned to the company and its Customer Value programme?

6. Outsourced services:

   - Are the call centres converted to action centres and easy to reach and fast in action?
   - Are all outsourced services providing Customer Value?

7. Products:

   - Are the products designed from a Customer's needs?
   - Are the products customized?
   - Are the products priced from Customer's needs, using Customer Value Pricing techniques?
   - Are the products designed from a Customer's needs? Are the products customized?

8. Customer Value Added and Customer metrics:

   - Is the company measuring Customer Value Added and satisfaction?
   - Is there a Customer Performance Management System, based on measuring Customer difficulty and Customer delight?
   - Are there other feedback mechanisms, complaint handling?
   - Are they acting on these?
   - Is there a continuous programme to capture data through Customer contact programmes?
   - Is there a Continuous Customer Improvement Programme?

9. Customer Circles:

  - Are these in place?
  - Are they being assessed?
  - Are they yielding Continuous Customer Improvement Programmes?
  - Are they monitoring the Customers' Bill of Rights and the Circle of Promises?

10. Departmental objectives:

  - Do the departments have Customer goals?
  - Are they measured or incented on these?

11. The Customer:

  - Is the Customer considered King?
  - Is the convenience of the Customer more important than the convenience of the Company?
  - Are the processes designed to be Customer-friendly?
  - Is their execution Customer-friendly?
  - Are the metrics Customer directed?
  - Are the websites and other interaction points Customer-designed and Customer-friendly?
  - Are the transactions Customer-friendly?
  - Are the touchpoints Customer-friendly?
  - Does the Customer find value in the products and the benefits, including price?
  - Is there systemic learning in the organization?
  - Does the company try to say it is right when it is wrong?
  - Does the company co-create Customer experience?
  - Is the Customer allowed to decide what segment he should be placed in?
  - Is there a Customer segmentation leading to a segment size of one?
  - Is the Customer in control?

The last point can be best shown from the following example (Box 11.1).

BOX 11.1
Is the Customer in Control?

In late 2008, an Indian citizen with a valid Schengen visa[1] was leaving from Manchester airport for Prague (Czekoslavia). Czekoslavia had become a signatory to the Schengen treaty and so had stopped issuing Czek visas because Schengen visas were valid there (for over a year at the time of this story). This passenger with a valid Schengen visa was denied boarding by Servisair, Czek Airline's ground handling staff, who were very rude and would not accept the Schengen visa, nor would they check if the Schengen visa was valid. After the flight left, they discovered their error. There was no apology. The passenger wrote to the President of Servisair, and the net upshot was that they were sorry, but these things happened because their computer was not upgraded. Not upgraded in one year? Heads should roll. But no, there is no concern, nor any systemic desire to correct such problems. Moreover, there is no move to avoid arrogant and rude handling of passengers.

If this was your company, what would you do?

Source Author.

Detailed assessment of the company from a Customer's point-of-view is necessary to certify companies. Customer Value Foundation does this.

CHAPTER SYNOPSIS

This is a key chapter on the certification of people and companies on how Customer-centric they are. What has to be taken into account in such certifications, and how can they

---

[1] A Schengen visa, issued by certain European countries who are Schengen signatory countries, allows the recipient to visit all the countries in the Schengen treaty with one visa.

be done? We look at various constituents that are to be assessed in Customer Circles. The company Customer certification programme examines:

- Management
- Strategic
- Does the company have a Customers Bill of Rights with back-to-back promises from various individuals and departments?
- Employees
- Channel partners
- Outsourced services
- Products
- Customer Value Added and Customer metrics
- Customer Circles
- Departmental Objectives
- The Customer

12

Epilogue: Total CVM at Glacier Products

Six months later, Doug, Jack and Shirley are discussing the Total Customer Value Management programme at Glacier.

Jack and Shirley agree that Doug has become more democratic and has allowed the two of them to work more independently and more strategically.

Doug compliments them, "I think you have also become less of bosses and more of team leaders now. The Customer seems to be becoming the boss. And this has not hurt us or our business in any way. On the contrary, it has helped our business to grow. There are fewer complaints, better teamwork and focus on the Customers. We seem to understand the Customer more and more. On-time arrival of goods, shorter lead times, better inventory and production control has materialised. It has forced our production people to address the perceived need of the Customer to get fresh product as opposed to having product that has been lying around for a long time. Our product development team is now bringing out Customer preferred products, which allow the homemaker to customise to her needs, and take away the feel of ready to eat meals! We are fast becoming the number one company in the business, as our market share is climbing."

Glacier had embarked on a programme of Total Customer Value Management, starting with a Customer strategy that re-iterated that the Customer and his needs would drive the company, and eventually its strategy and products. Customer service would be outstanding and promises would be kept. The Business strategy was driven from the Customer strategy keeping in mind the shareholders' needs. But for now, the goal was Customer focus. Top manager alignment and frontline alignment would be the steps. The company would incorporate Customer Circles at touch point levels and at the senior levels. These circles would be monitored through a Customer Circle monitoring system, so that top managers could review their progress, their effectiveness, and understand which Customer Circles were successful and which were not, and understand why some were meaningful and others not that effective, and then figure out corrective actions.

To ensure continuity, Glacier had decided to appoint a Chief Customer Officer, Doug's one-time job.

The programme started with the Customer Circles and with listening to the Voice of the Employee. They had learnt of the problems of the employees, how they felt when Customers were angry with them and how they felt when Customers were happy with them. They were then able to figure out why Customers were happy or unhappy, why they yelled, and why they smiled. And corrective action along with the Customer's DNA and delight factors were built. In subsequent meetings, many Customer-centric and Customer pleasing suggestions were created, along with co-creation of Customer Value, particularly on the products, and convenience. Employee loyalty had gone up, employee churn had reduced.

Complaints had come down, pressure on price had reduced.

Value measurements and CVA had continued. And Glacier's CVA scores were increasing as were market share and profitability. The Voice of the Customer and the Voice of the Competitor were captured on an ongoing basis.

Teamwork and the concept of internal Customers were better understood and followed.

Customer Bill of Rights and the Circle of Promises were put into place, putting accountability on the employees for the Customer's happiness and the company's well being.

Meetings and reporting systems had CVA and Customer and Employee Assets reported. Value of Customer dictated segments to be pampered, ignored, or nourished. There were sections on the Customer in weekly or monthly meetings.

Finally, the Customer was discussed at the Board level.

Doug comments, "As I understand it, many of our officers have put together Customer goals. Let me see if I can enunciate some of these:

- **Jack Griswold, COO and CCVC:**

  - Drive Employee Value and Customer Value in all departments
  - Work with finance to increase Shareholder Value, and
  - Balance convenience of company with convenience of Customer

- **Shirley Madison, CFO:**

  - Increase Shareholder Value
  - Understand relationship between Shareholder and Customer Value
  - Build a pricing matrix
  - Measure Return on Customer
  - Start a Finance Customer Circle

- **Jimmy Vaidya, Chief of Manufacturing:**

  - Reduce inventory to provide fresher product
  - Work closer with marketing, finance and logistics with a Customer Value goal, with an eye on cost

- **Rita Timko, Chief Marketing Officer:**

  - Focus on Customer needs using CVA
  - Design price justification template
  - Build better Customer relations
  - Start marketing Customer Circles
  - Implement Value Selling techniques

- **JoJo Mohindra, CIO:**

  - Build Customer-centric processes/Liaise with Customers
  - Elicit Customer metrics from data
  - Support customisation for Customer
  - Have members attend Customer Circles and support their work
  - Build systems that are easy to modify as Customer problems are noticed

- **Cindy Pandit, Chief of HRD:**

  - Increase Employee Value, self esteem, awareness, proactiveness and loyalty
  - Build employee's brand equity
  - Build a courtesy system
  - Start programme for building Customer and Business awareness
  - Start a HRD Customer Circle
  - Support other Customer Circles

- **Rohit Carson, Chief Technical Officer:**

  - Determine Customer needs for new products
  - Focus on Customer needs on existing products
  - Look at freshness of packaged food products and customisation of offerings
  - Support Customer Circles, as necessary

TOTAL CVM AND ORGANIZATIONAL TRANSFORMATION AT GLACIER PRODUCTS

What is required for Total CVM is an organization that is ready to transform itself in the quest for increasing Value for Customers. This transformation starts with the attitudes, mindsets, and learning (and self learning coming from increased awareness and pro-activeness. True transformation requires Business Excellence including Customer-led processes, a top down alignment and a bottom up focus on the Customer within the company. Using Business Excellence and Total Quality techniques to achieve change and transformation will yield faster and more permanent Total CVM solutions and lead to Customer Excellence, and higher profits. Doug is discussing the changes that have happened on the Customer front by using Total CVM.

When asked, the top managers of Glacier agreed the programme has been a success and should be followed more aggressively and become an ongoing one.

They all agreed that their objectives were taking root, and visible differences were being seen. The 'C' word was being heard more often, the Customer's point of view was being looked at, people were thinking of Continuous Customer Improvement. Hitherto sacred cows that led to the convenience of the company were being changed. Marketing was looking at price justification, and farming of Customers. Manufacturing and new products were being driven by the Customer.

The Last Mile

Doug takes Pam out for lunch

Doug has been able to reduce his workload by using the Task Assessment programme. He has cut out unnecessary emails, meetings and travels and has become a better organiser, a better delegator and has found time to institute Total CVM, and he has found more time for Pam.

Pam congratulates Doug on his successful start to Total CVM.

She says, "Doug, you seem to be more relaxed. Total CVM seems to have released time to you to think and have a family life, in addition to making Glacier more efficient and Customer focused.

"But what I do not understand is that all your Customer work has been within the company, and sometimes suppliers. You must try to use newer methods to interact with the Customer."

Doug responds, "You are right. This is the last mile I have been thinking of. We need to use social media and marketing and digital marketing to make this happen. This means Glacier Products must start a platform to have our Customers interact with each other. We can learn what they want and suggest solutions. This will work only when we are truly adding value, and Customers start to 'sell' us!"

Pam says, "Remember, a Customer is one whose satisfaction is key to the organization's success."

Appendix I
Total CVM: Barriers and Possible Solutions

More companies are recognising the importance of Customers, and yet few are able to institute measures such as Total CVM in their companies. What prevents them from doing this? Is it ignorance, indifference, or just a lack of motivation?

I can't imagine ignorance as a reason, except that CEOs may be lulled into thinking they are doing everything for the Customer (which means everything they know). However they may not be aware of all they can do.

Indifference cannot be a reason, because most CEOs are aware. Motivation can be another factor.

When Doug decided to incorporate Total CVM at Glacier Products, there was no open objection. There was cynicism, and many shrugged the initiative away, thinking the known way of doing business would prevail. Also, many of the non front-facing department heads, including Jack Griswold (COO), Shirley Madison (CFO), Jimmy Vaidya (Chief of Manufacturing), JoJo Mohindra (CIO), Cindy Pandit (Chief of HRD) and Rohit Carson (Chief Technology Officer) while being quizzical, also could not think through Customer tasks to institute in their departments, and had not lent pro-active cooperation. Thus the programme had not been able to take root company-wide, because the Customer mindset was not there.

The determination of Doug to transform the organization, and the help from the Customer Guru in educating them on what their departments could do, and his coaching on the Customer Circles and other Total CVM techniques and initiatives progressed the programme at Glacier.

Doug recalled that a recent executive poll at LinkedIn on impediments to Customer experience stated Customer strategy and lack of internal cooperation (or organizational silos) as the items (33 per cent and 28 per cent respectively) (see Figure AI.1).

FIGURE AI.1
Barriers to Customer Experience

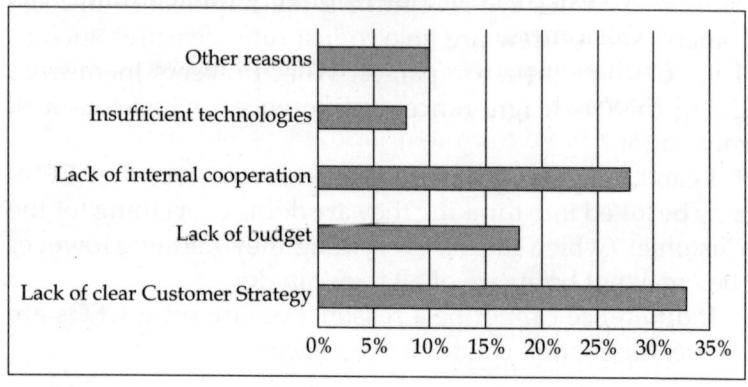

Source   LinkedIn.

Picking up on Doug's experience, given below are the reasons why a Total CVM programme could possibly have difficulty in a company:

- **Management, Employees and Attitudes as impediments to Total CVM**

    1. The CEO and his attitude
    2. The lack of clear Customer strategy
    3. The top managers and their attitude or lack of enthusiasm
    4. Experienced and educated front-line people, or part time front-line people, outsourced front-line people like call centres (why change?)
    5. A know-it-all attitude

6. Casual or apathetic attitude
7. We are too busy with other initiatives
8. Impatience and looking for instant results. There will be some, but Total CVM takes time and perseverance because we are impacting mindset changes

- **Customers and Channels as an impediment to Total CVM**

    1. No external Customers, or very limited number of Customers
    2. Channel partners as Customers or indirect Customer contact
    3. We have a limited amount of product to sell or we have captive Customers, or we have regulated prices

- **Business programmes or thinking as an impediment to Total CVM**

    1. We have Quality or Six Sigma, or a Business Excellence Programme in our company
    2. We have a successful brand
    3. We have a successful business or growth
    4. Profits drive our Company

Let us examine the possible impediments.

MANAGEMENT, EMPLOYEES AND ATTITUDES AS IMPEDIMENTS TO TOTAL CVM

1. The CEO as a Barrier to Total CVM

Barriers

- When he focuses on short-term returns, and not building a long term and sustained market or business leadership.

- When he cannot stop being a CEO god. This is often unconscious, but not being able to let the Customer become truly Number One in the organization is a barrier to Total CVM.
- He has too many competing priorities.
- The Customer priority is in the background (the Customer is important, but we are successful, and so we must be doing things right).
- The Customer priority is seen in a limited fashion (the Customer is important, and we are doing everything for the Customer). This means a lack of knowledge about what one could really do for the Customer.
- The CEO does not lead the Total CVM initiative himself. What happens is that top management alignment and interdepartmental Total CVM becomes difficult. Also by not insisting on having a section on Customers in his monthly reviews, and by not measuring Customer assets, or assigning bonuses for Customer related activities, the CEO becomes an impediment to Total CVM.
- By not asking for CVA (Customer Value Added) scores and Customer Assets added on his financial reports, he slows down the programme.

Solution

The CEO support is absolutely a necessity for any Total CVM programme to be a success. Therefore,

- The Board may have to suggest a CVM programme to him. In the Tata companies Business Excellence programmes were mandated from the top and were part of the top management review. This helped this programme to become a reality.
- Making Customer results as important metrics, and putting Customer assets on the balance sheet. Rewarding

the CEO for Customer results and increased Customer assets. Reviewing CVA results.
- Often, the CEO stays on the sidelines and waits for some successful results, before he becomes an evangelist. In one of the Tata companies, the CEO did not directly lead the programme, hoping his staff would manage the programme, before getting highly involved to give the programme body and longevity. Here the Total CVM programme was started in a limited fashion. Today, he has nominated himself the Chief Customer Officer and is directing the programme.

In another Tata company, the CEO started the initiative, but remained out of the day-to-day programme. But his tacit approval, and a note or two to the organization certainly helped. Their balanced scorecard now has Total CVM as the number one priority.

There is no real solution beyond this, unless some departments adopt some CVM programmes, as was done at Glacier and attracts the CEO's attention.

2. Lack of Clear Customer Strategy

Barrier

- This is symptomatic of the CEO and top management not focusing on Customers and therefore not building a clear Customer strategy.

Solution

The solution is for the CEO to recognise the Customer as important and also to ensure that all the executives have a Customer role so that they can build Customer-centricity and inter-departmental cooperation.

3. The Top Managers as a Barrier to Total CVM

Barriers

Top managers as Barriers:

- Often do not participate whole-heartedly in a Total CVM programme. They are sometimes bystanders.
- They believe they have a review role, and not a participatory role or a leadership role or a strategic role in Total CVM.
- They do not believe they have any role in Total CVM, or do not understand their possible roles.
- Most managers are operational rather than strategic in thinking. Some are not pro-active. Such managers have difficulty in making Total CVM their programme.
- They do not lead their departmental teams in Total CVM.
- They do not install Total CVM in their department.
- They are not prepared to learn.

Solution

There are several ways to get the buy-in of top managers:

- The best way is a Customer education and awareness programme. Without the CEO's intervention, this may not be enough. A Chief Customer Officer or a Customer Value consultant certainly helps in aligning the organization.
- Another approach is a top down tactic from the CEO. He insists on:

  1. Customer related Key Results linked to compensation
  2. Customer related discussions in each management review
  3. Putting Customer Circles in the department.

- Another method is to:
  1. Start an apex Customer Circle incorporating all the direct reports of the CEO or the department heads to oversee the functioning and roll-out of Customer Circles. This was first tried at Tata Power and brought in participation and buy-in of top managers.
  2. Make the top Managers assess the Circle of Promises and Customers Bill of Rights and ensure it is workable and warranting it's working.
  3. Getting their active participation in building the Customer strategy certainly helps. And even more so if the Customer strategy drives the Business strategy.

- Giving incentives for Customer related programmes can put a focus on Total CVM.

4. The Front-line Employees as a Barrier to Total CVM

Barriers

Experienced and educated front-line people, or part time front-line people, outsourced front-line people like call centres are often reluctant to change.

- When people have been around for some time and have been successful, they know it all, they've been there. Why change where they have been successful? These people tend to become casual about the Customer.
- Outside vendors and channel partners do not have the motivation insiders have unless they are brought into the Customer Circles. Converting call centres to action centres helps.
- When a company is successful, quick wins are limited.
- The company does not help front-line people to build their own self respect and self esteem.

- The company does not measure or build Employee Value.
- The company does not build the employee's brand equity.
- The environment is not employee-friendly, let alone Customer-friendly.

Solution

- The programme should be top-driven.
- There are other departments participating in such programmes through Customer Circles with good results.
- The department head must appear to be Customer-friendly and motivated, and lead the programmes.
- The Voice of the Customer and the difficulties old hands face within the company and outside with the Customers must be heard, and Employee Value programmes put into place. Build the employee self esteem and self-respect.
- Build a Customer awareness programme. The best way is through Customer Circles and CVA studies.
- Setting up Customer Circles, and making them see, through peers, the Customer Value consultant or the Chief Customer Officer, the value of changing to embrace Total CVM.

5. The Know-it-all Attitude as a Barrier to Total CVM

Barriers

Sometimes company management has a know-it-all attitude:

- We know what we need to do (The State Bank of India has a 32-item list they know they have to improve on for the Customer. "Why do we need Total CVM?" they ask. The reason is that you cannot work on 32 items; you need to prioritise and these priorities come from the Customer and Customer insight and a CVA study.

- We know what the Customer wants (though employees know it from their own vantage point, not the point of view of the Customer).
- We are doing everything for the Customer. We have nothing to learn here.
- We have a Quality or Business Excellence Programme.
- You can not teach us anything.
- We have Customer retention (mistaken for loyalty).

Sometimes we come across managers who are so sure of themselves, and know-it-all. They are not open to anything. They are sceptical of anything beyond known techniques. Innovation or change is smothered.

It is very difficult to change these people.

Solution

- By giving examples of what Total CVM can do and how the managers can improve their bottom line.
- By education with the help of a consultant or a Chief Customer Officer. Show them what their Customer related roles can be.
- By learning from others what can be done for the Customer beyond what is being done.
- By providing them incentives. Not learning or not changing will become detrimental to them.
- By putting Customer programmes in their Key Result Areas.
- Driving the business strategy from the Customer strategy.
- Putting them into Customer Circles and getting their involvement with the Circle of Promises.

6. The Casual or Apathetic Attitude as a Barrier to Total CVM

Barriers

Often we come across managers who are apathetic and not pro-active to the Customers. This could be because:

- We do not need to change.
- Customers will come and go, why worry?
- Our Customer share is stable, even though we are gaining new Customers. Why worry about Customer defection or Customer churn? (In India, there is a 5 per cent per month churn on prepaid telecom Customers. Isn't it worthwhile worrying about?)
- Our competition is doing the same things as us.
- Why rock the boat is a common reason why Total CVM cannot come into the picture.

Often apathetic people have low self-esteem or are over their heads. Awareness no longer drives them.

If there is someone in the organization with a positive outlook, he may be able to institute CVM but not Total CVM. One will continuously have to prove the benefits of the programme to them.

Solution

- Increasing employee self-esteem, awareness and making them more proactive. This requires education and hand holding
- Making them understand what Total CVM is all about, and how it can increase business metrics
- Ensuring that incentive systems and KRA's reflect Customer programmes
- Making them share Customer Circles and Customer strategy programmes with enthusiastic people

7. The "We are too Busy" Attitude as a Barrier to Total CVM

Barriers

We are too busy with other initiatives is a comment that leads to not initiating Total CVM in an organization.

- The CEO truly believes he has the right initiatives in the right priority.
- They have a Customer programme or a Customer Department.
- We are out of bandwidth.
- Customers are not a problem.

Solution

- An examination of the tasks through a task audit is necessary. A better understanding of what the Customer could mean to the organization is necessary.
- Getting rid of unnecessary and irrelevant tasks can open up time for more work.
- Ensuring Customer tasks have high priority.

CUSTOMERS AND CHANNELS AS AN IMPEDIMENT TO TOTAL CVM

Barriers

Sometimes having limited Customers, or captive Customers can be an impediment to adopt Total CVM. Often, you think of your Customers as only Channel partners, and so you do not take Customers seriously, since you are the principal!

1. We have no External Customers, or Very Limited Number of Customers

- We have a successful business and a limited number of Customers.
- We have a great relationship with them.
- Our internal and limited external Customers need us.

Too many of these companies go downhill when a competitor builds a strong presence or changes tactics, while your entire company is not Customer-centric.

Such companies can concentrate on internal Customers and build extremely robust Customer Value programmes and teamwork, efficiency and pride. The external Customers if any will also notice this.

Solution

- Educating employees to understand the true meaning of Total CVM. It builds Employee Value and Customer Value, and more efficient organizations.
- Render Total CVM a departmental task, and to look at a wider spectrum of Customers, including shareholders and suppliers.
- Showing them how even great companies can fall as competitors outstrip them.
- Making Customer goals congruent with departmental goals and incentives.
- Driving the business strategy from the Customer strategy.

2. The Channel Partners or Indirect Customer Contact as a Barrier to Total CVM

Barriers

Very often, the end Customer is ignored because the immediate Customer is the channel partner. Branding then seems to be the only way to attract the Customer.

We have seen in Glacier's case that touching the end Customer reduces reliance on the intermediary and increases value to the end Customer. In addition, the channel partner needs to be motivated to become a value creation partner with the parent company.

Channel partners or indirect Customer contact can be (but not always) an impediment to Total CVM.

- Often they see themselves as distinct from the company Total CVM programme.
- Have their own agenda, strategy and business imperatives, such as a distributor or retailer worrying about his ROI.
- Have never really been treated as a partner to build Customers and loyalty for the principal company they distribute for.
- Have been looked at as distributors or as a means or a pair of hands to get the product to the Customer, and subservient to the company.
- Channel partners have been so used to the company doing everything to improve their own brand and Customer loyalty. This is the company's job, not mine.
- Not used to building their own brand equity which requires an in-depth Customer focus.

For years, many channel partners have been just logistic partners. They ride the coattails of the brand or the company, and basically do a logistics job, without impacting the end Customer. Of course, there are others, like giant retailers, some mom and pop stores having a great Customer relation, or large distributors. In the food service business, for example, the large US distributors are Sysco Corp, Houston, with USD 22.6 billion in sales this past year, and US Foodservice, Columbus, MD, with USD 17.7 billion, and Unipro with USD 16 billion in sales out of Stockton, CA. They have brand equity and clout, versus a smaller logistics type distributors (there are many large logistic companies with clout the largest being DHL, others are UPS Supply Chain Solutions, Atlanta,

USD 4.1 billion; Exel, Westerville, OH, USD 3.9 billion; CH Robinson Worldwide, Eden Prairie, MN, USD 3.6 billion.

The larger ones may also not be providing the kind of value the end Customer wants, as they may cater more to their distribution chain.

Solution

- Getting channel partners involved and aligned to the Customer strategy by their being part of creating it, and catalysing them to help the parent company with Customer Circles and Customer Value are ways to get their attention.
- The smaller ones can see how their brand equity can be built by better Customer focus, and can thus be aligned by their participation in Customer Circles.
- Educating channel partners about Customer Value.
- Putting dealers and retailers into Customer Circles.
- Building with them one or more Customer related tasks.

3. We have a Limited Amount of Product to Sell or We have Captive Customers, or We are in a Regulated Industry

Barriers

The company or managers ask:

- Why do we need to be Customer-centric?
- We are regulated and Customer-centricity will not increase market share.

We have seen these companies become sloppy and when competition is allowed to enter regulated markets, they fail. Moreover, entry into new segments of business becomes difficult. The company's image becomes poor. The employees become apathetic.

Classic examples are monopoly companies in regulated industries, like telecom and airlines in India and elsewhere. Where are the leaders of the regulated period today?

Solution

Companies change because:

- They know or are made aware that competition will eventually come in.
- They should also know their present Customers in the regulated business could be future Customers for new businesses.
- Education on Total CVM as a builder of efficiency and teamwork, and improvement of profits.
- Total CVM helps reduce pressure on price.

Tata Power recognises that they have a presence in the Customer's premises. Eventually, they can use their wired electricity supply system to supply other services to the Customer. Alternatively, if they have excellent Customer Value, the Customer will find price to be acceptable (this was proven at Tata Power), and the Customer would be happy to do other business with them because of the value they receive and the trust they have got in the company.

Tata Crop Nutrition and Agri-Business also believes adding value to the Customer will give them different avenues of doing more business with their existing Customers, and that they could attract new Customers for new products.

Both these companies are in regulated industries.

BUSINESS PROGRAMMES OR THINKING
AS AN IMPEDIMENT TO TOTAL CVM

Business programmes or business thinking can be an impediment to Total CVM.

1. We have Quality or Six Sigma, or a Business Excellence Programme in our company.
2. We have a successful brand.
3. We have a successful business or growth.
4. Profits drive our Company.

1. Quality or Six Sigma Programmes or Business Excellence Programmes as Barriers to Total CVM

Barriers

Many companies believe that:

- If they have a quality programme or a Six Sigma programme or a Business Excellence programme, they are driven by the Customer and they do not need a Customer programme. Our work at GE Capital proved that CVA was the way to understanding Customers.
- Quality, and the business is more important than the Customer.
- Quality and Business Excellence make us understand the Customer and captures the Voice of the Customer.
- Quality and Business Excellence are building employee self respect.

This is the case with companies with strong Quality and Business Excellence programmes. Business Excellence programmes require that there be ever-increasing value for Customers, and normally need CVA to measure value. Often, only satisfaction is monitored, and processes are built from a company's needs and efficiencies.

Solution

- Quality and Business Excellence programmes provide a ready-made platform for the Customer Value programmes. The processes, monitoring and other thought processes make them ideal staging platform for Total CVM. Integrating these into a Total CVM programme is an ideal step. They do not have to be competing programmes but complementary ones.
- Understanding that Total CVM is more basic and is focused on Customers, and on mindsets and attitude changes. Also remembering Business Excellence is process driven.
- Total CVM will automatically build Business Excellence.
- Educating employees on the differences on Business Excellence and Total CVM. Total CVM tells you why Customers buy and do not buy from you. Total CVM leads to increased loyalty, market share, profitability and total Shareholder Value. Processes lead to efficiency gains, not necessarily market share, as GE found was happening in spite of aggressive Six Sigma programmes.

2. The Successful Brand as a Barrier to Total CVM

Barriers

When companies have a successful brand,

- They believe they are Customer-centric.
- The brand contact is more important than Customer contact.
- That the brand comes from Customer trust that comes from doing things right for the Customer, so why do more?
- They do not understand that the Customer experience has to be built and improved and the total company has

to stand behind this. Trust is a moving target and has to be won every day.

- If we measure brand metrics, why measure Customer metrics.

Reality is that Customer Value and other brand promotion measures build brand. Customer Value and brand building are not in conflict, they have to work congruently. However, turf becomes so important that brand builders believe in the brand first, just like business excellence people believe in business excellence first. In the hierarchy of business, the Customer must come first. The brand creates value, which we measure in a CVA exercise. In fact, we have been able to measure the value of the brand. Often, brand value is almost 50 per cent of the total value creation to the Customer, but not 100 per cent. Much depends on the definition of brand. Other Customer Value benefits create the rest of the value. Brand equity of employees impacts brand.

Solution

- For brand managers and Total CVM to work together in increasing Customer Value.
- Overall image of the company and the brand that contribute to Customer Value. Image is only one part of the Customer Value the Customer perceives. Price and Benefits are the important constituents of Customer Value.
- Customer Value will increase brand value.

3. The Successful Business or Growth as a Barrier to Total CVM

Barriers

Successful business or growth can become a barrier to Total CVM:

- We are too busy growing for Total CVM.
- We must be doing something right for the Customer, we do not need Total CVM.
- We have Customer retention and that is good enough. Mistaking Customer retention for loyalty.

Solution

- It is often possible that your company is truly adding Customer Value. However, it is also likely that the Customer Value delivered is substandard, and you are the best of the lot. This is the case with telecom companies in India. Any company that breaks the mould and starts to truly provide Customer Value will be the winner. Understanding this is a starting point.
- Also, you must understand success does not mean it is forever. You have to win success everyday. You can be reactive and react to competitive moves, or you can be proactive and be ahead of the game. That is why Next practices beat Best practices all the time.

Just see what is happening to the great and successful companies of 2008 in 2009. Many like Bear Stearns, and AIG had to be rescued and others just disappeared.

4. Profits Alone Drive Our Company

It is not unreasonable for profits to be important to a CEO, shareholders, the Board and even managers seeking to meet their profit goals. However, once these stakeholders realise that the long term profits will improve through Customer programmes, they will realise Customer goals and shareholders goals are congruent.

Please also note that most Total CVM concepts require no extra corporate investment other than changing attitudes.

That is why we say CVI (Customer Value Investment) equals increased ROI!

The solution is to understand that profits are short-term drivers. The solution is to add Customer Value through Total CVM and thereby drive profits and shareholder wealth for the long term.

Appendix II
TOTAL CVM at Godrej

Godrej is a well-respected, large Indian conglomerate whose businesses range from white goods to furniture, to agri-products, chicken, home care, FMCG, and services. Their HiCare division is a young three-year-old start-up to service the pest control business. This business has hitherto been a mom and pop business, in what in India is called the unorganized sector. This sector is epitomized by poor and unreliable service with low prices, and questionable chemical and environmental focus. A few years earlier, one organized player had entered this sector.

Customer Value Foundation (CVF) started a Total Customer Value Management programme and set up Customer Circles at the front-line level. We also conducted a Customer Value Added and Voice of Customer study. The following is the result of the Customer Circle work. We were also able to show how to change the rules of the game. The programme lasted about six months.

1. Customer Circles and employee alignment to the Customer and to make them more focused on the Customer. The Godrej HiCare programme actually became more elaborate than had been envisaged. The following was accomplished:

   a. Top managers' alignment to the Customer. They were exposed to the concept as a group and individually, with Customer related roles being defined. Their Customer focus remains defused, with one or two notable exceptions. The general attitude is, "I am present at reviews and so I do not need to take proactive action."

b. Operations managers, and IT have embraced Total CVM, and shown leadership here.
c. Front-line employees' alignment to the Customer: Customer Circles were instituted incorporating service centre employees including call officers and technicians, Field Sales Officers (FSOs) and technical officers, with help from IT and accounting.
d. Front-line employees have embraced the Customer, and Customer-centricity. Though early to generalise, they have seen results such as:

Customers

a. Less irritation of Customers.
b. Customer's DNA (do not annoy) methods working well.
c. Customer delight help in the relationship.
d. Customers being nice to them.
e. Fewer complaints.
f. Customers asking for technicians, call officers.
g. Referrals and repeat sales.
h. More on time service.

It is evident that Customers want to have a relationship and deal with people they like. The trick, which we are starting to achieve is to get liked and build trust, reliability and a relationship.

In the Service Centres

a. Incorporating the Courtesy system: greeting each other, smiling.
b. De-briefing meetings, where people are discussing problems and solutions.
c. Call officers are setting up meetings more efficiently, with correct addresses landmarks, etc.

d. More on time service (technicians get to destination when promised).
e. Better team work, so much so that technicians are giving referrals directly to the FSOs so that they could bag contracts with faster response. People are happier working with each other, fewer fights.

Call Officers

a. Referrals improved, by 30 per cent.
b. Better set up of technicians' visits and in contiguous areas to reduce travel time.
c. Better collection of addresses, telephone numbers and landmarks, making technician visit easier and on time.
d. Call officers are ready to talk to irritated Customers and defuse their anger, by better listening and better action.
h. Setting up repeat technician visits more efficient.
i. Scheduling service calls per contract or Customer need.
j. Call officers now getting into Goa club, trying for Bangkok club (these are employee recognition programmes).

Technicians

a. Wearing Customer Champion badges. Customers ask what this means, and are delighted to hear they are the focus of the business.
b. Better feedback in the office because technicians bring correct landmark/addresses/Customer feedback.
c. Consequently, on time arrivals have improved.
d. Technicians are leaving their names, chatting up Customers, telling them the Do's and Don'ts and are getting better cooperation. They are carrying calling cards and call sheets in folders so that Customers sign crisp sheets (also gives a sense of professionalism).

e. Happier Customers. Some even offer technicians tea and coffee. Often Customers ask for same technician.
f. Better discussions on grievances, and solutions.
g. Better and speedier dissemination of referrals.

Inspectors

a. The inspection reports are better made out and usable with drawings, allowing technicians to do a better job.
b. Reports are more timely.

Sales

a. More repeat business.
b. Better and speedier referrals from technicians. Referral business up to Rs 300,000 of sales per FSO.
c. Less pressure on price. An example is Reliance in repeat business.

2. Customer Bill of Rights were made with interlocking promises between various participants. This enforces a team focus on the Customer.
3. Roll out of Customer Circles: Santa Cruz and Vikhroli:

a. To members who did not attend initial Customer Circles.
b. To other service centres in Mumbai.
c. This has started in other cities, in the next phase.

4. Working out how future Customer Circles will function, including working agenda, leadership, follow up and Continuous Improvement Programme.
5. Convert call centres to action centres:

a. Better coordination between call centre and Godrej.

  b. Godrej listens to voice of call centre.
  c. Call centre reports focus on Customer and his happiness, not on call statistics. Number of complaints should come down.
  d. Call centres should talk about closure of Customers' problems not satisfaction.
 6. Discussion on building robust Customer focused systems and processes.

When Customer Value Foundation started work at Godrej, they were convinced that Godrej would have to change the rules of the game. The majority of Godrej people agreed that brand would play a role, but were unable to think that brand would reduce the importance of price. A Customer Value Foundation Total CVM study showed how it was possible to change the rules of the game, and how unconsciously, Godrej was actually doing this. We showed Godrej this through our study.

VALUE

Please note that the results are highly skewed towards the needs perceived by the unorganized sector (termed Others) in the study because their relative weight is high in the marketplace compared to PCI (the other player in the organized sector) and Godrej. Godrej has very low penetration in the two sectors studied.

 1. The questionnaire is based on Waterfall of Needs and attribute trees built by Godrej personnel.
 2. They felt that the Value to the Customer is the combination of the Overall Benefits the Customer perceives he gets from the service provider and the image of the service provider, versus what he perceives is the cost of the service.

3. Cost is 64 per cent in importance in the value equation, whereas the benefits are 33 per cent and the image a mere 5 per cent. The image being so small in importance is a reflection of the lack of brand, and trust in the pest control service providers (see Table AII.1). This is very important. Godrej must play on its brand, its ethics and the fact they are trustworthy, and they have safe products and processes.

In terms of Value, Godrej is at par with competition, and appears to be higher in cost.

In reality, Godrej is being compared with other unorganized service providers and PCI. The Customers of unbranded service providers are less demanding than those selecting Godrej. Their expectations are different and often lower. The Customers of unbranded service providers tend to rate their service providers better. In effect, the unbranded service providers cater to a different segment of Customers, and a segment to be weaned away towards using Godrej or branded services. Godrej has to upgrade the perception of such Customers.

In the marketplace, we see ourselves as we want to. And when we come up against a seemingly price conscious market, we tend to think the market works only on price. We are not willing to change the perception. But through a value study, we can start to understand how benefits can become more important than price. Table AII.2 vividly portrays this.

Even with limited Customers, the actual cost in the case of Godrej is less important.

What does this tell us?

It tells us that the majority of the Customers in the un-organized segment view cost as important as they do not see the benefit of pest control service as high. Godrej has to find a way of letting them know the importance of the pest control service and the advantages of using Godrej over competiiton.

TABLE AII.1

| Attribute | Impact Weight | Value | | | | Godrej vs. Industry | Ratio Company vs. Competitors | | | Ratio Godrej/... | |
| | | Scores | | | Industry Average | | | | | | |
		Godrej	PCI	Others			Godrej	PCI	Others	PCI	Others
Overall Benefits	33%	8	8.06	8.06	8.05	0.99	0.99	1.00	1.00	0.99	0.99
Overall Image	5%	8.06	8.2	8.06	8.11	0.99	0.99	1.02	0.99	0.98	1.00
Overall Cost	63%	7.63	7.94	7.91	7.90	0.97	0.96	1.01	1.00	0.96	0.96
Overall Value	100%	7.65	7.63	7.71	7.68	1.00	1.00	0.99	1.01	1.00	0.99

Source : CVF's Total Customer Value Management programme at Godrej.
Notes

means poor, irrespective of rating versus competition

means better than competition

means equal to competition

means worse than competition

TABLE AII.2

Attribute	Entire Industry	PCI and Godrej	Godrej Only
		Impact Weight	
Overall Benefits	33%	45%	64%
Overall Image	5%	0%	0%
Overall Cost	63%	55%	36%
Overall Value	100%	100%	100%

Source   CVF's Total Customer Value Management programme at Godrej.

In addition, this tells us that by adding value, you can make the price less important in the eyes of the Customer. Over a period of time, brand and image will be built up. Why is it not important now? The reason is that currently, service execution (that is the pest control service works to my satisfaction or elimination of pests) is more important than the HiCare brand, which has to be established.

Given below are the other important parameters:

OVERALL BENEFITS

The service execution forms 50 per cent of the benefits and the Customers see this as the most important benefit. The pest control package is the second most important parameter (see Table AII.3).

It is likely, as Godrej becomes more important a service provider, the package and people will become more significant. If we look at only the organized sector, we can see the weights (importance) change from the perception of the overall market (see Table AII.4).

The people become more important (34 per cent versus 19 per cent for the entire industry). Thus, teaching our front-line people Customer Value will help as the industry seeks more organized players.

TABLE AII.3
Profile: Food Processing Customers Overall Benefits

Attribute	Impact Weight	Overall Benefits								
		Scores				Godrej vs. Industry	Ratio Company vs. Competitors			Ratio Godrej/....	
		Godrej	PCI	Others	Industry Average		Godrej	PCI	Others	PCI	Others
Pest Control Package	34%	7.94	8.02	8.08	8.05	0.99	0.99	0.99	1.01	0.99	0.98
People	19%	7.88	7.98	8.17	8.08	0.97	0.97	0.98	1.03	0.99	0.96
Service Execution	47%	8.18	8.22	8.09	8.14	1.00	1.01	1.01	0.99	1.00	1.01
Overall Benefits	100%	8	8.06	8.06	8.05	0.99	0.99	1.00	1.00	0.99	0.99

Source   CVF's Total Customer Value Management programme at Godrej.

Notes

■ means poor, irrespective of rating versus competition

■ means better than competition

□ means equal to competition

■ means worse than competition

TABLE AII.4

Attribute	*Entire Industry*	*PCI and Godrej*
	Impact Weight	
Pest Control Package	34%	37%
People	19%	34%
Service Execution	47%	28%
Overall Benefits	100%	100%

Source   CVF's Total Customer Value Management programme at Godrej.

PEST CONTROL PACKAGE

Godrej comes out looking poor in the pest control package (see Table AII.5). The most important factor is that the processes and procucts are safe. Godrej does well here. Godrej should build on these. Is Godrej's service impersonal? In a desire to make the contact process uniform, are we losing the customization? In a mom and pop operation, the service provider seemingly bends over backwards to do what the Customer wants.

In an effort to understand what drives the pest control package, we went beyond what HiCare executives had suggested. The pest control package has to have a warranty and a service execution declaration or history that Customers can see and derive satisfaction from (see Table AII.6).

The pest control package should include people, service execution selling, warranty and, of course, show an understanding of the needs of the Customer. Is HiCare too rigid?

PEOPLE

Godrej's people are less knowledgeable (to do with age of service?) and accessible (by design more process directed)

TABLE AII.5

Pest Control Package

Attribute	Impact Weight	Scores			Industry Average	Godrej vs. Industry	Ratio Company vs. Competitors			Ratio Godrej/....	
		Godrej	PCI	Others			Godrej	PCI	Others	PCI	Others
Understands my Needs	17%	7.59	7.95	8.08	8.00	0.95	0.94	0.99	1.03	0.95	0.94
Customises Service	14%	7.59	7.78	7.9	7.83	0.97	0.97	0.99	·1.02	0.98	0.96
Monitors	23%	7.47	7.71	7.92	7.81	0.96	0.95	0.98	1.03	0.97	0.94
Process and Products are Safe	45%	8.06	7.85	7.89	7.89	1.02	1.02	0.99	1.00	1.03	1.02
Overall Pest Control Package	100%	7.94	8.02	8.08	8.05	0.99	0.99	0.99	1.01	0.99	0.98

Source CVF's Total Customer Value Management programme at Godrej.

Notes ▓ means poor, irrespective of rating versus competition

▓ means better than competition

�░ means equal to competition

▒ means worse than competition

TABLE AII.6
Pest Control Package Importance from Customers

Attribute	Impact Weight
Understands my Needs	23%
People	23%
Service Execution	33%
Warranty	21%
Overall Pest Control Package	100%

Source: CVF's Total Customer Value Management programme at Godrej.

than competition. So Godrej's people turn out to be poor versus others (see Table AII.7). Customer Circles will help their soft skills.

Actually, within PCI and Godrej, Customers want more skilled people (see Table AII.8).

In trying to understand the people equation (Table AII.9), one also sees that the actual service execution impacts the Customer wherein skilled people will execute the job better and be more responsive! And what does the Customer equate Sevice execution with? It is the lack of any pests during the contract. If this is not done properly, the service package and people are perceived to be poor.

People are reviewed on their service execution, something missed out in looking at how Customers perceive people.

SERVICE EXECUTION

Reliability and technical support along with crisis management are key to service execution. I think a question like "the service eliminates pest" would have been a a better one to ask rather than the service is effective or reliable. In any event, these last two make up 35 per cent of the importance of the service execution model (see Table AII.10).

Godrej is rated below par in effectiveness. Again, the question is one of expectation, or has Godrej oversold itself?

TABLE AII.7

Attribute	Impact Weight	Scores			Industry Average	Godrej vs. Industry	Ratio Company vs. Competitors			Ratio Godrej/....	
		Godrej	PCI	Others			Godrej	FCI	Others	PCI	Others
					People						
Skilled	24%	7.94	7.86	8	7.95	1.00	1.00	0.98	1.02	1.01	0.99
Responsive	22%	7.88	7.77	7.94	7.88	1.00	1.00	0.98	1.02	1.01	0.99
Knowledgeable	22%	7.65	7.78	7.97	7.88	0.97	0.97	0.98	1.03	0.98	0.96
Accessible	10%	7.65	8.11	7.98	7.99	0.96	0.95	1.02	1.00	0.94	0.96
Prompt	21%	8.12	7.88	8	7.97	1.02	1.02	0.98	1.01	1.03	1.02
Overall People	100%	7.88	7.98	8.17	8.08	0.97	0.97	0.98	1.03	0.99	0.96

Source CVF's Total Customer Value Management programme at Godrej.

Notes

means poor, irrespective of rating versus competition

means better than competition

means equal to competition

means worse than competition

TABLE AII.8

Attribute	Entire Industry	PCI and Godrej
	Impact Weight	
Skilled	24%	45%
Responsive	22%	0%
Knowledgeable	22%	18%
Accesible	10%	18%
Prompt	21%	19%
Overall People	100%	100%

Source CVF's Total Customer Value Management programme at Godrej.

TABLE AII.9
People Importance from Customers

Attribute	Impact Weight
Skilled	21%
Responsive	12%
Knowledgeable	18%
Accessible	6%
Prompt	9%
Service Execution	34%
Overall People	100%

Source CVF's Total Customer Value Management programme at Godrej.

Going further, crisis management is a very important part of the service execution, even more so in the organised sector (PCI and Godrej). We can see the market need shift from reliable and effective to crisis control, as the previously important factors become more common and expected in the organized sector (see Table AII.11).

OVERALL IMAGE

Image is currently not important but is bound to become so. The main items of importance in creating image are concerns for environment and ethics. Brand and trust will soon become important. In a limited analysis (given Godrej's sample size),

TABLE AII.10

		Service Execution									
		Scores					Ratio Company vs. Competitors			Ratio Godrej/...	
Attribute	Impact Weight	Godrej	PCI	Others	Industry Average	Godrej vs. Industry	Godrej	PCI	Others	PCI	Others
Reliable	22%	8	7.94	7.86	7.90	1.01	1.01	1.01	0.99	1.01	1.02
Effective	13%	7.65	7.95	7.79	7.83	0.98	0.97	1.02	0.99	0.96	0.98
Quality Assurance (process includes audit reports)	10%	7.88	7.71	7.84	7.80	1.01	1.01	0.98	1.01	1.02	1.01
Timely	10%	8.35	7.95	7.92	7.97	1.05	1.05	1.00	0.99	1.05	1.05
Technical Support	23%	7.94	7.77	7.88	7.85	1.01	1.01	0.99	1.01	1.02	1.01
Crisis Management	21%	7.94	7.85	7.72	7.78	1.02	1.02	1.01	0.98	1.01	1.03
Overall Service Execution	100%	8.18	8.22	8.09	8.14	1.00	1.01	1.01	0.99	1.00	1.01

Source CVF's Total Customer Value Management programme at Godrej.

Notes
means poor, irrespective of rating versus competition
means better than competition
means equal to competition
means worse than competition

TABLE AII.11

Attribute	Entire Industry	PCI and Godrej
	Impact Weight	
Reliable	22%	14%
Effective	13%	7%
Quality Assurance	10%	15%
Timely	10%	3%
Technical Support	23%	19%
Crisis Management	21%	43%
Overall Service Execution	100%	100%

Source   CVF's Total Customer Value Management programme at Godrej.

brand shows some importance. Godrej does well in brand itself. Table AII.12 is overshadowed by the unorganized players.

If we look at the organized sector, trust in the company becomes more important, showing that the Customers' latent need is coming out (see Table AII.13).

OVERALL COST

Non-price terms make up 60 per cent of the price and actual price is 40 per cent of the importance in the perception of overall cost (see Table AII.14). Godrej is rated better on cost, showing that people are willing to pay a price for dealing with Godrej.

Part of the reason is that Godrej may have better payment terms as shown in Table AII.15.

Payment terms become less important in the organized sector. Actual price is more important, because people suspect the organized sector will be more expensive (see Table AII.16).

Non-price terms are more important than the price terms. This includes training and safety and warranty. Strangely, Godrej is rated poorly on these (see Table AII.17). One has

TABLE AII.12
Profile: Food Processing Customers Overall Image

| | | Image | | | | Ratio Godrej vs. | Ratio Company vs. Competitors | | | Ratio Godrej/.... | |
| | Impact Weight | Scores | | | Industry | | | | | | |
Attribute		Godrej	PCI	Others	Average	Industry	Godrej	PCI	Others	PCI	Others
Brand	0%	7.94	7.55	7.58	7.60	1.04	1.05	0.99	0.99	1.05	1.05
Trust	5%	7.82	7.8	7.81	7.81	1.00	1.00	1.00	1.00	1.00	1.00
Ethics	44%	7.82	7.77	7.75	7.76	1.01	1.01	1.00	1.00	1.01	1.01
Concern for safety and environment	51%	7.76	8.02	7.81	7.87	0.99	0.98	1.03	0.98	0.97	0.99
Overall Image	100%	8.06	8.2	8.06	8.11	0.99	0.99	1.02	0.99	0.98	1.00

Source CVF's Total Customer Value Management programme at Godrej.

Notes

means poor, irrespective of rating versus competition

means better than competition

means equal to competition

means worse than competition

TABLE AII.13

	Entire Industry	PCI and Godrej
	Impact Weight	
Attribute		
Brand	0%	0%
Trust	5%	25%
Etics	44%	45%
Concern for safety	51%	30%
Overall Image	100%	100%

Source Customer Value Total Customer Value Management programme at Godrej.

TABLE AII.14

Profile: Food Processing Customers Overall Cost

Attribute	Impact Weight	Overall Cost						Ratio Company vs. Competitors			Ratio Godrej/....	
		Scores			Industry Average	Godrej vs. Industry		Godrej	PCI	Others	PCI	Others
		Godrej	PCI	Others								
Price Terms	40%	8.19	7.92	7.93	7.95	1.03		1.03	0.99	0.99	1.03	1.03
Non Price Terms	60%	7.71	8.06	7.90	7.94	0.97		0.97	1.02	0.99	0.96	0.98
Overall Cost	100%	7.63	7.94	7.91	7.90	0.97		0.96	1.01	1.00	0.96	0.96

Source (CVF's) Total Customer Value Management programme at Godrej.

Notes

    means poor, irrespective of rating versus competition

    means better than competition

    means equal to competition

    means worse than competition

TABLE AII.15

Price Terms

Attribute	Impact Weight	Scores			Industry Average	Godrej vs. Industry	Ratio Company vs. Competitors			Ratio Godrej/...	
		Godrej	PCI	Others			Godrej	PCI	Others	PCI	Others
Price itself	44%	7.76	7.8	7.97	7.90	0.98	0.98	0.98	1.02	0.99	0.97
Payment Terms	56%	8.12	7.9	7.72	7.81	1.04	1.04	1.02	0.97	1.03	1.05
Overall Price Terms	100%	8.19	7.92	7.93	7.95	1.03	1.03	0.99	0.99	1.03	1.03

Source CVF's Total Customer Value Management programme at Godrej.

Notes

     means poor, irrespective of rating versus competition

     means better than competition

     means equal to competition

     means worse than competition

TABLE AII.16

	Entire Industry	PCI and Godrej
Attribute	Impact Weight	
Price itself	44%	60%
Payment Terms	56%	40%
Overall Price Terms	100%	100%

Source CVF's Total Customer Value Management programme at Godrej.

TABLE AII.17

		Non-Price Terms					Ratio Company vs. Competitors			Ratio Godrej/...	
		Scores									
Attribute	Impact Weight	Godrej	PCI	Others	Industry Average	Godrej vs. Industry	Godrej	PCI	Others	PCI	Others
Crisis Support	12%	7.47	7.62	7.59	7.59	0.98	0.98	1.01	1.00	0.98	0.98
Partnership-Training, Updates, Safety, Health	37%	7.12	7.68	7.66	7.62	0.93	0.93	1.01	1.01	0.93	0.93
Warranty	47%	7.29	7.66	7.58	7.58	0.96	0.96	1.02	1.00	0.95	0.96
Price Justification	4%	7.69	7.68	7.75	7.72	1.00	1.00	0.99	1.01	1.00	0.99
Overall Non Price Terms	100%	7.71	8.06	7.9	7.94	0.97	0.97	1.02	0.99	0.96	0.98

Source CVF's Total Customer Value Management programme at Godrej.

Notes

means poor, irrespective of rating versus competition

means better than competition

means equal to competition

means worse than competition

to assess if the warranties are poor, or the execution of warranties are poor.

Price justification does not show up as being important. Yet when we look at the organized sector, price justification becomes a significant factor! Not as significant as warranties, but important enough (see Table AII.18). Figures AII.1 and AII.2) represent the loyalties (Slippery Slope) and the Value Map respectively.

TABLE AII.18

	Entire Industry	PCI and Godrej
Attribute	Impact Weight	
Crisis Support	12%	16%
Partnership-Training, Updates, Safety, Health	37%	13%
Warranty	47%	44%
Price Justification	4%	28%
Overall Non Price Terms	100%	100%

Source   CVF's Total Customer Value Management programme at Godrej.

FIGURE AII.1
Food Processing Customers: Slippery Slope

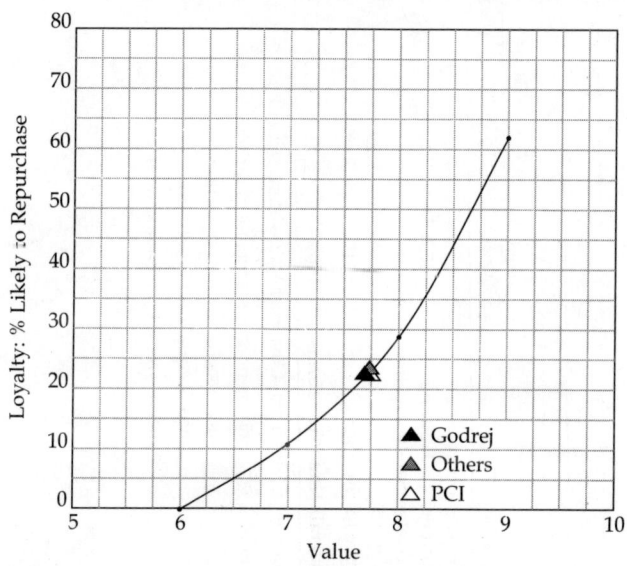

Source   CVF's Total Customer Value Management programme at Godrej.

FIGURE AII.2
Food Processing Customers: Value Map

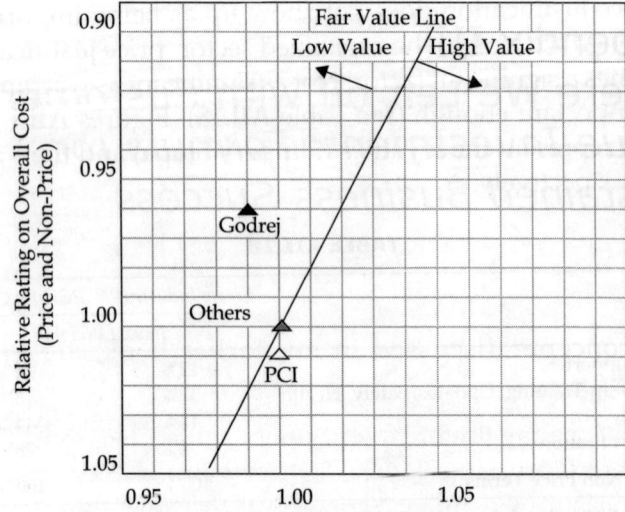

Source   CVF's Total Customer Value Management programme at Godrej.

Appendix III
Where We Left off with *Customer Value Investment: Formula for Sustained Business Success*

The concepts discussed in my earlier book, are given below:

Most management practitioners remember that Management Gurus like Peter Drucker wanted them to seek and measure Customer Satisfaction (because the purpose of any organization, according to him, was to have satisfied Customers). Few remember that many years later Drucker exhorted them to seek Customer Value and not mere satisfaction.

Marketing Gurus like Philip Kotler are advising that an emphasis be placed on co-creating a Customer experience, along with the 3Cs (Customer-in-Control, Customer convenience, and Choice). All this in addition to the traditional 4Ps (product, promotion, place and price).

First, everyone is now talking about the Customer in the same manner we talked about quality 20 years ago. In spite of all the talk, there is a limited focus on the Customer. In reality, the Customer revolution is just starting and *Customer Value Investment* is meant to contribute to making this revolution a true Customer movement.

Second, the Customer has to become the focus of any business. Creating value for the Customer will necessarily become a paramount strategy. This strategy has been proven to lead to increased shareholder value by Profit Impact of Marketing Strategies (PIMS) analysis of over a thousand

American companies' databases, and from the experiences of those companies practising Custcmer Value even in a limited form.

Third, Customer experience and interaction with the Customer in co-creating Customer Value will become even more important in the near future. Being Customer-driven and putting the Customer in control will improve loyalty. It's ironic that we wish to control our suppliers, but do not wish to allow our Customers (whose suppliers we are) to control their suppliers! (Incidentally, as companies we seek Customer Loyalty; how many companies are truly loyal to the Customers?)

Last, but not least, the various Customer and Customer concepts are not presently well understood. In fact, definitions of the key terms and concepts of major Customer-related initiatives vary widely from book to buok, from article to article, and even within companies. *Customer Value Investment* defines these. These are listed in Table AIII.1.

Although there are books dealing with various Customer-related initiatives, *Customer Value Investment* is a simple and concise book discussing the Customer, bringing to the fore the importance of the Customer and Customer-focus, and defining various Customer-related factors.

TABLE AIII.1
Customer Concepts

Customers as Assets	Putting Customer in Control
Customer-in-Center©	Stated and Implied Weights
Customer Champions	Customers' DNA
Customer Lifetime Value	Value Creation
Customer Share	Competitive Profiles
Value of Customer	Customer Waterfall of Needs
Customer Capital	People or Employee Value Add
Customer Franchise	Value Maps
Customer Momentum	Customer Reporting
Customer Circles	Organization of the Future
Customer Strategy	
CVA	
Customer Metrics	

Source Gautam Mahajan, *Customer Value Investment.*

Most executives and senior managers will be aware of many of these initiatives. They will feel they are practising many Customer concepts, and wonder what is new. What I find is that most companies have some form of Customer-focus, and some data or satisfaction measurement gathering. Using Customer Value Management (which includes the Customer-in-Centre© concept) will allow them to integrate all their various Customer efforts into a holistic way of making their Customers loyal; and by adding value to him, the company will add value to themselves.

These executives will also find that when they institute this kind of focus and effort, along with measurement of Customer Value Added, everyone will be marching to the same tune in their organizations, leading to a much wider spectrum of competitive advantage.

Customer Value Investment showed the increase of benefits to Customer-savvy companies who practised it, in terms of improving business results. The book seeks to increase the level of Customer awareness among a large body of people who are all Customers and deal with Customers.

However, without question, the ultimate goal of the book is to help you put your Customers in the centre of your business objectives and strategies, and let them drive your business to their satisfaction…and ultimately yours!

This new book, *Total Customer Value Management*, has many more principles (beyond the previous book) which will help organizations become Customeric and be Customer-led and build shareholder wealth.

Index

About the Author

Mr Gautam Mahajan is an internationally acclaimed expert and thought leader in strategy, general management (including Customer Value) and globalization. He is President of Inter-Link Services Pvt. Ltd., an international consulting firm operating since 1987 and helping clients from America, Europe, Asia, Australia and India. Inter-Link helps companies with marketing, business development, strategy, globalization, changing the mindset and thinking through the future. Gautam has started the Customer Value Foundation to help companies with **Total C**ustomer **V**alue **M**anagement (**Total CVM**). His book, *Customer Value Investment: Formula for Sustained Business Success*, is a bestseller. Mr Mahajan spoke to CEOs from 25 countries on Customer Value in Spain in January 2008, and in Florida in February; and in June introduced Total CVM to two US companies. In October 2008, he consulted for a pan-European company on Total CVM and spoke at Chester to 40 European companies. Total CVM is running successfully at the Tatas and Godrej. Tata Chemicals Crop Nutrition and Agri-Business and Tata Power have completed the second phase of a Total CVM programme. A major overseas BPO company is converting call centres to action centres. Mr Mahajan is conducting seminars for HRD, CFOs and CIOs on their Total CVM roles. Overseas companies where Mr Mahajan has worked with CVM associates are GE Capital, Stamford, CT; State Farm Insurance, Bloomington, IL; and Wisconsin Energies, Milwaukee, WI, along with Castrol (BP).

Customer Value Foundation is arguably the only company in the world consulting in Total CVM. Everyone practices Customer Value in bits and pieces.

Mr Mahajan has global affiliates in Customer Value Management in North and South America, Europe and Australia/New Zealand.

Mr Mahajan worked in the US for 17 years with Continental Group, the world's largest packaging company (then a Fortune 50 company), and ran a division. He is one of the inventors of the PET bottle base and noise control kits. He spent time in California in 1998–2000 helping British dotcom companies.

Mr Mahajan is the National President of the Indo-American Chamber of Commerce, and was Chairman, PlastIndia Committee; Vice President, All India Plastics Manufacturers Association; Trustee, Plastics Institute of America. He was a member of the US-India think tank. Among his honours is a Fellowship from Harvard Business School and Illinois Institute of Technology. He also has 18 US patents. He was honoured by the Illinois Institute of Technology with its Distinguished Alumni award. He was written up in the *Wall Street Journal* for his study on the *American Business Experience in India*.

Mr Mahajan is a graduate of IIT Madras, where he was an Institute Merit Scholar. He has a Master's degree in Mechanics from the Illinois Institute of Technology, and has an MBA from Suffolk University.

He can be contacted at Mahajan@CustomerValueFounda tion.com (telephone +91 98100 60368).